本译丛受到宁波大学科学技术学院重点学科（翻译专业学位硕士点）培育项目资助，为译行丝路•翻译研究与语言服务中心系列成果之一

Translating Ningbo
Editors   Xia XIANG   Anfang HE

A Thousand Years of Academic Heritage in Eastern Zhejiang

千年文脉　浙东学术文化

Author

Tongyi FANG

Translators

Wentao ZHANG

Xia XIANG

Reviewer

Tiezhu DONG

ZHEJIANG UNIVERSITY PRESS
浙江大学出版社
·杭州·

宁波出版社
NINGBO PUBLISHING HOUSE
·宁波·

图书在版编目（CIP）数据

千年文脉：浙东学术文化 = A Thousand Years of
Academic Heritage in Eastern Zhejiang / 方同义著；
张文涛，项霞译. — 杭州：浙江大学出版社；宁波：
宁波出版社，2023.12
　（宁波文化译丛 / 项霞，贺安芳总主编）
　ISBN 978-7-308-24387-2

　Ⅰ. ①千… Ⅱ. ①方… ②张… ③项… Ⅲ. ①浙东学
派—研究 Ⅳ. ①B244.995

中国国家版本馆CIP数据核字(2023)第218901号

千年文脉：浙东学术文化

A Thousand Years of Academic Heritage in Eastern Zhejiang

方同义　著　张文涛　项　霞　译　董铁柱　译审

策划编辑	黄静芬
责任编辑	黄静芬
文字编辑	黄　墨
责任校对	仝　林
封面设计	周　灵
出版发行	浙江大学出版社
	（杭州市天目山路148号　　邮政编码　310007）
	（网址：http://www.zjupress.com）
排　版	杭州林智广告有限公司
印　刷	浙江新华数码印务有限公司
开　本	710mm×1000mm　1/16
印　张	19.5
插　页	4
字　数	390千
版 印 次	2023年12月第1版　2023年12月第1次印刷
书　号	ISBN 978-7-308-24387-2
定　价	88.00元

A View of the Moon Lake

A Corner of Tianyi Pavilion Architecture

A Pool in Front of Tianyi Pavilion

A Tiger Statue in Tianyi Pavilion Museum

A Lion Statue in Tianyi Pavilion Museum

The Bizhi Pavilion

The Fragrant Grass Islet on the Moon Lake

Former Residence of the Shi's Family of Yongshang (Ningbo)

Mansion of Fan Sima (Fan Qin)

Pingzi Tablet

Shuibei Pavilion of Xu Shidong

Temple of He Zhizhang

The Front Gate of Tianyi Pavilion

Statue of Fan Qin, the Owner of Tianyi Pavilion

Tianyi Pavilion

Where Yang Wenyuan (Yang Jian) Gave Lectures

总　序

　　宁波历史悠久，文化璀璨；宁波历史文化研究著述丰富，成绩斐然。然而，如何让宁波文化走出国门，如何向世界讲好宁波故事，却一直是个薄弱环节。这与宁波自古以来就崇尚开放的城市禀性不够合拍，也与今天"滨海宁波，扬帆世界"的时代追求不相协调。

　　有鉴于此，宁波大学科学技术学院人文学院翻译专业教师团队大胆提出：将宁波出版社 2014 年精心推出的"宁波文化丛书"（第一辑）翻译成英文版，让这套丛书作为文化使者，把宁波历史、宁波文明、宁波精神、宁波智慧带到四面八方。

　　"宁波文化丛书"（第一辑）共 8 本，出于一些原因，我们替换了其中 1 本，因此这套"宁波文化译丛"也是 8 本。具体是：王耀成著《商行四海：解读宁波帮》，黄定福著《奇构巧筑：宁波建筑文化》，谢安良著《丝路听潮：海上丝绸之路文化》，黄渭金著《东方曙光：宁波史前文明》，涂师平著《羽人竞渡：宁波发展史话》，方同义著《千年文脉：浙东学术文化》，虞浩旭、张爱妮著《甬藏书香：宁波藏书文化》，郁伟年著《阿拉宁波人》。

　　得益于原作者在挖掘、整理和研究宁波历史文化方面所做出的艰苦努力，文质兼美的文本为我们的翻译工作奠定了良好的基础。

　　但是，要忠实地翻译原著并不是一件容易的事情。以古文翻译为例，上述著作都或多或少征引了古代文献，有的不仅数量很多，而且专业性很强。对于古代文献，中文著作往往直接引用原文，至于古文如何解读可以让读者自己去琢磨。译著则不同，必须做到字字落实，不能含糊，所以翻译起来特别费时费力。我们还经常碰到引用的古文有文字错讹的情况，那就更加考验译者的学问和识见了。一边做翻译，一边查资料，一本书翻译下来，硬是把英语老师磨炼成古文通了。

　　这只是翻译三要素"信、达、雅"中"信"的问题。而译者追求的不仅仅是"信"，还有"达"与"雅"。翻译不是简单的语言转换，而是一种再创造。为了向读者奉献一套质量上乘的译丛，我们采取译者精心打磨、同事互相切磋、专家审读把关等措施，把精品意识贯穿于翻译工作的全过程。我们希望我们的译作对得起优秀的宁波文化，也对得起自己的职业操守。

在译丛即将面世之际，我们衷心感谢原作者的创造性劳动，感谢浙江大学出版社和宁波出版社的大力支持，感谢审稿专家和责任编辑的辛勤付出，感谢项霞、贺安芳两位总主编的精心组织和策划。

限于时间和水平，这套译丛也可能存在这样那样的不足甚至错误，欢迎专家和读者提出批评意见。

本译丛受到宁波大学科学技术学院重点学科（翻译专业学位硕士点）培育项目的资助，由译行丝路·翻译研究与语言服务中心出品，是宁波大学科学技术学院翻译团队"翻译宁波"（"Translating Ningbo"）的第一步。万事开头难，有了第一步就可以有第二步、第三步……我们将继续努力，为传播宁波历史文化做出自己应有的贡献。

周志锋

2022 年 11 月 11 日

于宁波大学科学技术学院

CONTENTS

Resplendent Moon Lake:
The Cradle of Zhedong Scholarship

The Moon Lake, the mother lake of Ningbo people, gave birth to Zhedong (eastern Zhejiang) scholarship, which has a long history of more than a thousand years in Ningbo.

I. The Moon Lake and Zhedong Scholarship

In some sense, I can be regarded as a native of Ningbo, Zhejiang, for I have worked here in Ningbo for 17 or 18 years, although my hometown is Zhuji, Zhejiang. Among all the cultural relics and tourist attractions of such a famous national historical and cultural city, what impresses me most is the Moon Lake.

Different from the famous West Lake in Hangzhou featuring natural scenery and breathtaking beauty, the Moon Lake is a manually excavated lake in the urban area of Ningbo, with both natural flavor of pastoral style and elegant beauty of Jiangnan gardens[①]. Although not as well-known as the West Lake, the Moon Lake captivates me, drawing me close to her and allow me to indulge in the pleasure of her company.

As a scenic spot, the Moon Lake, also known as Ningbo West Lake, is located in the southwest corner of the old urban area of Ningbo. Its surface

---

① Jiangnan (江南), literally the south of Yangtze River, refers to a region in the south of the lower reaches of the river. It is a beautiful and prosperous area. Jiangnan gardens are featured with exquisiteness, grace and tranquility.

looks like a full moon at the round part and a crescent at the curved part, hence the name. The current area of the scenic spot covers 96.7 hectares, including a water area of 9 hectares. The Moon Lake was firstly excavated during the Zhenguan period (627–649) of the Tang dynasty (618–907), and its ten scenic islets were formed during the Shaoxing period (1131–1162) of the Southern Song dynasty (1127–1279), when such buildings as pavilions, terraces and open halls were finished with seasonal trees and flowers planted around. The ten islets are the Zhuyu Islet[①], Moon Islet and Chrysanthemum Islet on the east shore of the lake, the Flower Islet, Bamboo Islet, Willow Islet and Fragrant Grass Islet in the middle, and the Mist Islet, Snow Islet and Lotus Islet on the west shore. Besides, there are three causeways on the lake, namely, Yanyue Causeway, Guangsheng Causeway and Taohua Causeway. There are also seven bridges over the lake, namely, Huxin West Bridge, Huxin East Bridge, Chongchong West Bridge, Chongchong East Bridge, Hongqiao Bridge, Gunxiu Bridge and Siming Bridge. All these constitute the wonderful general picture of the Moon Lake.

Walking along the lake, I can feel the love and care of Ningbo people for the lake everywhere. It is said that the Moon Lake is the eye of Ningbo, which means that local people love the lake as much as they love their own eyes; it is also said that the lake is the living room of Ningbo, where visitors to the city are usually invited to have a sit. Therefore, the "living room" must be dressed up beautiful, elegant and tasteful, so as to bring the guests a moment of pleasure and a feeling of being at home. Indeed, when a visitor enters the scenic spot renovated in 1998, he/she will strongly feel the careful design of the Moon Lake in each detail. Everything there is naturally and well organized, and each building, whether it be a restored old house or a newly-added building, is appropriately designed. Wandering along the grass, the trees, the bridges and

---

① Zhuyu Islet (Zhuyu, 竹屿) and the Bamboo Islet (Zhuzhou, 竹洲) are both named after the bamboo growing on them. Their Chinese names are distinguished from each other simply by the different characters for the same English word "islet". Therefore, the former is transliterated here so as to avoid confusion.

the lanes while enjoying the graceful scenery, a tourist will be totally pleased.

I have sightseen and experienced the beauty of the lake for quite a few times. For me, its beauty is presented in four aspects: elegance, tranquility, leisure and profoundness.

The Moon Lake is a place of elegance. The lake has indescribable beauty of elegance penetrating your heart. Its elegance is embodied everywhere, in colorful flowers, green trees, verdant gardens, sparkling water, rippling waves, and even in withered trees and old vines, as well as in the buildings like pavilions and terraces. The Moon Lake is like a large private garden, with winding paths to the secluded places or diverse scenes; it is also like a Jiangnan girl, full of fresh, refined and elegant style.

The beauty and elegance of the Moon Lake creates a year-round enchantment. In spring, visitors can see newly sprung grasses and flowers accompanied by willows and poplars with rippled leaves in breeze. In summer, they can find trees in full shade, pleasure boats on the green surface of the lake, and flowers in full blossom. In autumn, tourists can experience the serenity in the bamboo forests, smell the fragrant chrysanthemum, appreciate the moon over the tranquil lake, and enjoy the fine weather with thin clouds and light breeze. In winter, they might meet romantic snow or rain in a beautifully tranquil and cool day. Apparently, compared with the lake in the daytime, the lake at night is my preference. For the night lake, everything is dimmish, especially the reflection of the trees in the water, just like an oil painting or a gouache painting, with ink-like darkness mixed with the green water.

The Moon Lake is a location of tranquility. The lake water is waveless, just like a bright mirror, reflecting everything around the lake. After a blast of breeze, ripples appear, regularly and gradually spreading outward. Thereafter, the surface of the lake restores its quietude and then trees and flowers, again, appear on the surface.

The scenes on and around the lake are all in calmness, a kind of calmness in clamor. Around the lake are Zhongshan Road, Tianyi Square and City God Temple Market, the most hustling and bustling places in downtown Ningbo with dense traffic and noisy crowds, while the lake itself is tranquil with smooth ripples, accompanied by trees of lush and shady leaves and flowers in blossom. As soon as a visitor enters the serene lakeside park, his/her annoyance on the mind would be dispelled along with the noise outside.

When the night falls, the lake in the moonlight looks dimmish. With the moon reflected on the lake and the old trees and buildings around being vague, silence is especially experienced. I, here and now, really want to become a little lotus in the lake, touched by the breeze, swayed by the waves, and nurtured by the dew, merging into unity with the night, the lake and the moon.

The Moon Lake is a resort of leisure. Ningbo is a bustling city, a world-famous oriental port city and a city of brands, and the people here have a very tight schedule, whether they be white-collar workers, civil servants or ordinary workers. As one who has been living in Ningbo for many years, I find that each one here has a lot more work to do owing to manpower shortage. Therefore, the Moon Lake is the right place for them to slow down their pace of life, to get relaxed, and to enjoy leisure. The lake, as a scenic spot, is not enclosed, and no tickets of admission are needed, so people can pay a visit at will. On weekdays, the lake is slightly deserted, with fewer visitors. However, comparing it with the crowded the West Lake where visitors are likely to merely see people instead of the scenes, I prefer the Moon Lake for its quietness. On Sundays, it takes on a bustling look. People flock here to enjoy their leisure moments. Some sing Beijing Opera, some sing Yue Opera, and others sing modern popular songs. They are grouped into different circles, noisy but joyful. The old sit together to have a chat on the issues at home and abroad, and the young enjoy their romantic moments, appreciating flowers or taking photographs. Also, there are some people doing gym, practicing Taichi, playing chess or poker, or strolling along the lake. People visiting here can always enjoy their fun and pleasure. The lakeside park is not only a large garden, but also a great land of pleasure.

The Moon Lake is a place of profoundess. It is a place full of stories, with profound cultural and academic accumulation. Each scene of the lake, and even each corner of the scenic spot has its own background story. For example, the Pine Islet (alias the Bamboo Islet), where the Ningbo No.2 High School is located now, was once home to Lou Yu (楼郁) 1,000 years ago, in the Qingli period (1041–1048) of the Northern Song dynasty (960–1127). During the period, the "Five Masters of the Qingli Period", namely, Yang Shi (杨适), Du Chun (杜醇), Lou Yu, Wang Zhi (王致) and Wang Yue (王说), actively held various academic activities. For more than 30 years, Lou Yu taught batches of local students in the public schools of Mingzhou (now Ningbo), including prefecture and county schools, with the support of Wang Anshi (王安石), the magistrate of Yinxian County. He set up a lecture hall on the Bamboo Islet to disseminate Confucian teachings, and it was said "all the talents of those days were his students". The educational and academic activities of the five masters led to the new atmosphere of Confucian learning in Siming (another name for Mingzhou), laying the foundation for the subsequent development of Zhedong scholarship.

The Fragrant Grass Islet is a small but exquisite place. On the east of the islet is the ancient Huanjin Bridge, while on the west is a newly-built suspended bridge of pine wood, connecting the islet with the outside. On the present islet, visitors can sightsee winding paths, delicate artificial rockeries, pavilions under shade as well as branches reflected in the water. There are two tea houses on both the north and south ends. In the middle are Bizhi Pavillion and Xiangzu Pavilion, while on the waterfront stands Yishui House, which is the most comfortable, feeling like a graceful private courtyard. Historically, the islet was a site for academic education, where the scholars of Siming School[1] held academic and educational activities from the Qingyuan period (1195–1201) to the Jiading period (1208–1224) in the Southern Song

---

[1]   Siming School, a philosophical school focusing on the learning of Lu Jiuyuan's *xinxue* (心学, Neo-Confucian philosophy of the mind).

dynasty. The representatives of Siming School, the "Four Masters"[1], Yang Jian (杨简), Shu Lin (舒璘), Yuan Xie (袁燮) and Shen Huan (沈焕), all gave lectures there. Besides, the reading buildings of book collectors Shi Shouzhi (史守之) and Feng Fang (丰坊) were built there, too. The islet was also a window for Mingzhou scholars to communicate with those from other places. For example, Shen Huan and Lou Yao (楼钥) once invited Lü Zujian (吕祖俭), a representative of Jinhua School, to give lectures at Shi Shouzhi's Bizhi Pavilion. For these events, Quan Zuwang (全祖望) gave a vividly description in his "An Account on the Academy of Three Masters of the Bamboo Islet" (《竹洲三先生书院记》): In the early morning, someone shouted, "Master Lü is here." Then, everyone ran to the bank of the lake to greet him. During his stay, Lü Zujian either gave lectures in the hall, talking with the audience for a whole day, or had a good time in a boat, cruising on the lake. It could be imagined that the academic atmosphere on the islet was active and prosperous, and the life there was full of fun and pleasure. What an attractive thing! At that time, Lü was *jiancang* (监仓)[2] of Mingzhou, living in the east of the city. He made friends and had a close relationship with the Shen brothers, Shen Huan and Shen Bing (沈炳), who often invited him to give lectures there. That's how the scene described above happened.

With so many ancient houses and anecdotes, the Moon Lake is indeed a right place for the people of the present time to have a soul conversation with those from ancient times. If possible, I would like to travel through the time tunnel shown in the science fiction novels, to have a deep conversation with Lou Yu, the forerunner of Mingzhou Confucian education, on his statement "learning is based on exhaustive inquiry into principle (*li*, 理)", and to show him my respect as a modern Ningbo scholar; I would pose questions to Quan

---

[1] The "Four Masters" refer to the "Four Masters of the Chunxi Period" in the reign of Emperor Xiaozong (1162–1198) of the Southern Song dynasty. They were representatives of Siming School which focused on the learning of Lu Jiuyuan's *xinxue*. They were also called the "Four Masters of Yongshang".

[2] *Jiancang*, grain warehouse supervisor.

Zuwang, such a productive historian with sincere affections for the Siming landscape and culture, about the history of the Moon Lake, so as to continue the writing of "Dialogues at the Moon Lake" (《湖语》).

In this sense, the Moon Lake is not only exquisite, with the extrinsic beauty of Jiangnan gardens, but also with profound culture and unique intrinsic beauty.

The Moon Lake has a long history of more than 1,200 years, even longer than the history of Ningbo city. It is justifiably called "the mother lake of Ningbo people", as it is closely tied to their life and social production.

The formation of the pristine Moon Lake was closely related to the construction of water conservancy projects in Ningbo.

Ningbo is located on a coastal plain, with Yaojiang River, Fenghua River and Yongjiang River converging in its town. However, in ancient days, the fresh water here was difficult to store because it drained easily. Therefore, partial droughts happened every year, during which pools and wells all dried out and fresh water was scarce. So it was very difficult to feed people and animals with enough fresh water, let alone the irrigation of farmland. According to *The Siming Book Series: Water Conservancy of Yongshang* (《四明丛书·甬上水利志》), "Ningbo is on the lowest land of saline-alkali soil, and the people here always have difficulty irrigating their farmland", which clearly demonstrates the special geographical environment and the predicament of drought of the Ningbo area. Therefore, generations after generations, people there usually paid much attention to "resisting salinity, storing fresh water, discharging flood and draining waterlogged farmland" by building dams and water gates and by enclosing water of lakes or pools with embankment, so as to reduce the damages from drought or floods. In the Tang dynasty, Ningbo farmland was getting larger along with the increase of population, so it was necessary to carry out water engineering projects in a large scale, so as to meet the needs of economic and social development. In the tenth year of the Zhenguan period (636), Wang Junzhao (王君照), the magistrate of Maoxian County, started building the lake for the first time, but the related details are pitifully unknown today. According to the "Water

Diversion of Ningbo West Lake" (《西湖引水记》) by Shu Dan (舒亶)[1] of the Northern Song dynasty, "Two li[2] to the south of Yinxian County, there was a little lake built by Magistrate Wang Junzhao in the middle of the Zhenguan period. It was probably in the place that is called Xihutou by today's locals. The lake disappeared long ago except its west corner which is now named Ningbo West Lake". In fact, the lake built by Magistrate Wang consisted of two lakes, namely, the Sun Lake and the Moon Lake, and the two lakes had two headstreams: One was from Tuoshanyan Weir in southwestern Yinxian County, and the other from Dalei Village and Lincun Village in eastern Yinxian County. The water from the two sources converged in the southwest of urban Ningbo, forming the two lakes which were together called the South Lake. From the Song dynasty (960–1279), the southern part of the South Lake was called the Sun Lake, and its northwest part Ningbo West Lake or the Mirror Lake. Meanwhile, Ningbo West Lake was also called the Moon Lake because its original shape was said to be like the moon (crescent). Besides, the Sun Lake had long been silted up before it was turned into land.[3]

It can be seen that the original purpose of building the South Lake was to solve the problems of water conservancy and water source in Ningbo.

Nearly 200 years later, in the first year of the Changqing period (821) of the Tang dynasty, Han Cha (韩察), the governor of Mingzhou Prefecture, moved the prefecture office from Xiaoxi Town to Sanjiangkou[4] under the approval of Tang imperial court, where official buildings were constructed along the line from Haishu Tower (now Drum Tower) to where today's Zhongshan Square is, and the core area was enclosed with walls so that the inner city was formed. In the late Tang dynasty, governor Huang Sheng (黄晟) built *luocheng* (the outer city), which is the area within the Ring Road

---

[1]　Shu Dan (舒亶 , 1041–1103), courtesy name Xindao, literary name Lantang, a native of Dayin in Cixi (now in Yuyao, Ningbo).

[2]　The term li (里), a unit of distance, is a half of one kilometer.

[3]　Today's Sun Lake in Ningbo is not the one mentioned above.

[4]　Sanjiangkou, literally the mouth of three rivers. It is where Yongjiang River, Yaojiang River and Fenghua River converge in Ningbo.

of Haishu District today. This marked the formation of the basic pattern of urban Ningbo with "three rivers plus six canals, and a lake at the core".

During the Five Dynasties (907–960), Qian Hongyi (钱弘亿), the tenth son of King Qian Yuanguan (钱元瓘) of the Wuyue State, was appointed the prefect of Mingzhou in the second year of the Qianyou period (949). Later, the Wuyue State was merged into the Song dynasty, and thereafter Qian Hongyi was appointed as the local military governor of Fengguo Army, but he still resided in Mingzhou. During his administration of more than 10 years in Mingzhou, Qian made the Moon Lake take on a new look through large-scale dredging engineering.

During the Yuanyou period (1086–1094) and Shaosheng period (1094–1098) of the Northern Song dynasty, prefect Liu Shu (刘淑) and his successor Liu Cheng (刘珵) dredged the Moon Lake, meanwhile built pavilions and terraces, planted trees and flowers of four seasons, and constructed seven bridges and three causeways to connect the islets with the banks. All these well-proportioned buildings constituted the scenes of the ten islets of the Moon Lake. As a stanza goes, "Enjoying wine and sunny spring days in the well-decorated boats, just as in a jade fairyland with glistening lights of waves." The Moon Lake at that time boasted its prominent function of sightseeing, attracting both men and women tourists. In addition, its function of water conservancy was continually strengthened during the Northern Song and Southern Song dynasties. During the Yuanfeng period (1078–1085) of the Northern Song dynasty, when the lake was dredged, water from Tuoshanyan Weir was diverted to the lake through the Wangjing Gate in the west of the city, so that more than 100,000 urban residents were offered fresh water. In the fifth year of the Baoyou period (1257) of the Southern Song dynasty, in order to regulate the lake water, Xingchun Qi and Baofeng Qi[①] were built to the north and south of the Moon Lake. At present, the former is called Shi Qi, while the latter Yongfeng Qi. Thereby, the residents inside Mingzhou City were provided with

①   Qi means sluice gate.

a complete water supply system for their transportation, irrigation, drinking and washing.

The most famous and oldest relic of water conservancy facilities on the Moon Lake is Shuize Tablet (水则碑)[1]. It is located on the former Pingqiao River along the Chrysanthemum Islet, i.e., beside the crossroads of Zhenming Road and Yingfeng Road today. It is under the stone pavilion in the Pingqiao River with its lower part in water. On the front side of the tablet, there is a Chinese character "平" (*ping*, literally, level), so it is also called Pingzi Tablet. The stone tablet was actually a hydrological observation station in Ningbo more than 700 years ago, founded by Wu Qian (吴潜)[2], the governor of Mingzhou, in the first year of the Kaiqing period (1259) in the Southern Song dynasty.

Ningbo is on a plain with a crisscross river network. In old times, when it rained too much, there would be waterlogging; meanwhile, as a city close to the sea, it had limited fresh water. Therefore, if the fresh water was discharged excessively, it would affect irrigation. That's why Wu Qian set up Shuize Tablet to measure day and night the level of water in Ningbo, so as to decide when to open or close the water gates: water to be discharged when the character *ping* is covered by water and to be stored when it is uncovered. In the name of Shuize Tablet, *ze* means "scale" or "criterion". Sluice gates were the fundamental facilities for the water conservancy of Ningbo, because precious fresh water resources couldn't be discharged randomly. By sluice gates, people discharged water against flood when it overflowed, and they stored water against drought when it became less. Importantly, the time for opening and closing of the water gates must be appropriate, so as to drain or store water accordingly; if the sluice gates were not timely opened or closed, disasters would happen. After the establishment of Shuize Tablet, Wu Qian wrote an inscription titled "On Pingqiao Shuize Tablet" (《平桥水则记》), explaining the reason for engraving *ping* on the stele, and pointing out that the use of sluice gates was the key to

---

[1] Shuize Tablet, used as a water level measuring instrument.

[2] Wu Qian (1196–1262), an expert of water conservancy of the Southern Song dynasty, who was also a national hero and influential poet.

Ningbo water conservancy. He wrote, "So the tablet was positioned under the Pingqiao Bridge, with *ping* on it as a measuring scale. Please keep it there!" In doing so, he earnestly warned the future generations to act in accordance with the tablet so as to ensure the regional safety whether it is in flood or drought.

During his 3 years of administration in Ningbo, Wu Qian was diligent in his work, careful to the people, active in water conservancy, and made great contributions. In the fourth year of the Baoyou period (1256), he presided over the construction of Hongshuiwan Dam as an important causeway against flood in the river. In the same year, Wugong Dam[①] was built. In the next two years, sluice gates and dams were thoroughly maintained in every part of Ningbo. Water conservancy facilities such as Daxi Dam, Beiguo Weir and Chenglang Weir were finished, all of which were directly connected with the water system of the Moon Lake. All these projects were used for blocking salt water and storing fresh water, flood discharge and drainage, and boat transportation. Some of these water conservancy projects, although built more than 700 years ago, are still playing a role today. It can be said that they have brought benefits to the people for generations.

Wu Qian deserves the eternal memory of Ningbo people, and the meritorious deeds of such an outstanding man of talent will forever coexist with the beauty of the Moon Lake.

The benefits of the Moon Lake to Ningbo people also lay in its function as the departure or transit port of boat shipping, the cheapest ancient transportation, due to its connection with the water network around Ningbo, including rivers, ponds and sea. Embarking on a boat from the Moon Lake, one could travel not only to the nearby places in Ningbo, but also to far-away domestic places like Hangzhou and Beijing via the Xitang River, Daxi Dam, Yaojing River and the Grand Canal, and even to foreign countries for international trade. That is just the reason why the former Koryŏ Embassy was built in Baokui Lane near the Moon Lake. Besides, the embassy, an important

---

① Wugong Dam, named after Wu Qian who was respected as Wugong (Master Wu).

relic of the Ningbo Maritime Silk Road, witnessed the cultural exchanges between China and the Korean Peninsula in history.

According to documentary records, in the Tang and Song dynasties, Ningbo "was not a metropolis, though; it was a place where the sea routes converged. Therefore, business ships brought abundant goods from Fujian and Guangdong provinces of the south, from Japan of the east and from Koryŏ of the north". In the Song dynasty, Mingzhou had become one of the three major foreign trade ports alongside Guangzhou and Quanzhou. Although not as busy as Guangzhou, it was the center of trade with Koryŏ and Japan. At that time, tribute ships from Koryŏ and Japan first arrived at Dinghaikou (now Zhenhai) in Mingzhou, entered the Moon Lake after their goods were inspected by *shibo si*[①] and taxes were paid, then reached Hangzhou via the Yuyao River, Cao'e River and Qiantang River, at last got to Kaifeng by canal, and even to Beijing in the Ming dynasty (1368–1644). The tribute ships went to the capital and presented the tributes to the imperial court, which would give a large number of rewards to the visitors. On their way back by the original route, the visitors would transport the rewards to the warehouses at the Moon Lake before they returned to their own countries through the Yongjiangkou (mouth of the Yongjiang River) in the monsoon season. It can be said that the Moon Lake was a transit center for tributes storage and international trade between China and countries like Koryŏ and Japan in ancient times.

In view of the high frequency of tributary trade between Koryŏ and the Song dynasty, Lou Yi (楼异), a Mingzhou native, advised the emperor to set up a Laiyuan Bureau[②] and establish a Koryŏ Embassy in Mingzhou for the trade between the two countries every year. Emperor Huizong adopted his advice and assigned him to Mingzhou as the governor for this mission. After

---

① *Shibo si* (市舶司, Maritime Trade Supervising Department), also known as the Trading-ship Office, functioned as customs at that time.

② Laiyuan Bureau, literally, a bureau for visitors, traders and envoys from afar, especially for those from foreign countries. Now in Ningbo, the relic of Laiyuan Pavilion can still be seen in Jiangxia Park.

Lou Yi took office, he built Koryǒ Embassy near the Moon Lake in seventh year of the Zhenghe period (1117) under the reign of Emperor Huizong. The main function of the embassy was to offer board and lodging for envoys from Koryǒ and provide them with warehouses for storing goods. The establishment of Koryǒ Embassy fully demonstrated the key position of the Moon Lake in foreign trade at that time.

It might be said that from here, the Ningbo people good at business and trade started their glory of Ningbo *bang* (宁波帮)[①] and "Grand Oriental Port".

The Moon Lake is not only a beautiful water area, but also a gathering place of talented people, with profound cultural accumulation and high taste. Therefore, it was praised as "Southeastern Zou-Lu"[②] by Quan Zuwang.

In my opinion, it is moderately realistic to describe the Moon Lake as the "cradle of Zhedong scholarship" for their relationship.

Some claimed that the Moon Lake was "the vital place of Zhedong scholarship". I myself once named it "the sacred place of Zhedong scholarship". It seems that neither of the above ideas is appropriate enough. Now, I prefer to adopt the expression "the cradle of Zhedong scholarship", which might be closer to the truth. My reasons are as follow. As a lake in city, the Moon Lake has beautiful scenery and convenient water transportation, attracting generations of officials and scholars to settle here; meanwhile, the culture and education flourished around the lake along with the establishment of academies, poetry societies and book-collecting buildings (private libraries). A great variety of cultural activities were held one after another, such as academic teaching and discussion, scholarly gathering, poem composing and painting. Diverse cultural activities converged there, involving the studies of Confucianism and Buddhism, writing of prose and poetry, as well as book

---

① Ningbo *bang* (Ningbo Commercial Group) refers to the group of Ningbo merchants who conduct their business at home and abroad.

② Zou, the Zou State in the Warring States Period (475 BCE–221 BCE), was the homeland of Mencius; and Lu, the Lu State in the Spring and Autumn Period (770 BCE–476 BCE), was the homeland of Confucius. "Zou-Lu" is usually used to refer to a place with prosperous culture and education.

collecting. Thereby, within such a small area around the Moon Lake, an excellent atmosphere was formed for academic innovation and development. In modern words, the Moon Lake created various conditions for academic development, including both "hardware" and "software" conditions. These conditions were particularly conducive to scholars' academic innovation. Therefore, it is appropriate to call the Moon Lake "the cradle of Zhedong scholarship".

Moreover, the word "cradle" is both dynamic and static. Zhedong scholarship, like an infant, experienced a process of emergence and formation before growing mature, while it was the profound cultural accumulation around the Moon Lake that provided the basic environment for its growth. However, according to the timeline in history, the development process of Zhedong scholarship was full of ups and downs, and thereby unable to be generalized simply. It is necessary to analyze in detail the academic performances, representatives and achievements of each specific development period of Zhedong scholarship, because each period has its own unique characteristics.

In the Moon Lake scenic spot, what specially impresses me is He *mijian ci* (Temple of He Zhizhang) located beside Ludian Bridge on the Willow Islet. The Moon Lake was excavated in the tenth year of the Zhenguan period (636) under the reign of Emperor Taizong of the Tang dynasty. It is said that He Zhizhang (贺知章), a famous poet of the Tang dynasty, once lived in seclusion here. He's ancestral home was Yongxing (now Xiaoshan) in Yuezhou. In the first year of the Zhengsheng period of the Tang dynasty (695), he was enrolled as *jinshi* (进士)[①] and promoted to the position of *mishujian* (秘书监)[②] in the middle of the Kaiyuan period (713–741). In the third year of the Tianbao period (744), he returned home after his retirement and lived at Xiaoxi Lake (the Creek Lake) of Siming. He Zhizhang was good at poetry and calligraphy and

---

① *Jinshi*, literally, advanced scholar, a title for the nominees who passed *dianshi* (殿试 , the imperial court examination), the highest-level imperial civil service examination.

② Typically, *mijian* (秘监) is short for *mishujian*, director of the Palace Library. That's why He Zhizhang was addressed He *mijian*.

highly praised for his noble character and free lifestyle. Eloquent and fond of drinking, he had a good relationship with famous poets like Du Fu (杜甫) and Li Bai (李白). Li Bai praised him as "Siming yilao" (四明逸老)[①]. He was open-minded and uninhibited, especially in his later years. Thereby, he called himself an "unrestrained man of Siming". The word "Siming" in the self-given title was actually adopted from Siming Mountain in Mingzhou. It reflected his close relationship with the land where he lived. His great affection for his hometown could also been felt in the lines of his poem "On My Way Home" (《回乡偶书》):

> While I left young, old I am back at home.
>
> My accent the same, but my hair is graying.
>
> Children don't know me, a smile in greeting,
>
> "Hello, my dear guest, where are you from?"

He Zhizhang was a big celebrity. Naturally, a monument would be built to commemorate him over his relationship with the Moon Lake. Therefore, the local officials of Mingzhou built the Yilao Hall to honor him. Another monument about him was the Temple of He Zhizhang rebuilt in the fourth year of the reign of Emperor Tongzhi (1865) in the Qing dynasty (1616–1911), which is still kept well today. This is a wonderful story about the famous poet He Zhizhang and the Moon Lake.

Nevertheless, Mingzhou in the Tang dynasty did not enjoy high cultural status. It was in the Northern Song and Southern Song dynasties that the Moon Lake culture saw its prosperous development and rapid rise.

In the middle of the Jiayou period (ca. 1060) under the reign of Emperor Renzong of the Song dynasty, the governor Qian Gongfu (钱公辅) rebuilt the Willow Islet on a large scale and built Zhongle Pavilion on it. Sima Guang (司马光), an important imperial official, composed a poem named "Zhongle Pavilion" (《众乐亭》) to Qian Gongfu for his effort on the scenes of the lake:

---

①   Siming yilao, an old man of leisure in Siming.

The bridge turns the otherwise waste islet into an attraction,

And splendid buildings appear out of the overgrown grass.

With good friends meeting here in such a wonderful scene,

The islet so charming is no more as deserted as it was.

Better to have more visitors come here and have fun,

Cause it's annoying for others just to enjoy yourself along.

Wonder how your achievements are known?

Music and songs are here and there on the waterfront.

By this poem, Sima Guang highly praised the scenery and atmosphere of the lake rebuilt by Qian Gongfu. So it can be seen that the Moon Lake had already become a popular place for sightseeing by that time.

In the third lunar month of the second year of the Qingli period (1042), Wang Anshi was enrolled as *jinshi*, and then appointed as *jiedu panguan* (节度判官)[①] of Huainan. Later, he was transferred to Yinxian County as the magistrate. As a man of integrity, he was strict in law enforcement and did lots of deeds beneficial to the local people of Ningbo. For example, he organized local workers to build causeways and dig ponds so as to improve irrigation system and facilitate transportation. In times of famine, he ordered to loan the grain stored in the official storehouse to farmers at a low interest rate to solve the difficulties of the people in getting through the famine. During his tenure as the magistrate of Yinxian County, Wang Anshi set up a county school on the Bamboo Islet to greatly promote education, and assigned Lou Yu, one of the "Five Masters of the Qingli Period", to work in it as a lecturer. Wang Anshi's measures and the teaching activities of the "Five Masters" could be viewed as the starting point of the great development of Confucian education in Siming, and also laid the early foundation for the emergence and formation of "Zhejiang scholarship" featured with unique academic style.

In the middle and late years of the Northern Song dynasty, Mingzhou's economy got a higher status, much more developed than that of the Tang

---

① *Jiedu panguan*, assistant to the Military Commissioner.

dynasty and the Five Dynasties. Along with the economic development, the population of Mingzhou largely increased, and a large number of mansions appeared around the Moon Lake. During this period, the function of recreation of the lake was highlighted. Bridges and pavilions were built on causeways, trees and flowers were planted on the bank, and buildings like Honglian Pavilion, Zhongle Pavilion, Chongchong West Bridge and Chongchong East Bridge were successively completed. During the Yuanyou and Shaosheng periods in the reign of Emperor Zhezong of the Song dynasty, the prefect Liu Shu and his successor Liu Cheng rebuilt the lake and enlarged the numbers of islets to ten, laying a foundation for today's scale.

In the Southern Song dynasty, the imperial court moved to the south, and settled the capital in Lin'an. Therefore, Mingzhou and Yuezhou, the close areas, became the backyard of the imperial capital, and the Moon Lake thereupon witnessed the great prosperity of its own culture.

During this period, libraries, academies and poetry societies were successively established on the north and south of the Moon Lake, and Buddhist temples, Taoist temples and folk temples also appeared around the lake. In particular, those great royal and aristocratic families, including the Shi family, played an important role in promoting the prosperity of the Moon Lake culture.

The Shi family lived in today's Baokui Lane and nearby. Shi Hao (史浩) was appointed prime minister twice, in charge of court administration. He became a very important minister trusted by the emperor for his great achievements in decision-making. Advocating flexible administration in his tenure, Shi Hao firstly defended the innocence of Zhao Ding (赵鼎) and Li Guang (李光)[1], and then claimed that Yue Fei (岳飞)[2] had been wronged for a long time, suggesting to rehabilitate them, restore their original titles, and

---

[1] Zhao Ding, Li Guang, Li Gang (李纲) and Hu Quan (胡铨) were together called the "Four Famous Ministers of the Southern Song Dynasty". All of them belonged to the warring faction in the war against nomadic Jurchen (the Jin dynasty, 1115–1234).

[2] Yue Fei (岳飞 , 1103–1142), one of China's greatest generals in the Song dynasty.

take care of their descendants. When Shi Hao retired, Emperor Xiaozong of the Song dynasty granted him a piece of music named "The Bamboo Islet of the Moon Lake", and constructed Zhenyin Temple with a small fortune for him. Meanwhile, Shi Hao himself built Huaguo Temple on the Moon Islet. He also built Chenkui Pavilion (later called Baokui Temple) to hold imperial edicts and inscriptions from the emperor. Besides, he built a mansion on the Chrysanthemum Islet as his own residence. Many of his sons and grandsons also built mansions around the lake. By this, it can be seen that the Shi family was powerful and greatly influential at that time. In addition, Shi Hao was a high-ranking official of high cultural literacy, enthusiastic about Confucianism. At that time, the leading representatives of *Zhuxue*[①], *Luxue*[②] and Yongjia School[③], such as Zhu Xi (朱熹), Lu Jiuyuan (陆九渊)[④] and Ye Shi (叶适)[⑤], were all recommended by Shi Hao to serve the imperial court. Shi Hao invited Shen Huan and Yang Jian to give lectures in his residences on the Bamboo Islet or the Chrysanthemum Islet. In particular, with the great support from the Shi family, Yang Jian taught and propagated *Luxue* in Siming for more than 20 years, cultivating a large number of Confucian talents. He also made great achievements in his *xinxue*[⑥] theory. Under the initiative of Shi Hao,

---

① *Zhuxue* (朱学), Zhu Xi's Neo-Confucianism.

② *Luxue* (陆学), Lu Jiuyuan's Neo-Confucian philosophy of the mind.

③ Yongjia School, aka. Yongjia School of Practice or Yongjia School of Utility, was a Confucian school formed in Yongjia (now Wenzhou) of eastern Zhejiang during the Southern Song dynasty. It was led by Ye Shi.

④ Lu Jiuyuan (陆九渊, 1139–1193), respected as Master Xiangshan, was a *xinxue* scholar of the Southern Song dynasty. He was a rival of his contemporary Zhu Xi, a great Neo-Confucian, whose academic focus was the learning of heavenly principle (*lixue*, 理学). Lu's thought was revised and refined three centuries later by Wang Yangming (王阳明), a *xinxue* scholar of the Ming dynasty, and then evolved into a systematic academic school called Lu-Wang School. It was opposed to the other great and dominant school called Cheng-Zhu School, which was named after its leading philosophers Cheng Yi (程颐), Cheng Hao (程颢) and Zhu Xi.

⑤ Ye Shi (叶适, 1150–1223) was a presentative of Yongjia School. He stressed the philosophy of practice and benefits.

⑥ *Xinxue* means the learning of heart-mind. It refers to the Neo-Confucian philosophy of the mind, one of the two major branches of Neo-Confucianism. The other major branch is *lixue*, the learning of heavenly principle.

academies around the Moon Lake were well and fully developed. Along with the emergence of Siming School represented by Yang Jian, Shu Lin, Shen Huan and Yuan Xie, Ningbo became the national center of *Luxue* in China.

Shi Mengqing (史蒙卿) was one of Shi Migong (史弥巩)'s grandsons, and their family was a gentry clan of Siming. Most of the decedents of the Shi family were the disciples of *xinxue* scholar Yang Cihu (杨慈湖)[1] until Shi Mengqing's turn to *Zhuxue*. Shi Mengqing's academic turn was associated with the trend of the era during the reign of Emperor Lizong (1224–1264) of the Song dynasty, when *Zhuxue* was treated as the orthodox study. In the process of spreading *Zhuxue*, Shi Mengqing fostered numerous Confucian talents in Siming area, among whom were the well-known brothers Cheng Duanli (程端礼) and Cheng Duanxue (程端学).

Wang Yinglin (王应麟) and Huang Zhen (黄震), contemporaries of Shi Mengqing's, also tended towards *lixue* and *Zhuxue*. Wang Yinglin, who lived in the present-day Shangshu Street near the Moon Lake, was a knowledgeable scholar and master of textual research (*kaojuxue*, 考据学) in Mingzhou during the Song and Yuan dynasties. Deriving from the ideas of Lü Zuqian (吕祖谦), a representative of Jinhua School, Wang's scholarship was "broad in horizon", and "not limited to just one school". He comprehensively integrated the ideas from Confucian classics, history, as well as commentaries and records, from the various pre-Qin schools of thought, and even from Buddhism and Taosim.

As a famous scholar in the late years of the Southern Song dynasty, Huang Zhen was the founder of Dongfa School, a branch of Zhedong *Zhuxue* School. Huang once stayed temporarily near the Moon Lake before he led a secluded life in the Baozhuang[2] Mountain. Although Huang Zhen was a follower of *Zhuxue*, his study covered a larger and broader academic area. Proficient in Confucian classics and historical studies, he made great contributions to the

---

[1]   Yang Cihu is the literary name of Yang Jian.

[2]   It is literally supposed to be pronounced as "Baochuang" (referring to the stone columns engraved with Buddhist scriptures). It is here transliterated as "Baozhuang" according to the local pronunciation of Ningbo natives.

study of Confucian classics, Neo-Confucianism and history. Huang's studies were then spread by his disciples such as Yang Weizhen (杨维桢) and Cheng Jing (陈樫).

In the Ming and Qing dynasties, the Moon Lake culture showed a trend of expansion in its development, although its status was no more as high as that in the Southern Song dynasty. Meanwhile, from the view of a larger range of Ningbo, Zhedong scholarship, as a national leading academic school, reached its new peak due to the rise of Wang Yangming[1] and Huang Zongxi (黄宗羲)[2].

In the Southern Song dynasty, the Shi family played a leading role in the rise and development of the Moon Lake culture, while in the Ming and Qing dynasties, the role of small and medium-sized aristocratic families became more and more prominent; the Moon Lake culture was no longer limited to the surrounding areas of the ten islets of the Moon Lake, and its spatial scope was greatly expanded. Besides, due to the adjustment of the national political and economic pattern, along with the economic development and cultural popularization in every local area of Ningbo, the Moon Lake was no more as influential as it had been in the Southern Song dynasty when it was viewed as a national cultural and academic center (of *Luxue*, for example). However, the status of the Moon Lake in the culture and scholarship of this period still could not be underestimated, in view of the great role of Tianyi Pavilion[3] established near the Moon Lake and the influential activities of academic scholars like Huang Zongxi and Quan Zuwang at the Moon Lake and in other areas of

---

[1] Wang Yangming (王阳明, 1472–1529), also known as Wang Shouren, is well-known for his interpretation of the Neo-Confucianism based on the *xinxue* theory. His philosophical doctrines, emphasizing understanding of the world from within the mind, were in direct conflict with *lixue* espoused by Zhu Xi, the outstanding and highly esteemed Neo-Confucian philosopher of the twelfth century (*cf.* Chapter Three).

[2] Huang Zongxi (黄宗羲, 1610–1695), respected as Master Lizhou after his literary name, was one of the foremost Chinese scholars in history studies during the transitional period between the Ming and Qing dynasties (*cf.* Chapter Five).

[3] Tianyi Pavilion (天一阁), an important representative of Ningbo's historical value. It is the oldest existing private library in China, with a collection of approximately 300,000 volumes of various ancient books, including more than 80,000 volumes of rare ones. It has exerted a profound influence on other libraries in China.

Ningbo.

Siming scholars and officials had a traditional hobby of collecting books. In the Song dynasty, there were book-collecting buildings (private libraries) like Lou Yao's Donglou Building and Shi Shouzhi's Bizhi Pavilion at the Moon Lake. During this period, Siming became one of the national centers for the block printing of books, and the books of high quality were mostly printed in Yinxian and Yuyao. In the Qing dynasty, many famous book-collecting buildings had an enormous collection of books, including Huang Zongxi's Xuchao Hall, Zheng Xing (郑性)'s Erlao Pavilion, Huang Chengliang (黄澄量)'s Wugui Building, Lu Zhi (卢址)'s Baojing Building, and Xu Shidong (徐时栋)'s Shuibei Pavilion. Up to the modern times, there were still such buildings, and one of them was Feng Mengzhuan (冯孟颛)'s Fufu Room. In particular, Tianyi Pavilion near the Moon Lake was established by Fan Qin (范钦) of the Ming dynasty, and it is now known as the earliest private library in existence in China. In the pavilion, there are over 300,000 volumes of ancient books, including 70,000 volumes collected by Fan Qin himself. It has been more than 400 years since it was established in the forty-fifth year of Emperor Jiajing (1566) of the Ming dynasty. It is inconceivable how much it experienced through so many wars, chaos and changes. Up to today, the library is still standing there, within which the books are well preserved with book scent. Obviously, it is impossible for the library to remain well-protected without the deep love for books—the main carrier of human civilization in those ages—or the strictest regulations to be practically followed.

Well matched with the Moon Lake, Tianyi Pavilion, the world-famous private library also played an important role in the cultural and academic construction of Siming. Scholars like Huang Zongxi, Wan Sitong (万斯同), Quan Zuwang, Qian Daxin (钱大昕)[1] and Ruan Yuan (阮元) all paid a visit to it, and enjoyed their extensive reading there; besides, when the *Complete*

---

[1]   Qian Daxin (钱大昕, 1728–1804), courtesy name Xiaozheng/Jizhi and literary name Xinmei, is a historian, educator and representative of Qian-Jia School, an academic school during the reign of Emperors Qianlong and Jiaqing of the Qing dynasty.

Library in the Four Branches of Literature (《四库全书》)[1] was compiled in the Qing dynasty, a large number of ancient rare books were picked from this library for reference.

Huang Zongxi was a great scholar of innovative spirit. As a Yuyao native, he achieved great success in Ningbo by establishing and running the Yongshang Zhengren Academy with his good friend Wan Tai (万泰). Meanwhile, he created a brand-new school of history studies in eastern Zhejiang. He traveled between Yuyao and Ningbo, giving lectures at Wan's residence near the Moon Lake. Many of his disciples were also living near the lake, including Zhang Ruyi (张汝翼), Chen Xigu (陈锡嘏), Chen Ruxian (陈汝贤), Zhang Shixun (张士埙), Zhang Shipei (张士培), Zhang Xikun (张锡锟), Wan Sida (万斯大) and Wan Jing (万经). Surely, the traces of the activities of the early-Qing Zhedong School founded by Huang Zongxi can still be found around the Moon Lake today.

Quan Zuwang was born in the north of the Mist Islet at the Moon Lake. As a famous historian in the middle of the Qing dynasty and an important representative of Zhedong School, Quan inherited and carried forward the academic thoughts of Huang Zongxi and Wan Sitong. After reading *Jieqiting Collection* (《鲒埼亭集》) he wrote and *Continued Collection of Ancient Yongshang Poems* (《续甬上耆旧诗》)[2] he compiled, readers could feel the author's incomparable love and affection for his hometown and the Moon Lake. Many articles in *Jieqiting Collection* were written to memorize or trace the history of a fact or a thing in his hometown, like a temple, a tablet, a pavilion, a family, a historical event or even a tree. As a man of great gift and talent, he devoted himself to the collection of the anecdotes of his hometown as well as the poems and essays of his excellent fellow-townsmen in the past. About

---

[1] The book series *Complete Library in the Four Branches of Literature* is composed of the books of four branches, namely, *jing* (经 , Confucian classics), *shi* (史 , historical records), *zi* (子 , philosophical writings) and *ji* (集 , miscellaneous works).

[2] It is a sequel to the *Collection of Ancient Yongshang Poems* (《甬上耆旧诗》) complied by Hu Wenxue (胡文学) and Li Yesi (李邺嗣) of the Qing dynasty.

the famous historical relics or anecdotes at the Moon Lake, he wrote a large number of accounts: "The Stele Inscription on the Yilao Hall of He Zhizhang" (《贺公逸老堂碑铭》), "The Stele Inscription on the Longshen Temple on Bizhi" (《碧沚龙神庙碑铭》), "The Tablet Inscription on Yan Dunfu Temple on the Bamboo Islet" (《竹洲晏尚书庙碑》), "An Inscription on the Back of the Tablet for the Temple of Four Masters of the Chunxi Period" (《淳熙四先生祠堂碑阴文》), "An account on the Academy of Three Masters of the Bamboo Islet", "An Account on Yang Wenyuan Academy on Bizhi" (《碧沚杨文元公书院记》), "An Inscription on the Back of Wu Qian's Shuize Tablet" (《吴丞相水则碑阴》, "On Shuiyun Pavilion" (《水云亭记》), "On the Relic of Siming Dongtian/Zhenyin Temple" (《真隐观洞天古迹记》), "An Account on the Rebuilding of Zhongle Pavilion" (《重修众乐亭记》), "An Account on the Rebuilding of Shizhou (Ten Islets) Pavilion" (《重修十洲阁记》), "Taohua (Peach Blossom) Causeway" (《桃花堤记》), "On the Ten Islets of Xihu Lake (the Moon Lake) at Yinxian County" (《鄞西湖十洲志》), "Dialogues at the Moon Lake", etc. Especially in the "Dialogues at the Moon Lake", Quan Zuwang, in form of dialogues of two persons, clearly depicted the picture of the Moon Lake with his deep love for it—its formation and headstreams, its interesting places and anecdotes, its local products, its water conservancy and its related historical figures—leaving a wealth of documents for the studies on the Moon Lake.

During the late Qing dynasty and the Republican period (1912–1949), China was a semi-colonial and semi-feudal society, in which the government, naturally, had no time to take into account the protection and dredging of the Moon Lake. Meanwhile, the aristocratic families, as a folk force protecting the Moon Lake before this period, tended to decline. Therefore, the Moon Lake, encountered with threats of siltation, lakebed shallowing and area shrinking, lost its otherwise gorgeous scenery, although some new mansions were built along the side of the lake such as Yintaidi Mansion, Jiang's Mansion, Lu's Mansion and Weng's Mansion.

However, during this period, some experienced patriots in Ningbo, who were concerned about the situations of the country and the people, were attempting to introduce into China the advanced Western culture, while inheriting the Chinese traditional culture, so as to save the nation from risks and to urge China onto the road of modernization towards strength and civilization. Their efforts were also clearly reflected in the construction of Moon Lake culture, and the prominent landmark event was the establishment of Bianzhi Academy and Yuehu Academy. In the fifth year under the reign of Emperor Guangxu (1879) of the Qing dynasty, Zong Yuanhan (宗源翰), the governor of Ningbo, established Bianzhi Academy, where six disciplines were taught: *Hanxue* (the Han studies)[①], *Songxue* (the Song studies)[②], art of writing, history, geography, and astronomy & calendar. These disciplines included both traditional Chinese culture and Western new knowledge. That was the first step towards modern education, although traditional culture was still very influential at the moment. But after all, people started to accept the things from Western culture. In the thirty-first year of Emperor Guangxu's reign (1905), educators like Zhang Meiyi (张美翊) and Chen Xunzheng (陈训正) changed Yuehu Academy into Ningbo Normal School. In the first year of the Republican period (1912), the county-owned Women's Normal School was founded on the original site of Bianzhi Academy. In this way, the academy system, which had been brilliant for thousands of years in the history of the Moon Lake, was replaced by the modern school system. Obviously, this change also indicated the transformation of Ningbo into a modern society.

"Along with the breeze on the Moon Lake, the scent of books wafted for thousand years." The Moon Lake culture has a long history and rich connotation, breeding the excellent humanistic spirit of Ningbo. Quan Zuwang, who had a deep love and understanding for the lake, once said, "The lake

---

① *Hanxue* (汉学), literally, the Han studies, focuses on the interpretation of the Confucian texts mainly with philological methods (*xungu*, 训诂). It relies exclusively on the originals of the transmitted Confucian Classics that were created during the Han dynasty (206 BCE–220 CE).

② *Songxue* (宋学), literally, the Song studies, is also known as *daoxue* (道学, the learning of the way) or Neo-Confucianism of the Song dynasties. Different from *Hanxue*, it focuses on the analysis of main ideas, righteous principles and normative principles in Confucian classics.

is so still and deep, enough to wash the *daoxin* (the heart-mind of *dao*); so clean, enough to purify the moral integrity; and so subtly misty, enough to understand the heavenly mystery." Accordingly, *daoxin* is moral idea, the "moral integrity" is the practice of moral ideas, and the "heavenly mystery" refers to the "opportunity in the changing times". "Understand the heavenly mystery" could be interpreted as the pioneer spirit in a new era. For centuries, this kind of humanistic spirit bred in the Moon Lake culture has been influencing the value orientation of future generations. The belief of Ningbo *bang* in honest commercial operation and active donation to their hometown, Ningbo people's spirit of venerating learning and encouraging the good, as well as their opening-up consciousness all demonstrate the spiritual essence of eastern Zhejiang culture. The people of Ningbo, closely associated with the Moon Lake, will definitely continue to promote this spirit, going forward ceaselessly for a brilliant future, whether it be hardship or difficulty ahead.

II. Origin and Characteristics of Zhedong Scholarship

The term "Zhedong scholarship" is not coming from nowhere. It is a concept with rich connotations. It is rooted in a profound economic, social and cultural base.

Zhedong is a geographical term. The names of Zhedong (eastern Zhejiang) and Zhexi (western Zhejiang) originated in the Tang and Song dynasties. It is related to the name of "Zhejiang River" (Qiantang River today). Originally, Zhejiang as a province was named after a river called Zhejiang River in its boarders. It was in the territory of the Yue State in the Spring and Autumn Period (770 BCE–476 BCE). Later it was merged into the Chu State in the Warring States Period (475 BCE–221 BCE), and then it became a region of Kuaiji *jun* (郡)[①] before it was merged into Minzhong *jun* in the Qin dynasty (221 BCE–206 BCE). Thereafter, it was governed by Yangzhou *cishi bu* (刺史 部, department of regional inspection)[②] in the Han dynasty, and it was divided into two *dao* (道) in the Tang dynasty: eastern Zhejiang *dao* and western Zhejiang *dao*. Up to the Song dynasty, it belonged to *Liangzhe lu* (路) before it was divided into eastern Zhejiang *lu* and western Zhejiang *lu*. In the Yuan dynasty (1206–1368), it was a part of Jiangzhe *xingzhongshu sheng* (行中书 省), while in the Ming dynasty, it became Zhejiang *buzhengshi si* (布政使司). Finally, it got its present name Zhejiang Province in the Qing dynasty. What is called Zhedong generally refers to the area in the east of Qiantang River, covering present-day Ningbo, Shaoxing, Zhoushan, Taizhou, Wenzhou, Lishui, Jinhua and Quzhou. In the past, these areas were called "Upper Eight *fu* (府)"

---

① *Jun*, prefecture. The Qin empire was divided into 36 *jun*, under which were a number of *xian* (县 , counties).

② The *cishi* system was created during the Former Han dynasty (206 BCE–25 CE) in order to control and supervise the officials in the 13 *zhou* (州).

by Zhejiang folks in accordance with their eight administrative divisions (*fu*), namely, Ningbo *fu*, Shaoxing *fu*, Taizhou *fu*, Wenzhou *fu*, Chuzhou (Lishui) *fu*, Wuzhou (Jinhua) *fu*, Yanzhou (Jiande) *fu* and Quzhou *fu*, while the areas of Zhexi, namely, Hangzhou, Huzhou and Jiaxing, were called "Lower Three *fu*".

China is a large country of a vast territory with vastly different regional characteristics. But in general, the main way of living for Chinese people is farming. Thereby, China is defined as an agricultural society. In this farming-dominated country, it is natural to see the dominance of Confucian culture featured with gentleness and honesty.

However, in spite of the overall pattern of economy, society and culture of this country, the differences among various regions cannot be ignored.

Located on the southeast coast of China, eastern Zhejiang in the past had plains, basins, mountains and coasts in its terrain. It was a marginal zone in ancient China when the middle and lower reaches of the Yellow River were regarded as Central Plains. Correspondingly, its culture was also marginal in the larger culture picture of China dominated by Confucianism. Most inland areas of China were suitable for plantation industry, and that's why the farming-dominated culture was formed. However, in eastern Zhejiang the ways of production and living were diversified because it had a complex terrain featuring many mountainous and coastal areas. Especially in its plain areas, the commodity economy and trade were well developed due to its smooth water transportation and convenient coastal ports. Therefore, the traditional views of emphasizing agriculture and restraining commerce had little influence upon the people there who, on the contrary, agreed with the idea that "both agriculture and commerce are essential". Thus, different from the inland area with an agriculture-dominated culture, eastern Zhejiang had a "mixed culture of agriculture and commerce".

Moreover, due to its marginal location, eastern Zhejiang was culturally lagging behind the Central Plains in the north, and it was just a receiver of the culture disseminated and transplanted from the latter. Therefore, the academic culture of eastern Zhejiang was not a pure original culture, but an "innovative transplanted culture".

Located in a mountainous and coastal area, Siming area boasted crisscross river networks and fertile farmlands. The locals there made a living by planting crops, fishing in the sea and conducting trade activities. With an open mind and a broad vision, they flexibly and proudly received both continental and marine cultures. The stronger the contrast is, the more the people would think. Siming people, half from mainland and half from ocean, were particularly enlightened and inspired by such a great contrast between the two heterogeneous civilizations. In today's fashionable words, "innovation" was the main "melody" of traditional Siming culture. That is to say, Siming had an advantageous foundation for the creative development of its regional culture. This could be viewed as Ningbo's unique "blended land-sea culture" resulting from the interaction between land and marine cultures.

To sum up, for eastern Zhejiang, including Siming region, the basic pattern and inherent characteristics of its cultural formation and development were based on the convergence of marginal culture, agriculture-commerce culture, innovative transplanted culture and blended land-sea culture.

The concept of Zhedong scholarship indicates some similarity and consistency in academic tendency. In ancient China, due to the inconvenient traffic, communication was difficult, so were the exchanges of information among scholars. However, without necessary academic discussion, it would be uneasy for scholars to exert mutual influence upon each other's academic tendencies, or to reach a certain agreement. In this case, exchanges between teachers and students became the most convenient way. Therefore, the schools based on similar or consistent views were usually formed through teacher-student relationship. Besides, geo-social relationship was another significant factor. In history, Zhu Xi was the first to put forward the concept of *Zhexue* (Zhejiang scholarship). He once argued that Zhejiang scholars had a similar academic tendency, i.e., they paid much attention to historical studies, and had a preference for practical pursuits. For example, Lü Zuqian in his own studies combined Chen Liang (陈亮)'s[1] learning with Ye Shi's. Whereas Ye Shi's Yongjia School paid attention to the textual research of historical governing systems, Chen Liang of Yongkang School focused on the kingly way of ruling and the political supremacy of sovereignty based on its observation on the events of previous dynasties. And both of their ideas were adopted by Lü Zuqian. Obviously, Zhu Xi noticed that the similar academic tendency of Zhejiang scholars resulted from their more chances of discussions and exchanges due to their geographical proximity.

The concept of *Zhexue*, since it was put forth by Zhu Xi, had exerted great influence upon the scholars such as Ye Shi, a contemporary scholar, and Liu Xun (刘埙), a Jiangxi scholar of the late Song and early Yuan dynasties, who both accepted this concept. Besides, this expression was repeatedly mentioned in Quan Zuwang's *Scholarly Annals of the Song and Yuan Dynasties* (《宋元学案》). So it could be said that this term had long been accepted by scholars.

The term "Zhedong scholarship" also means a special style in academic learning. The scholars in eastern Zhejiang did not copy thoroughly all the theories introduced from the outside. Instead, they emphasized innovation with local features based on their own independent thinking and better mastery of them.

According to the existing documents, the concept of "Zhedong scholarship" was formally put forth and demonstrated by the Qing scholar Zhang Xuecheng (章学诚)[2], who himself was a follower of *Zhexue*. He argued:

> Although Zhedong scholarship derived from Wuyuan[3], most of its scholars, from the time of Yuan Xie and his two sons Yuan Su (袁肃) and

---

[1]　Chen Liang (陈亮, 1143–1194) was the founder of Yongkang School in the Southern Song dynasty. He stressed a more practical application of philosophical thought.

[2]　Zhang Xuecheng (章学诚, 1738–1801), given name Wenbiao/Wenmao, courtesy name Shizhai, literary name Shaoyan, was a historian and litterateur in the Qing dynasty and a native of Kuaiji (now Shaoxing).

[3]　Wuyuan, the name of Zhu Xi's hometown, here is used to refer to Zhu Xi and his learning of *lixue*.

Yuan Fu (袁甫), began to follow Lu Jiuyuan and his brother Lu Jiuling
(陆九龄) of Jiangxi Province. Zhedong scholars were proficient in Confucian
classics, familiar with traditional culture but unwilling to talk about virtue and
human nature in empty words, so their learning was still compatible with Zhu
Xi's teachings. However, the ideas of Wang Yangming started to deviate from
Zhu Xi's theory in the process of developing Mencius's concept of *liangzhi*
(良知)[1]. Thereafter, Liu Zongzhou (刘宗周)[2] of Jishan (now in Shaoxing)
developed *liangzhi* into *shendu* (慎独)[3], which was different from, but not
totally contradictory with, Zhu Xi's doctrines. Liu's disciple, Huang Zongxi
of Lizhou (now in Yuyao), who was the teacher of Wang Sitong (万斯同)
and his brother Wan Sida in Confucian classics and history, also followed
the learning of Lu Jiuyuan without contradicting Zhu Xi's thought, so that
later scholars like Quan Zuwang still held Huang's ideas. However, Mao
Qiling (毛奇龄)[4] of Xihe (now Xiaoshan), in spite of his great achievements
in the learning of *liangzhi*, excessively criticized Zhu Xi's theory due to his
academic sectarianism. Therefore, even Zhedong scholars disapproved of
his views. (Excerpted from "Zhedong Scholarship" [《浙东学术》], Vol.
V of *General Interpretation of Historiography* [《文史通义》] by Zhang
Xuecheng.)

As seen from above, all the learning that belonged to the Zhejiang
academic system during the Ming and Qing dynasties was generally named
as "Zhedong scholarship" by Zhang Xuecheng. He listed a series of its
representatives, including Wang Yangming, Liu Zongzhou, Huang Zongxi,
Wan Sitong and Quan Zuwang, and demonstrated their common academic
characteristic: "Following Lu Jiuyuan's ideas without deviating from Zhu

[1] According to Wang Yangming, "*liangzhi*" means the "innate knowledge of the good". The term
was derived from Mencius's expression "*liangzhi*" as "innate, ethically relevant knowledge".
[2] Liu Zongzhou (刘宗周 , 1578–1645), courtesy name Qidong, literary name Niantai, respected as
Master Jishan, was a Neo-Confucian of the late Ming dynasty.
[3] *Shendu*, vigilant solitude. Liu Zongzhou put forward the concept of *shendu*.
[4] Mao Qiling (毛奇龄 , 1623–1716), courtesy name Dake, respected as Master Xihe, was a philosopher
of the early Qing dynasty.

Xi's theory." Zhang Xuecheng made a great academic impact for his precise interpretation on the concept of "Zhedong scholarship" and his accurate summary of its academic characteristic.

In modern times, to generalize the studies in Zhejiang academic system, scholars proposed concepts such as "Zhedong historical studies" and "Zhedong School". For example, in 1932, He Bingsong (何炳松), a scholar of Jinhua in eastern Zhejiang, published *The Origin of Zhedong School* (《浙东学派溯源》), which could be viewed as a landmark achievement in the systematic reviewing of Zhedong scholarship. In 1993, a book named *A Study on Zhedong School* (《浙东学派研究》) was published by Zhejiang scholars Wang Fengxian (王凤贤) and Ding Guoshun (丁国顺), and in 1996, Fang Zuyou (方祖猷) published the *Collected Papers on the Early-Qing Zhedong School* (《清初浙东学派论丛》), in which the author introduced quite a few Zhedong scholars of the Qing dynasty. It can be seen that the term "Zhedong School" was popular in the 1990s.

Whether it be *"Zhexue"*, "Zhedong scholarship", "Zhedong historical studies" or "Zhedong School", all these titles refer to the learning system that originated, spread and evolved in eastern Zhejiang. Generally, this system was distinctive from any other academic schools or paradigms in other areas of China. It was only out of research needs that the scholars named it differently, so as to make a distinction based on the focuses of different periods or the scholars of different academic backgrounds. The term "school" focused on the description of inheritance, specialization, and systematization of knowledge. Therefore, it had great limitations in its use in view of the restricted sense of "knowledge inheritance". Nevertheless, in a loose way, the concept of "Zhedong School" was available, maybe more convenient, especially when outside scholars viewed Zhejiang academic and cultural system as an integrated, homogeneous cognitive object. However, researchers in Ningbo tended to use the term "Zhedong scholarship" which, in a wider range, covered each different aspect of the learning system in eastern Zhejiang. In this sense, "Zhedong scholarship" was a more accurate and appropriate concept to refer to the ancient learning system in Zhejiang.

From above, the so-called "Zhedong scholarship" is a general name for various systematic and specialized learning or knowledge that has emerged, formed, and evolved with ups and downs in eastern Zhejiang.

"Zhedong scholarship", as well as its representative scholars and schools, played an important role in the intellectual and cultural history during the Song, Ming and Qing dynasties, and also exerted a great impact on the development of Modern China. He Bingsong argued, "In my opinion, Zhedong School was the most glorious in the academic history of China." Zhedong scholarship is not only regional, but also national, and could be viewed as the essence of Chinese scholarship. The study on the Zhedong academic history is a cornerstone for the research of Chinese academic history.

In terms of its development process, Zhedong scholarship went through a long period before it began to rise in the Southern Song dynasty. In the Ming and Qing dynasties, it became top-ranking in China with its great academic achievements created by a large number of talented scholars in eastern Zhejiang.

As early as 6,000 or 7,000 years ago, the ancestors of Zhejiang people lived in Hemudu area beside the Yaojiang River, where they created the world-known "Hemudu Culture". From then on to the Spring and Autumn Period, Shaoxing area became the birthplace of ancient Yue culture, where there appeared famous politicians, thinkers and reformers such as Goujian (勾践), Fan Li (范蠡), Wen Zhong (文种) and Ji Ran (计然).

Regionally, Zhedong scholars mainly gathered in Kuaiji and nearby areas in the Han and Tang dynasties, and culture in other areas was less developed. During this period, the main representatives of Zhedong scholarship were Wang Chong (王充), Yu Shinan (虞世南), Zhi Ji (智觊), etc.

In the Song and Yuan dynasties, the academic culture of eastern Zhejiang achieved considerable development, which was reflected in the fact that this area became an academic center where scholarly groups started to form. During this period, eastern Zhejiang earned a very important academic status, and gradually became an indispensable part like other culturally prosperous regions in China. Benefiting from the Song imperial court's policy of valuing intellectuals and encouraging education, Zhedong scholarship, thereafter, developed into a regional academic center featuring a teacher-student relationship based on academy education. During the Qingli and Yuanfeng periods of the Northern Song dynasty, Mingzhou and Yongjia became the centers of academic activities in eastern Zhejiang because of a group of famous Confucian scholars' early appearing in these areas. For example, the "Five Great Scholars of Mingzhou" gave lectures in Mingzhou in the Qingli period under the rein of Emperor Renzong of the Song dynasty, while the "Nine Masters of Yongjia"[1] subsequently held academic activities in the Yuanfeng period under the reign of Emperor Shenzong of the Song dynasty. In the Southern Song dynasty, Zhedong academic culture started to develop independently with its spirit of self-innovation. During the period, four academic schools were formed, namely, Jinhua School led by Lü Zuqian, Yongkang School by Chen Liang, Yongjia School by Ye Shi, and Siming School by the "Four Masters of Yongshang". By that time, *Zhexue* had already developed into a mainstream academic school on an equal status with *Minxue* (闽学 , Fujian scholarship) in Fujian and *Luxue* in Jiangxi.

Rising in the Ming dynasty, Wang Yangming's *xinxue* became a nationwide learning through his preaching in academic and educational activities. Thereafter, seven Yangming schools focusing on *Wangxue* (studies on Wang Yangming and his *xinxue*) were formed in China, namely, Zhezhong *Wangxue* (in central Zhejiang), Jiangyou *Wangxue* (in Jiangxi), Nanzhong *Wangxue* (in the area near Nanjing), Chuzhong *Wangxue* (now in Hubei and Hunan), Beifang *Wangxue* (in Northern China), Min-Yue *Wangxue* (in Fujian and Guangdong), Taizhou *Wangxue* (in Jiangsu). In eastern Zhejiang,

---

[1]   Nine Masters of Yongjia is also known as "Nine Masters of the Yuanfeng Period", namely, Zhou Xingji (周行己), Xu Jingheng (许景衡), Liu Anije (刘安节), Liu Anshang (刘安上), Jiang Yuanzhong (蒋元中), Shen Gongxing (沈躬行), Dai Shu (戴述), Zhao Xiao (赵霄) and Zhang Hui (张辉). They were greatly influenced by Cheng Yi's learning (*Luoxue*).

Yangming *xinxue* evolved into Yaojiang School led by Shen Guomo (沈国模), Jishan School by Liu Zongzhou, and Tao Shiliang School by Tao Shiliang (陶石梁) who was a third-generation disciple of Wang Ji (王畿)[①]. At the turn of the Ming and Qing dynasties, Jishan School achieved a great development. As far as eastern Zhejiang is concerned, Liu Zongzhou and Huang Zongxi were two key figures in the academic development of this region. Based on the differentiation, explanation and rectification of the doctrines of Cheng-Zhu *lixue* (Cheng Hao/Cheng Yi and Zhu Xi's Neo-Confucianism) and Lu-Wang *xinxue* (Lu Jiuyuan and Wang Yangming's philosophy of the mind), Liu Zongzhou put forward the concept of "*shendu*" which was of great practical significance. By then, Liu's Jishan School had been ranked one of the most influential academic schools. As Liu's authentic academic follower and successor, Huang Zongxi not only accepted Liu's theory, but also extended the new academic possibilities with his outstanding creativity. From (Zhu Xi's and Lu Jiuyuan's) learning of *xinxing* (heart-mind and human nature), to (Wang Yangming's and Liu Zongzhou's) doctrines on practice, and then to (Huang Zongxi's and Wan Sitong's) historical studies, Huang Zongxi developed a new approach for the development of Zhedong scholarship. Great scholars of this period, such as Huang Zongxi, Wan Sitong, Quan Zuwang, Zhang Xuecheng and Shao Jinhan (邵晋涵), wrote a new chapter in the development of Zhedong scholarship, leading it to a new high.

During the evolution of Zhedong scholarship, among the eight regions in eastern Zhejiang, Wuzhou (now Jinhua), Yongkang, Wenzhou and Mingzhou (Qingyuan, now Ningbo) were its academic bases in the Southern Song and Yuan dynasties, while Ningbo and Shaoxing were the ones in the Ming and Qing dynasties. In particular, Yuyao and Yinxian in Ningbo were viewed as the most important academic bases in eastern Zhejiang at that time.

At present, most researchers define "Zhedong" based on the related

---

① Wang Ji (王畿 , 1498–1583), courtesy name Ruzhong, literary name Longxi, respected as Master Longxi, was a native of Shanyin of Shaoxing Prefecture (now Shaoxing). He was a disciple of Wang Yangming and the founder of Zhezhong *Wangxue* School.

statements from the *Annals of Zhejiang* (《浙江通志》) published in the period of Emperor Yongzheng (1723–1735) of the Qing dynasty, i.e., the "Upper Eight *fu*" in the east of Qiantang River in the past constituted the "Greater Eastern Zhejiang". Furthermore, some researchers make a further division, putting forward the concepts of "Middle Eastern Zhejiang" and "Lesser Eastern Zhejiang". The former refers to Ningbo and Shaoxing area in the Ming and Qing dynasties, while the latter covers the area of present-day Ningbo. Here in this book, Zhedong is actually in the sense of "Lesser Eastern Zhejiang", including the eleven county-level regions subordinate to Ningbo, namely, Haishu, Jiangdong[1], Jiangbei, Yinzhou, Zhenhai, Beilun, Ninghai, Xiangshan, Cixi, Yuyao, and Fenghua.

　　From the perspective of historical development of Zhedong scholarship in Siming area, the academic activities of Siming scholars in early years were mainly about the spread of Central Plain culture in Siming area where the academic studies were unsystematic and scattered in different regions, because Siming was far from the political and cultural center of Central Plains in northern China; in the Southern Song dynasty, along with the move of the imperial court to the south, the culture and education in Siming area gradually developed into a higher level, with more academic activities and higher academic status; in the Ming and Qing dynasties, due to the efforts of great scholars like Wang Yangming and Huang Zongxi, Siming region became a center of academic innovation, where influential academic schools were formed. In terms of academic nature and characteristics, the important academic schools that influenced Siming area included Cheng-Zhu School of Neo-Confucianism[2], Lu-Wang School[3] of *xinxue*, and Zhedong School of historical studies that was created during the period from Liu Zongzhou's

---

[1]　Jiangdong, a former district of Ningbo, was merged into Yinzhou District in 2016.

[2]　Cheng-Zhu School, the dominant philosophical schools of Neo-Confucianism, based on the theories of the Neo-Confucian philosophers Cheng Yi, Cheng Hao, and Zhu Xi.

[3]　Lu-Wang School, a school of Neo-Confucian philosophy of the mind (*xinxue*), named after its two representatives Lu Jiuyuan and Wang Yangming.

Jishan School to Huang Zongxi's Yongshang Zhengren Academy.

In the Han and Tang dynasties, the academic development of Siming area was in its initial period, during which early-Tang scholar Yu Shinan made a great impact in his historical studies. Born in the great Yu family of Yuyao, Yu Shinan was a counselor of Li Shimin (李世民)[①] in the early Tang dynasty. He was also a calligrapher and poet. Yu Shinan's academic achievements involved many fields, including history, literature and calligraphy. Particularly, he sorted out and recorded his conversations with Emperor Taizong (Li Shimin), and compiled them into a book named *Accounts and Evaluations of Monarchs* (《帝王略论》), which was of high historical value.

During the Qingli period under the reign of Emperor Renzong in the Northern Song dynasty, Yang Shi, Du Chun, Wang Zhi, Wang Yue and Lou Yu mainly introduced into eastern Zhejiang the thought of the "Three Masters of the Early Song Dynasty" (Sun Fu [孙缚], Shi Jie [石介] and Hu Yuan [胡瑗]), especially the ideas of Hu Yuan's. Besides, they all gave lectures in Mingzhou during this period, so they were honored as "Five Masters of the Qingli Period" or "Five Great Scholars of Mingzhou". All the five scholars took education as their career and engaged in the spread of Confucian teachings all their lives. For example, Wang Zhi, Wang Yue and Yang Shi taught Confucian classics and history in Miaoyin Academy in the west of Yinxian County, and later they established Taoyuan Academy where they taught their students Confucian doctrines. In the seventh year of the Qingli period (1047), they were invited by Wang Anshi, the magistrate of Yinxian County, to give lectures in the County School. As founders of Siming scholarship, the five scholars fostered numerous intellectual talents for this area.

In the Southern Song dynasty, Siming School mainly focused on the

---

①   Li Shimin (李世民, 599–649), the Prince of Qin in the early Tang dynasty. During the period before Li ascended to the throne, Yu Shinan was successively appointed as Li's *canjun* (参军, administrative assistant), *jishi* (记室 , secretary), *Hongwenguan xueshi* (弘文馆学士 , member of the Institute for the Advancement of Literature), and *taizi zhongsheren* (太子中舍人 , attendant of Crown Prince).

learning and spread of Lu Jiuyuan's *xinxue*. Its representatives were the "Four Masters of Yongshang", namely, Shu Lin, Shen Huan, Yuan Xie and Yang Jian, among whom Yang Jian was the one who made the most remarkable achievements in *xinxue* studies. Advocated and promoted by the four masters, *xinxue* took root in Zhedong scholarship, and laid a firm foundation for the rise of Yangming *xinxue* in the Ming dynasty.

At the turn of the Song and Yuan dynasties, under the influence of the theories of Zhu Xi, Lü Zuqian and Lu Jiuyuan, four scholars rose in Siming area, namely, Shi Mengqing, Cheng Duanli, Huang Zhen and Wang Yinglin.

Shi Mengqing is the the author of *Guozhai's Instructions on Learning* (《果斋训语》). Quan Zuwang remarked in his "An Account of Jingqing Academy" (《静清书院记》), "The spread of Zhu Xi's Neo-Confucianism in my hometown (now Ningbo) started from Jingqing (Shi Mengqing)." Nevertheless, although Shi "taught his disciples with Zhu Xi's daily doctrines", he was also influenced by Lu Jiuyuan's *xinxue*, arguing that "when one reaches the pure state of his own heart-mind, he would know the heavenly principles". It could be said that Shi Mengqing was one of the early scholars in Siming area who combined Zhu Xi's *lixue* with Lu Jiuyuan's *xinxue*.

Cheng Duanli's ancestral family originally lived in Poyang, Jiangxi Province, before they moved to Yinxian County, where Cheng Duanli received education as a disciple of Shi Mengqing's. Cheng Duanli is the author of *Graded Learning Schedule* (《读书分年日程》) and *Weizhai Collection* (《畏斋集》). The former one, deriving from "Zhu Xi's Principles of Reading" (《朱熹读书法》), caused a huge impact due to its reasonable reading arrangement, which was acknowledged as the guidance of reading in the Song and Yuan dynasties.

Huang Zhen's works include *Huang Zhen's Daily Records* (《黄氏日抄》), *Brief chronicles of Ancient and Contemporary Dynasties* (《古今纪要》), *Records of History Compiling in Wuchen Year* (《戊辰修史传》), etc. It could be said that the prevalence of *Zhuxue* in Siming started from Huang Zhen. According to Huang Zongxi, "Among the scholars spreading Zhu Xi's

Neo-Confucianism in Siming, Dongfa [Huang Zhen's courtesy name] was the best." Thus, one could arguethat Huang Zhen, as a *Zhuxue* successor and representative, made greater contributions than Shi Mengqing did.

A native of Yinxian County, Wang Yinglin was respected as Master Houzhai. His writings covered a broad thematical range, including encyclopaedical books *Jade Sea* (《玉海》) and *Yutang Encyclopaedical Manuscripts* (《玉堂类稿》), collected text-research note *Reading Notes about Difficulties in Learning* (《困学纪闻》), historiographical writing *Text-critical Commentaries on the Bibliographical Treatises of The Book of Han* (《汉艺文志考证》), textual researches on poems *Textual Researches on the Three Versions of The Book of Songs* (《诗考》), comprehensive writing *Collected Works of Shenning* (《深宁集》), etc. Wang Yinglin's philosophical thought derived from many scholars such as Zhu Xi, Lü Zuqian and Ye Shi. As Quan Zuwang argued, "Although Shenning [Wang Yinglin]'s learning was from different scholars, his ability of collecting and analyzing academic literature was in fact based on the approach of Donglai [Lü Zuqian]." In terms of literature or historical studies, Wang learnt from Lü Zuqian and was, thereby, called "great master of Lü's studies"; while in philosophy, Wang was mostly influenced by Yang Jian (one of the "Four Masters of the Chunxi Period").

In the early years of the Ming dynasty, Fang Xiaoru (方孝孺) and Huang Runyu (黄润玉) were two scholars mainly influenced by Zhu Xi's Neo-Confucianism.

Fang Xiaoru received education from Song Lian (宋濂)[1], a disciple of Jinhua School with the studies of Lü Zuqian and Zhu Xi as its academic focus. A Ninghai native in the early Ming dynasty, Fang Xiaoru, courtesy name Xizhi, was respected as "Master Zhengxue". He was dismembered to death because of his refusal to draft an imperial edict of inaugural address for Zhu Di (朱棣)—Emperor Chengzu in the subsequent years. In the late Ming dynasty,

---

[1] Song Lian (宋濂, 1310–1381), courtesy name Jinglian, literary name Qianxi, was one of the principal figures in Jinhua school of Neo-Confucianism.

Fang was rehabilitated and granted a posthumous name "Wenzheng". His writings are seen today in *Xunzhizhai Collection* (《逊志斋集》). Academically following Zhu Xi, Fang Xiaoru emphasized moral introspection in his learning, focusing on "*zhengxin*" (正心, rectifying mind), "*chijing*" (持敬 , maintaining reverence) and "*guayu*" (寡欲, reducing desire), but meanwhile he valued the importance of the practical use of knowledge. When commenting on Fang Xiaoru's academic status, Huang Zongxi claimed that he was the "Father of the Scholarship of Ming".

A native of Yinxin County, Huang Runyu wrote books like *Records of Daily Remarks on Diverse Issues* (《海涵万象录》)[1] and *Supplementary Annotations to Confucian Classics* (《经书补注》). Huang's philosophical thought derived from, but was not just a copy of, Zhu Xi's Neo-Confucianism (*Zhuxue*), and it had a trend of combining *Zhuxue* with *Luxue*, serving as a bridge between the two academic schools.

In the middle of the Ming dynasty, Wang Yangming's *xinxue* rose in Yuyao, unprecedentedly making Siming area the national academic center.

Wang Yangming's *xinxue* inherited Mencius's theory of the mind, developed the *xinxue* theory of such scholars as Lu Jiuyuan, Yang Jian and Chen Xianzhang (陈献章)[2], and thereby established his own refined and complete *xinxue* system, which integrated the *xinxue* achievements of the Song and Ming dynasties. At the same time, Yangming *xinxue* advocated human subjectivity, emphasizing the development of human's subjective initiative, which was of immeasurable positive significance for the establishment of human subjectivity and autonomy. In doing so, Yangming *xinxue* eliminated the rigidity and fragmentation of the dogma of Cheng-Zhu School of Neo-Confucianism and advocated a new style of study.

Through Wang Yangming's decades of unremitting educational activities

---

[1]   It is also known as *The Records of Nanshan's Remarks* (《南山杂录》).

[2]   Chen Xianzhang (陈献章, 1428–1500), courtesy name Gongfu, literary name Shizhai, was respected as "Master Baisha". As the founder of Jiangmen School, he was a famous Confucian philosopher, educator, poet, and calligrapher in the Ming dynasty.

and the vigorous promotion of his disciples all over the country, Yangming *xinxue* developed into many schools of *Wangxue*. In eastern Zhejiang, especially in Siming area, the schools mainly included Zhezhong *Wangxue* School, represented by Xu Ai (徐爱), Wang Ji, Qian Dehong (钱德洪), Huang Wan (黄绾), Zhang Yuanbian (张元忭), etc.; Yaojiang Academy School, represented by the "Four Masters"[1] headed by Shen Guomo in the early stage, Han Kongdang (韩孔当) in the middle stage, and Shao Tingcai (邵廷采) in the late stage; and Jishan School, founded by Liu Zongzhou, with Huang Zongxi and Chen Que (陈确) as its core members, which was viewed as a school of rectified *Wangxue*, because it required to rectify *Wangxue* in spite of its close association with Yangming *xinxue*.

At the turn of the Ming and Qing dynasties, the academic development of Siming and even of the whole eastern Zhejiang area was marked by the rise of "Zhedong School of historical studies" represented by Huang Zongxi. A dominant academic theory in the middle of the Ming dynasty, Wang Yangming's *xinxue* exerted great impacts upon both Chinese and foreign scholars in modern history. During this period, Huang Zongxi was ranked among the three great masters along with Wang Fuzhi (王夫之) and Gu Yanwu (顾炎武), but in terms of his creativity in history and political philosophy, Huang Zongxi was indeed on an incomparable position in the academic circle at that time, superior to both Gu Yanwu and Wang Fuzhi.

The scholars of "Zhedong School of historical studies" advocated the combination of *Zhuxue* and *Luxue*, the unity of *dao* (ideal method) and *qi* (definite thing)[2] and the association between Confucian classics and historical studies. Thus, Zhedong scholarship embarked on a unique academic road featured with wide adoption and open-mindedness and truly reached an

---

① Four Masters, namely, Shen Guomo, Guan Zongshen (管宗圣), Shi Xiaoxian (史孝咸) and Shi Xiaofu (史孝复), were the founders of Yaojiang Academy School.

② Unity of *dao* and *qi* (道器合一), derived from the sentence "是故，形而上者谓之道；形而下者谓之器" ("Hence that which is antecedent to the material form exists, we say, as an ideal method, and that which is subsequent to the material form exists, we say, as a definite thing." A translated version by James Legge, 1815–1897).

unprecedented stage of maturity. In addition to Huang Zongxi, who complied *The Records of Ming Scholars* (《明儒学案》) and *Scholarly Annals of the Song and Yuan Dynasties*, scholars like Wan Sitong, Quan Zuwang, Shao Tingcai, Zhang Xuecheng and Shao Jinhan all had achieved their higher consciousness on "scholarship", which, along with the deep love for the academic forerunners of their hometown and their inclusion for and reflection on the different academic schools, led to the formation of the unparalleled "Zhedong School".

At the turn of the Ming and Qing dynasties, "Zhedong School of historical studies" was formed along with Huang Zongxi's efforts in giving lectures. Its members were very active in Siming and nearby areas, so were the subsequent figures like Wan Sitong, Wan Sida, Quan Zuwang, Zhang Xuecheng and Shao Jinhan. Still, there were more scholars, including Zhu Shunshui (朱舜水), Chen Que, Pan Pingge (潘平格), Huang Zongyan (黄宗炎), Xu Shidong, Huang Shisan (黄式三) and his son Huang Yizhou (黄以周).

Zhu Shunshui (1600–1682), given name Zhiyu, was a native of Yuyao. He was the author of *Collected Works of Master Zhu Shunshui* (《朱舜水先生文集》). After the troops of the Qing dynasty went through the Shanhai Pass in 1644, Zhu went into exile and participated in the campaigns to rebel against the Qing and re-establish the Ming. After the fall of the Southern Ming regime, he settled down in Japan where he gave lectures in Nagasaki and Edo (now Tokyo) to spread Confucianism, and won the high respect of both Japanese officials and scholars. As Zhu claimed, "an expensive fur coat is not made of the fur from only one fox", therefore, his learning absorbed the ideas of many scholars. For his academic orientation, he advocated "practical principles and learning for practical use".

Chen Que (1604–1677), courtesy name Qianchu, was born in Haining, Zhejiang Province. Like Huang Zongxi, he was also a disciple of Liu Zongzhou's. He authored *Chen Que Collection* (《陈确集》). In his writings like "On Books of Burials" (《葬书》), "Criticism on The Great Learning" (《大学辨》) , and "Unreasonable Remarks" (《瞽言》), he made bold criticism on social customs and Cheng-Zhu Neo-Confucianism.

Pan Pingge (1610–1677), a native of Cixi, was a philosopher with unique thoughts. He believed that Neo-Confucians had been affected by the ideas of Buddhism and Taoism, and made a comment that "Zhu Xi was associated with Taoism, while Lu Jiuyuan with Buddhism". Claiming that all the great Confucians, since the Song dynasty, were a group of Buddhist monks and Taoists with astonishing statements, Pan put forward his philosophical thought of pursuing benevolence. However, Pan's thought was strictly criticized by Huang Zongxi, who viewed Pan's learning as "elimination of Neo-Confucian *qi*, *xin* and *ti*"①.

Huang Zongyan (1616–1686) was a younger brother of Huang Zongxi's. He was proficient in the study of *The Book of Changes* (《易经》) and wrote 21 volumes of *Interpretations of the Hexagrams of The Book of Changes* (《周易象辞》). He was highly praised in the *Descriptive Catalogue of the Complete Library in the Four Branches of Literature* (《四库全书总目提要》) for his "unprecedented commentaries" and "convincing evidence" in the study of *The Book of Changes*.

Xu Shidong (1814–1873), courtesy name Dingyu, literary name Liuquan, was respected as "Master Liuquan". It was he, together with Huang Shisan and his son Huang Yizhou, who ceased the trend of declination of Zhedong scholarship subsequent to the period of Quan Zuwang and Shao Jinhan. Focusing on the study of Confucian classics, Xu expressed his unique opinions in books like *Textual Criticism on the Lost Speech of Tang in The Book of History* (《尚书逸汤誓考》) and *Textual Criticism on the Three Chapters of Great Declaration in The Book of History* (《三太誓考》).

Huang Shisan and his son Huang Yizhou were born in Dinghai (now in Zhoushan, Zhejiang), which was under the governance of Ningbo Prefecture in

---

① "Elimination of Neo-Confucian *qi*, *xin* and *ti*" refers to the elimination of *qi* (vital force), *xin* (heart-mind) and *ti* (original substance). It means that Pan Pingge denied these essential Neo-Confucian concepts because he believed that Neo-Confucianism was affected by Buddhism and Taoism.

the Qing dynasty. They were both famous scholars of Confucian classics and history of eastern Zhejiang in the late Qing. Therefore, they were categorized as members of Zhedong School by the great scholar Zhang Binglin (章炳麟)[1]. Huang Shisan, courtesy name Weixiang, literary name Jingju, was the author of *Jingju Posthumous Writings* (《儆居遗书》), which included works like *Interpretation of The Book of Changes* (《易释》), *Basic Knowledge of The Book of History* (《尚书启蒙》), *Interpretation of The Spring and Autumn Annals* 《春秋释》), *Commentaries on The Analects of Confucius* 《论语后案》) and the most valuable *A Brief Chronicle of the Late Zhou Dynasty* (《周季编略》). In addition, he had three writings on the study of *The Book of Songs* (《诗经》), and one of them was *Commentaries on The Book of Songs* (《诗丛说》).

Huang Yizhou, courtesy name Yuantong, literary name Jingji, was the author of *Elucidation on the Ten Commentaries in The Book of Changes* (《周易·十翼后录》), *General Interpretation of Confucian Classics* (《经义通诂》), *Jingji Miscellaneous Writings* (《儆季杂著》), *Notes on Reading* (《读书小记》), *Accounts and Commentaries on History* (《史说略》) and the most well-known *The History of Life Rituals* (《礼书通故》). Huang Yizhou, Yu Yue (俞樾), and Sun Yirang (孙诒让) were together called "Three Masters of the Late Qing Dynasty".

Past and present scholars have different views on the nature and characteristics of the Zhedong (both "Greater Zhedong" and "Lesser Zhedong" included) scholarship. Qing scholar Zhang Xuecheng summarized the two academic characteristics of Zhedong scholarship: 1) The integration of Confucian classics and history, i.e., Zhedong scholars believed "those who study human nature and destiny must resort to history"; 2) The combination of *Zhuxue* (Zhu Xi's *lixue*) and *Luxue* (Lu Jiuyuan's *xinxue*). They thought that "to follow *Luxue* doesn't mean to contradict *Zhuxue*". Surely, Zhang's statement was an accurate description of the essence of Zhedong scholarship. Meanwhile,

---

[1] Zhang Binglin (章炳麟, 1869–1936), well-known by his given name Zhang Taiyan (章太炎), was born in Yuhang, Zhejiang Province.

he defined Zhedong scholarship as "specialized learning" so as to distinguish it from Zhexi scholarship which focused on "extensive learning". As he argued, "Zhedong scholars value specialized knowledge, while Zhexi scholars exalt extensive learning."

From the perspective of modern civilization and scholarship, the characteristics of Zhedong scholarship can be summarized from five aspects.

1. Pursuit of Practical Efficacy and Utility; Advocation of Learning for Practical Use

Zhedong scholarship stressed practice and strived for practical efficacy and utility, aiming at the practical use of learning, and thereby formed its distinctive characteristics. For example, in the Han dynasty, Wang Chong oriented his learning at "eliminating empty words", "fighting against exaggeration", "valuing truth and sincerity" and "stressing efficacy", so as to object Han scholars' deification of Confucius and to oppose the falsity and emptiness in the learning of Confucianism. In the Southern Song dynasty, Zhejiang scholars held up the banner of pursuing practical efficacy and utility as a theoretical base, which was in sharp contrast to the empty Neo-Confucian (*daoxue*)[1] talks on mind and human nature. Zhedong scholars like Chen Liang, Ye Shi, Lü Zuqian and the members of Siming School all paid attention to the practical social problems and studied practical learning. What they were concerned about were the recovery of lost land, the unification of the country and the realization of national rejuvenation, so that they consciously shouldered the responsibility of "eliminating the trouble under heaven" and "bringing peaceful life to the people".

In the Ming dynasty, Yangming *xinxue* rose up. The reason why Wang Yangming vigorously advocated *xinxue* lay in the fact that Cheng-Zhu Neo-Confucianism deviated from the true spirit of Confucianism because of its

---

[1] The term *dao* (道) is a major concept of Cheng-Zhu Neo-Confucianism. It literally means "the way". That's why Cheng-Zhu Neo-Confucianism is also called *daoxue* (the learning of way). Conventionally, Neo-Confucianism is mainly composed of *lixue* and *xinxue*.

formalization, rigidity and emptiness after it became an official learning. The rise of *xinxue* was an opportunity for Confucianism to change from *xu* (emptiness) to *shi* (reality), which in essence was to restore the social morals and ethics, save the decadent scholarship and stabilize the society. In line with the Confucian spirit of *"rushi"* (入世)① of Confucius and Mencius, *xinxue* was the learning for practical use.

In the Qing dynasty, Huang Zongxi initiated Zhedong historical studies with "learning for practice use" as its clear academic orientation. He believed that Confucianism was a study on governance and Confucian scholars were intellectuals who studied for the worldly affairs, rather than those deceiving the public to earn their own fame by showing off confusing pedantical words or making high-sounding speeches.

According to Zhang Xuecheng, the expression *"ge you shi shi"* (各有事事)②, seen from the spirit of learning for practical use, means that the one who is involved is supposed to deal with social problems practically based on practical social situations. *"shi shi"* literally means "to tackle one's own affairs" or "to do the things that one is supposed to do", and generally refers to the creative practice in a certain social situation. Specifically, "for Wang Yangming, it means practical utility; for Liu Zongzhou, it means righteousness; for Huang Zongxi, it means seclusion; for Wan Sida and Wan Sitong, it means studying Confucian classics through historical studies"③. By this, Zhang Xuecheng profoundly interpreted the Zhedong academic spirit of "pursuit of practical efficacy and utility; advocation of learning for practical use".

2. Extensiveness and Inclusiveness

Although eastern Zhejiang was the birthplace of Yue culture, it was not

---

① *Rushi*, concerning the worldly affairs.
② *Ge you shi shi*, literally, every scholar has his practical affairs to tackle.
③ According to their respective background, Wang Yangming embodied Zhedong academic spirit (learning for practical use) by his deeds of calming rebellions; Liu Zongzhou did so by his martyrdom to the Ming dynasty; Huang Zongxi by choosing a secluded life for his moral integrity; and the Wan brothers by resorting to historical studies for the interpretation of Confucian classics.

an academic and cultural center. Instead, due to its marginal location, it was culturally influenced by the Central Plains. Therefore, its scholarship was inclusive, witnessing various academic schools or thoughts well positioned in this region. Meanwhile, through absorbing different academic cultures, Zhedong scholars realized their personal acquisition and made outstanding innovations. Therefore, extensiveness and inclusiveness can be viewed as a major academic tradition of Zhedong scholarship.

From the Northern Song dynasty to the Southern Song dynasty, along with the move to the south of the Song royal family and other eminent families of high-ranking officials and prestigious scholars, the thoughts of such academic schools as *Huxue* (胡[瑗]学)[①], *Wangxue* (王[安石]学)[②], *Shuxue* (蜀学)[③], *Luoxue* (洛学)[④] and *Guanxue* (关学)[⑤] were spread mostly from the Central Plains into Zhejiang which, thereby, became a center for the exchanges among various schools of thought. Therefore, it became a natural thing for Zhedong scholars to adopt and integrate the advantages of these thoughts.

In the Northern Song dynasty, the "Five Great Scholars of Mingzhou" were influenced by Hu Yuan's learning. In the Southern Song dynasty, most Zhedong scholars were also influenced by the scholarship of the Central Plains. For example, Jinhua School was associated with Cheng Yi's learning, because Lü Zuqian, the leader of Jinhua School, "inherited the thought from the documents of the Central Plains"; Yongjia scholar Zheng Boxiong (郑伯熊) and his brother Zheng Boying (郑伯英) continued the academic thought

---

① *Huxue*, the learning of Hu Yuan, who was one of the "Three Early-Song Confucian Scholars" . Traditionally, Hu Yuan's learning was named as "*Huxue*" (湖学), the learning of Huzhou.
② *Wangxue*, the learning of Wang Anshi. Wang Anshi (1021–1086), courtesy name Jiefu, literary name Banshan, was a Chinese poet and prose writer.
③ *Shuxue*, the learning of Shu (around today's Sichuan) School, which was a school initiated by Su Xun (苏洵) and his two sons Su Shi (苏轼 , well-known by the name Su Dongpo) and Su Zhe (苏辙).
④ *Luoxue*, the learning of Yiluo School, a branch of Neo-Confucianism, represented by Cheng Hao and his brother Cheng Yi.
⑤ *Guanxue*, the learning of Guanzhong (now in Shaanxi) School. Zhang Zai (张载) was one of its main representatives.

of Zhou Xingji[①], and printed the books of great Neo-Confucian scholar Cheng Yi whose theories were followed by Yongjia scholars like Chen Fuliang (陈傅良) and Ye Shi. Therefore, it can be seen how much the Yongjia scholars were influenced by the Cheng brothers' learning (*Luoxue*).

The learning of Zhedong scholars had numerous common elements with the theory of *Zhuxue*, which promoted the formation of Jinhua School of *Zhuxue* represented by He Ji (何基) and Wang Bai (王柏), and Siming School of *Zhuxue* represented by Huang Zhen and Wang Yinglin. When it was spread into eastern Zhejiang, *Zhuxue* gradually formed its characteristics of *Zhexue*, and its tradition of broad knowledge was also maintained and developed.

At the same time, Lu Jiuyuan's *xinxue* was widely spread and creatively developed in eastern Zhejiang. As followers of Lu Jiuyuan, the "Four Masters of Yongshang" spared no efforts to preach *Luxue* and made it a study prevailing in Siming, so that eastern Zhejiang gradually turned into the base of China's *xinxue* studies.

Statements like "following the learning of Lu Jiuyuan without contradicting Zhu Xi's thought" and "those who study human nature and destiny must resort to history" exactly illustrate the academic characteristics of Zhejiang scholars: extensiveness, inclusiveness and self-centeredness.

3. Seeking Truth and Reality; Believing Diversity Begotten by One Origin

Zhedong scholarship had an excellent tradition of seeking truth and reality and believing diversity begotten by one origin. For example, Wang Chong, a former prominent Zhedong scholar, held up the banner of pursuing truth and avoiding falsity/empty words, and he "explored the difference between *shi* and *xu*" in his work *Disquisitions or Discourses Weighted in the Balance* (《论衡》). Zhejiang scholarship in the Southern Song dynasty claimed the materialist views like "reciprocal causation of *dao* (ideal method) and *qi* (definite thing)" and "*qi* is dispensable to *dao*", and therefore showed the tendency of seeking

---

① Zhou Xingji (周行己 , 1067–1125), courtesy name Gongshu, respected as Master Fuzhi, was a disciple of Cheng Yi's and a member of the "Nine Masters of Yongjia".

truth and reality.

During the Ming and Qing dynasties, Wang Yangming was devoted to the research of *xinxue*. His theory of "*zhiliangzhi*" (致良知)[1] contains reasonable factors like valuing practice, emphasizing the unity of *benti* (本体)[2] and *gongfu* (工夫)[3], and seeking *benti* through *gongfu*. Especially, he advocated human subjectivity, which laid the foundation of subjective initiative for seeking truth and reality. Later, another Ming scholar Liu Zongzhou claimed "unity of *li* (principle) and *qi* (vital force)", while Zhang Xuecheng advocated "to realize *dao* through *qi*" and "*dao* is demonstrated through *qi*", both of which include the factors of seeking truth and reality.

In the eyes of Zhedong scholars, seeking truth and reality was their academic goal, and there were many different approaches to meeting it. The academic truth couldn't be monopolized by one school or one way. The concept that "*yiben wanshu*" (一本万殊)[4] put forth by Huang Zongxi contains profound methodological principles. It is an academic proposition with the spirit of the times. "*Yiben*" refers to the way of the sages in Confucianism, while in a broad sense it is the totality or whole of academic truths. "*Wanshu*" means Confucian scholars' diverse comprehensions of the way of the sages. It also refers to the various methods or approaches adopted in the pursuit of truth. According to Huang Zongxi, scholarship is a public instrument under heaven, not limited to private use. Everyone is entitled to the pursuit of academic truth and every scholar can do his best to explore and understand it. With enough efforts and time, he will reach the truth. "The more the efforts, the clearer the truth." Different academic schools may have different degrees of understandings on truth, but they are all on their way to truth. The outlook of academic truth conveyed by "*yiben wanshu*" is of profound significance in theoretical enlightenment, and in the process of seeking truth, it is not only a

---

[1] *Zhiliangzhi*, extension of the innate knowledge of the good.
[2] *Benti*, original substance.
[3] *Gongfu*, conscious effort.
[4] *Yiben wanshu*, diversity begotten by one origin.

sharp weapon, but also an inevitable requirement.

4. Emphasizing Both Confucian Classics and Historical Studies; Stressing Both Righteousness and Interest

Essentially, the views of "emphasizing on both Confucian classics and historical studies" and "stressing both righteousness and interest" were the unique opinions of Zhedong scholars on the issue of value (and the good). They were obviously not in line with the dominant orthodox Confucian values of ancient China, but closer to the modern ones, and thereby concordant with the development direction of the times. Zhedong scholars consistently valued historical learning, regarded it as of equal importance to Confucian classics, and thereby avoided the biased idea of the latter being superior to the former. Propositions like "historical studies for the worldly affairs" (by Zhang Xuecheng), "Six Classics are all history" (by Ye Shi, Wang Yangming, and Zhang Xuecheng), "history is a must for the study of human nature and destiny" (by Zhang Xuecheng), and "learning must derive from Confucian classics, and it is not for groundless fiction; it must be proved in historical records before it is used in practice" (by Huang Zongxi) all require that historical studies be raised to a higher position, that the interpretation of Confucian classics be organically combined with historical studies, and that the analysis on principles of human nature, the summary of historical experience, and the responses to practical affairs be unified. All these requirements would lead to a more comprehensive orientation in academic value and a broader academic horizon.

The expression "stressing both righteousness and interest" was originally a comment by Zhu Xi on Chen Liang's academic characteristics in an academic debate between the two scholars. In spite of its derogative sense, this statement was actually an appropriate summary for the academic features of Zhedong scholars who usually took in account both "righteousness" and "interest" in their learning, never shying away from the latter.

Ye Shi claimed "promoting righteousness by interest", Chen Liang put forward "Neo-Confucian learning for practical utility", and Huang Zongxi affirmed the authenticity of individual interest. All these scholars held positive attitudes towards the unity of righteousness and interest. For the perspective of values, Zhedong scholars' views of "promoting righteousness by interest" and "stressing both righteousness and interest" would inevitably lead to the conclusion that "both industry (handicraft)[①] and commerce are foundations". They called for "trade to be unimpeded and industry (handicraft) to be favored" and "support for merchants and currency circulation", and claimed that "Government is connected with people, and agriculture and commerce are equally essential. There should be mutual understanding and exchanges between two parties." As Huang Zongxi argued, "Due to their poor understanding, some scholars usually demote industry (handicraft) and commerce and falsely propose to restrict them. In fact, both the two sectors are what our enlightened monarch wants and they are equally foundational."[②] Actually, all of the above proposals were calling for the development of commodity economy of capitalist sprout.

5. Specialized Learning and Innovative Scholarship

Zhedong scholars thought highly of "learning of personal acquisition", "learning through various approaches and considerations", and "specialized learning", emphasizing that all learning must have an "orthodox idea", thought must be practically experienced, and scholarship must be creative. They opposed copying, parroting or echoing others' words, and refused the pedantic learning just with sage quotes as the ultimate knowledge. The formation of

---

① In ancient China, the vast bulk of manufacturing activity took place in small units—the homes of craftsmen and farmers. Therefore, industry mainly referred to handicraft industry at that time.

② The citation is from *Waiting for the Dawn: A Plan for the Prince* (《明夷待访录》) by Huang Zongxi, who criticized the false interpretation by others over the imperial policy on the social economical foundation, pointing out that what the government referred to by "*mo*" (末, the subordinate sectors) were not the sectors of industry (handicraft) and commerce, but the ones involved with wedding, funeral, and other rituals. That's why Huang Zongxi asked his family to hold a simple funeral for him after his death (*cf.* Chapter Five). In Huang's opinion, industry (handicraft) and commerce were as fundamental as agriculture, the "*ben*" (本, the fundamental sector), and all of them were the foundations of the social economy.

these beliefs is related to the deep influence of *xinxue* on Zhedong scholars. For example, from Wang Yangming's "*liangzhi*" to Huang Zongxi's "*benxin*" (本心)①, and then to Zhang Xuecheng's "*xingqing*" (性情)②, all these *xinxue* terms were put forth successively with their unique emphasis and continued for 100 years without a slight decline, and it is actually an obvious characteristic of Zhedong scholarship.

Wang Yangming claimed that "my own *xin* (heart-mind)" is the highest authority and standard of learning, that scholarship is a public instrument under heaven, and that the value of scholarship lies in the unique creation based on the "knowledge obtained from mind" and this creation is higher than any given authority. His theory indeed laid a foundation for the academic orientation and creation of Zhedong scholars in the Ming and Qing dynasties.

Huang Zongxi advocated "learning through various approaches and considerations", and stressed "personal acquisition" and "learning with orthodox idea", which was in line with Wang Yangming's theory. "Diversity of mind" refers to not only the infinite possibility in the development and evolution of individual consciousness and the physical world, but also the particularity of the physical world and mental world caused by the interaction of each individual's *gongfu* and *benti*, which leads to the infiniteness of academic creation based on the idea that "diversity begotten by one origin" and "learning through various approaches and considerations". Therefore, he put forward that "scholars should pay attention to the differences when they meet one-sided views③ or opposite statements. That's what 'diversity begotten by one origin' means".

"Specialized learning" in Zhang Xuecheng's remark is a profound summary of the characteristics of Zhedong scholarship. This concept refers

---

① *Benxin*, original mind.

② *Xingqing*, nature and emotion.

③ According to the "Tianlun" ("Discourse on Heaven") in *Xunzi* (《荀子·天论》), "The myriad things embody only a part (side) of heavenly way, and a certain thing is only a part (side) of myriad things." (万物为道一偏，一物为万物一偏。) Here the concept of "one-side views" indicates that a scholar should be clear about the limit of his knowledge.

to the studies of writing to reach *dao* through *qi*. It is an innovative study that starts from true nature and ends up with ultimate principle based on broad knowledge. With its practical utility like correcting errors and avoiding one-sided views, it opens up a new trend of the times.

Along with the development of the times, deeper researches on the nature, spirit and characteristics of Zhejiang scholarship would be carried out and more new researchers would join in so there would be continuous changes on the form of discourse and the emphasis of study. The nature and characteristics of Zhedong scholarship are not only summarized through the research on historical documents, but also discovered and constructed by researchers and their successors. This is not only because of the long history and large size of Zhedong scholarship, but also because of its connotation, value and spirit connecting with and inspiring modern civilization, which is the significance of studying Zhedong scholarship.

Chapter One

Origination from Education: The Initial Making of Zhedong Scholarship

About ten kilometers to the west of downtown Ningbo is Hengjie Town. On the east of the town is an alluvial plain based on the ancient Guangde Lake, and on its west are winding hills and mountains. In its confines are fertile fields, dense forests, abundant products, hence the name of "Land of Taoyuan", meaning a place of peace and happiness. On the west of the Hengjie Town lies a village called Lincun Village, right at the foot of the branch of Siming mountain on which green bamboos and pine trees are everywhere, beautiful and pleasant. According to a study, the village was home to Wang Yue, one of the "Five Masters" of the Qingli Period well-known in Ningbo history.

Nine centuries ago, Wang Yue changed his residence named "Zhuogu Tang" into a lecture house, and named it "Taoyuan Academy". In the ninth year of the Xining period (1076), Wang Xun (王勋), Wang Yue's grandson, had access to making statements to the emperor after his enrollment as *jinshi* (进士)[1] after the imperial examination , and was granted by Emperor Shenzong of the Song dynasty an inscribed board with Taoyuan Academy on it. The board from the emperor brought brilliant honor to the academy, and people around were all full of pride and excitement, spreading the news broadly. Therefore, students nearby flocked there for their study.

Taoyuan Academy could be viewed as one of the academies of eastern Zhejiang with the biggest scale, the longest history, and the greatest influence. It fostered numerous talents for Zhejiang with teachers like Yang Jian, a disciple of Lu Jiuyuan who was a famous philosopher and educator of the Southern Song dynasty. At Taoyuan Academy, Yang created "Cihu School", a

----

[1] *Jinshi*, advanced scholar.

philosophical school on the study of mind. At the end of the Zhizheng period (around 1370) of the Yuan dynasty, Taoyuan Academy was rebuilt under the application of a local Confucian Zhang Wenhai (张文海) whose following relegation, however, led to its gradual decline. Later, the academy was caught in a big fire in the first year under the reign of Emperor Jiajing of the Ming dynasty (1522).

For a long period of time, the once glorious Taoyuan Academy was in ruins. However, a group of scholars were reluctant to see it in a poor state, and decided to make a better digging into such a wonderful historical and human resource. On April 9th, 2010, "The First Seminar on Improving the Cultural and Historical Study of Taoyuan Academy and Guangde Lake" was held at Siming Shanju, a resort at Hengjie Town, Yinzhou District, Ningbo, where experts from different fields got together, exploring the past and present of Taoyuan Academy. They made the initial decision of rebuilding the academy and making it an educational base of *guoxue*[①]. It would be a latter-day "Tianyi Pavilion" in some sense. What a good outcome if done!

[①] *Guoxue* (国学), the study of ancient Chinese culture, especially Confucian culture, including language, literature and etiquette, etc.

I. Life and Experiences of the Five Masters of the Qingli Period

Zhedong scholarship at Siming area started from the Northern Song dynasty with Yang Shi, Du Chun, Wang Zhi, Wang Yue and Lou Yu as its forerunners. These five masters took education as their career mainly in the Qingli period under the reign of Emperor Renzong of the Song dynasty, and thus they were called the "Five Masters of the Qingli Period".

The beginning of Zhedong scholarship at Siming area benefited from the era of the Northern Song dynasty when culture and education were highly valued and well promoted.

Before the Northern Song dynasty, Mingzhou's economic, social and cultural development was not at a high level for its isolated location along the seaside. As Wang Yinglin, a famous scholar from the Southern Song, remarked, "It had been already a city since the Tang dynasty, while its academic development was not yet well developed." According to a statistic study, among the famous Tang poets, none was from Mingzhou. Up to the middle of the Northern Song dynasty, eastern Zhejiang cities like Mingzhou and Yongjia (now in Wenzhou) grew in terms of their status for the movement of popularizing culture and education in the Song dynasty.

The Song dynasty is the first period when *wenjiao* (文教)[①] was valued. Its court adopted the policy of "encouraging intellectual education, while restraining martial events", attached great importance to intellectual education, and urged young scholars to immerse themselves in reading, concentrate on

---

[①] In the Song dynasty, *wenjiao*, literally intellectual education, mainly focused on the teaching of Confucian classics and history, literature, etc. It is a concept relative to *wujiao* (武教, literally, martial training/education).

studies, and accept the ethical and moral doctrines of Confucianism. As for the cultivation and selection of talents, intellectual ability was considered before to all other standards. Meanwhile, *keju* (科举)[①] was expanded in its scale, and became the main approach to selecting officials of different levels.

The court's policy of valuing intellectuals and encouraging education exerted a positive influence upon the development of Mingzhou's educational culture. In particular, from the fourth year of the Qingli period (1044) under the reign of Emperor Renzong of the Song dynasty to the last years of the Northern Song dynasty, the court promoted three movements of large scale to facilitate the flourishing of education, leading the educational scene of Mingzhou into a new era. Echoing the national movements of educational flourishing, Magistrate Li Zhaowen (李照文) of Cixi County built a county-run school on the west of Cixi in the first year of the Yongxi period (984); the official registrar of Dinghai County (now Zhenhai) created a Confucian school in the second year of the Yongxi period (985); Magistrate Su Jicheng (苏季成) of Fenghua County established a county-run school in the Jingyou period (1034–1038); Magistrate Wang Anshi of Yinxian County started a county-run school in the eighth year of the Qingli period. At the time, another sign for the prosperity of Mingzhou education was the rise of private academies, among which were the most famous Taoyuan Academy, Chengnan Academy, and Wang Yinjun Lecture Hall. The establishment of academies and the devotion from a group of scholars to education greatly promoted the academic atmosphere in Mingzhou area and also directly improved the formation of talents groups there.

Nationally, it was in the Northern Song dynasty that the Neo-Confucianism philosophy was formed. The scholars in the early years of the Song dynasty, such as Hu Yuan, Sun Fu and Shi Jie, were all the forerunners of Neo-Confucianism, while the founders of the systematic Neo-Confucianism were Zhou Dunyi (周敦颐), Shao Yong (邵雍), Zhang Zai, Cheng Hao and Cheng Yi. The development of eastern Zhejiang academic thought had a

---

① *Keju*, the imperial civil service examination.

similar trend to that of Neo-Confucianism. For example, the academic focus of the "Five Masters of the Qingli Period" was especially associated with the thought of Hu Yuan, one of the "Three Masters of the Early Song Dynasty", while during the Yuanfeng period of Emperor Shenzong, the "Nine Masters of Yongjia" introduced into eastern Zhejiang the ideas of "*Luoxue*" represented by Cheng Yi. By this period, Zhedong scholarship, mainly focusing on spreading Confucian doctrines, had not formed its systematic academic thought with enough creativity. Thus, this could be defined as the primitive period of Zhedong scholarship.

Quan Zuwang, in his "An Account of the Academy of Five Masters of the Qingli Period" (《庆历五先生书院记》)[①], introduced the life experiences and educational activities of the five scholars.

Yang Shi, courtesy name Andao, from Cixi, was respected as "Master Hermit" by local residents for his modesty and solitude. He made a living by farming and teaching, far away from the vanity fair, and never minded the honors or blames upon him. His profound knowledge from years of study in seclusion brought him great fame in the capital city. Court officials like Sun Mian (孙沔) and Fan Zhongyan (范仲淹), as well as local officials like Governor Bao Ke (鲍轲) and Governor Qian Gongfu, successively recommended him to serve as an official, but all of them were refused. After his death at the age of 76, he got the inscription "The Tomb of Song Hermit" on his tombstone.

Du Chun, initially a hermit in Yuezhou, moved to Cixi, where he was respected as "Master Shitai" after his literary name. With the idea of "learning for oneself", he lived in seclusion and didn't have any request of being known by others. He supported his family by farming-related work, and won high praise in his hometown for his filial piety to parents and his harmonious relationship with brothers. In the middle of the Qingli period, he was invited

---

① To commemorate the great achievements of the Five Masters of the Qingli Period, Quan Zuwang built an academy and named it after their honorary title. This article was to make a record about the academy and related academic affairs.

by Wang Anshi, the magistrate of Yinxian County, to work as a teacher at the newly-established county-run school. Then he was employed in the same position in the Cixi county-run school by magistrate Lin Zhao (林肇). Wang Anshi appreciated very much Du Chun's morality and learning, and encouraged him to teach with in mind the responsibility of "propagating the Confucian doctrines, imparting professional knowledge, and resolving doubts"[1].

Lou Yu (1008–1077), courtesy name Ziwen, was respected as "Master Xihu". Initially, his ancestral family had been in Dongyang County of Wuzhou before they moved to Fenghua County during the late Tang dynasty. Up to the generation of Lou Yu, the family moved into the town of Mingzhou where he lived in Yuqing Fang on the east of Sun Lake. Lou Yu was ambitious and diligent, and he indulged in reading so much that his reading ranged from the Six Classics[2] to the works of various schools of thought during the period from pre-Qin eras to the early years of the Han dynasty, by which he got profound knowledge, and won high respect from the people around. In the eighth year of the Qingli period when the county-run school of Yinxian County was established, he was employed as a teacher working there for many years. Later, he was invited to teach for more than 10 years at the prefecture-run school established in the middle of the Huangyou period (1049–1054). In the fifth year of the Huangyou period (1053), he was transferred to Lujiang (now in Anhui Province) as *zhubu* (主簿)[3] after he was enrolled as *jinshi* in the imperial examination, but subsequently he went back to Mingzhou after an accusation against him. Later, he stopped his official career as a judge, and refused any official positions owing to his low salary not enough to support his family. In his hometown, he went on with teaching as a chief in the prefecture-run school for more than 10 years, mainly teaching the students from nearby areas. Among

---

① The quote is from "On Teachers" (《师说》) by Han Yu (韩愈) who summed up the duties of teacher in this article, and whose argument on teaching was widely acknowledged in traditional Chinese society.

② Six Classics, or *liujing* (六经), including *The Book of Changes*, *The Book of History*, *The Book of Songs*, *The Book of Rites*, *The Book of Music* and *The Spring and Autumn Annals* (《春秋》).

③ *Zhubu*, official registrar, in charge of secretarial affairs.

the 30 years of work, he was well-known in Mingzhou area and respected as "Master Lou".

Wang Zhi (985–1055), courtesy name Junyi, resided in Taoyuan Town of Yinxian County. His ancestral family moved to the town from Tonglu, Muzhou (an ancient prefecture, covering present-day areas of Tonglu, Jiande, and Chun'an) when his grandfather Wang Renhao (王仁镐) was transferred to Mingzhou as *yatui* (衙推)[1]. There he made friends with Yangshi and Du Chun from the same prefecture, and all of them were known by the local people for their integrity and respected as masters by their disciples. During the reign of Emperor Renzong, he was appointed as *jiaoshu* (校书)[2] of the Imperial Library, but he refused the position and led a secluded life in Zhuangjia, Huanxi Village (now Zhuangjiaxi Village, Hengjie Town) west to the town of Yinxian County, where he built a lecture house called Yinjiang Academy, hence the honorific title "Master Yinjiang" for him.

Wang Yue (1010–1085), courtesy name Yingqiu, was a native of Yinxian County, a nephew of Wang Zhi and a disciple of Yang Shi. Teaching in his hometown for over three decades, Wang Yue took education as his life career, without any farming things for food or clothing. Excellent in teaching, he was followed by numerous students. In the ninth year of the Xining period, he was additionally granted the title of *jiangshilang* (将仕郎)[3] and appointed as *zhangshi* (长史)[4] of Mingzhou Prefecture. But he declined the post. Then, the emperor inscribed "Taoyuan Academy" for his teaching house at Lincun Village. His descendants passed his learning down from generation to generation.

According to the life experiences of the above "Five Masters", except Du Chun who was originally a native of Yue Area close to Mingzhou, all of them were settlers from other places during the end of the Tang dynasty and later the

---

[1] *Yatui*, subordinate of local governor.
[2] *Jiaoshu*, collator.
[3] *Jiangshilang*, a low-level official rank.
[4] *Zhangshi*, subordinate of the governor.

Five Dynasties. Although Mingzhou was isolated at the time with relatively backward culture, it had a relatively stable society. It, therefore, became a destination of the settlers of those aristocratic families from northern China. Groups of them were well-educated.

II. Academic Status of the Five Masters of the Qingli Period

All of the five masters took education as their life career. Education, as the basic factor, functioned as the main approach to spreading cultural values at that time. At the beginning of Song dynasty, the development of civilization and the formation of Neo-Confucianism depended upon the combination of academic study and education. After the Eastern Han dynasty (25–220), the *boshi* (博士) system[①] of the imperial court went in decline, and there was no more atmosphere of giving lectures to the public, so that academic activities were merely confined between masters and their disciples. Therefore, in the period from the end of the Tang dynasty to the Five Dynasties, Buddhist temples were cherished, functioning as the institutions for education. That was why Buddhism prevailed over Confucianism. It was not until the beginning of the Northern Song dynasty that Confucianism saw a resurgence. At the time, the court established the Imperial Academy (*Taixue*[②]), and the prefecture-run and the county-run schools were gradually rebuilt. Meanwhile, state-run schools and private ones were both rejuvenated. The "Three Early-Song Confucian Scholars" all worked in the profession of education. Among them, Hu Yuan was a famous educator, and for 20 years he had run schools in Suzhou and Huzhou. His pedagogy was adopted by the court's *Taixue*. The pedagogy of the "Five Masters" and its basic spirit wonderfully matched the educational and academic ideas of Hu Yuan, who could be said to have greatly influenced the former ones. For example, Wang Yue and his uncle Wang Zhi, together with

---

① *Boshi* (literally, an erudite man), in the Han dynasty refers to an academic title granted to those erudite scholars who were proficient with the Confucian classics. The *boshi* system was set up to strengthen the dominance of Confucianism in education, governance and other fields.
② *Taixue* (太学), the Imperial Academy, the highest education institution of ancient China.

scholars like Lou Yu, Yang Shi and Du Chun, "set up the statue of Confucius at Miaoyin Academy, teaching classic Confucian works and historical books, advocating the study of practical service. Thereby, they had many followers." What the five masters did was in line with the idea of Hu Yuan, who advocated the "learning of Confucian doctrines for practical service". It could be seen from the above that the five masters spread Neo-Confucianism, and rebuilt the authority of Confucius, valuing both philosophy and morality and practical service. Arguably, what they did for Zhedong scholarship mainly focused on the cultivation of talents through education, laying the academic foundation.

The teaching and academic researching of the five masters originated from a civil foundation, and was encouraged by the local authorities, which formed a beneficial interaction between the both parties in the meantime. Their achievements in education were greatly associated with Wang Anshi's support because he, as a well-known official, had his unique perspective on respecting teachers, valuing education and building schools. Seen from the experiences of the five masters, only Du Chun and Lou Yu had the teaching experiences in official schools, and the other three were all teachers of private schools. Originally, their pursuit was not for being famous or influential. Among them, only Lou Yu and Wang Yue had the experience of being low-ranking officials; and only Lou Yu was enrolled as *jinshi*. The educational flourishing movements during the Qingli period directly pushed them to the society, and subsequently made them become the mainstay of Mingzhou education. During the period, they stuck to their own personalities and independence on their scholarship, and gained the respect from the court and local officials because of their friend-like but not hierarchical relationship with the authorities, in spite of their lower social status. It was just because of their civil foundation and independence in education and scholarship and the healthy interaction with the authority that the independence and openness of Zhedong scholarship were founded.

The education and scholarship of the five masters had the following common features: their thoughts and theories all corresponded to the learning of Master Anding (Hu Yuan)[1], both belonging to the field of the study for practical service; they "discarded Buddhism and Taoism", and opposed the influences of the two religions on people's thoughts; their methodology in the studies of the Confucian classics and historical books was in accordance with the requirements of Neo-Confucianism. That is to say, they broke through the barriers set by the scholars from the Han and Tang dynasties who just focused on the interpretation of words and sentences, and devoted themselves to the insight into the inner meaning of Confucian classics; they emphasized the combination on the study of Confucian classics and historical works, valuing the practical use of learning.

They studied both Confucian classics and history. For example, Yang Shi "was good at the research of governance and fund of investigating the root cause of the administrative disorders in different dynasties", and in his own words, "I spent 13 years in researching Confucian classics and history"; Du Chun "followed the steps of Ban Gu and Sima Qian[2] in historical writing", and put the historical studies on a very important position. The trend in what they did can be regarded as the origin of the idea of the later Zhedong scholarship that "those who study human nature and destiny must resort to history". On this base, they started to write books and developed their theories consciously. For example, Lou Yu, in his later years, "wrote and talked with his disciples everyday". Wang Anshi praised Wang Zhi as the "forerunner of Siming scholars to expound their ideas by writing". Their academic thoughts were oriented to reality, featured prominently with the focus on practice. Although they spent their whole life on education, they still "supported their family by farming-related work", that is to say, they could base their consideration on the real facts, viewing others with benevolence and caring about the local development.

---

[1] Hu Yuan's learning was named "*Huxue*" after the name of Huzhou, where he conducted studies and gave lectures.

[2] Ban Gu (班固) and Sima Qian (司马迁) were two famous historians in ancient China. The former authored *The Book of Han* (《汉书》), and the latter *Records of the Grand Historian of China* (《史记》). Both works were listed in "The Twenty-four Histories" ("二十四史") of China.

As for their cultural contributions, a summary could be made from the following aspects: Firstly, they promoted the educational and academic development of Mingzhou area. Because of their lifetime efforts, the educational career there developed rapidly, schools of various levels with different natures appeared in a fast way, and the number of students increased. Secondly, they cultivated a great number of talents qualified for social services. In particular, Lou Yu, as an educator of official school, made great achievements. Within his academic circle, "all of the excellent talents were gathered". In Quan Zuwang's words, with the efforts of the five masters, "our town was named as Zou-Lu several decades later".

Chapter Two

Recognition of Principle and Nature: The Rise of Zhu Xi's Neo-Confucianism in Eastern Zhejiang

In the Southern Song dynasty, Zhu Xi's Neo-Confucianism (*lixue*), similar to Lu Jiuyuan's Neo-Confucian philosophy of the mind (*xinxue*), had a nationwide influence. It considerably impacted the scholarship of eastern Zhejiang, especially that of Ningbo, although it was not as high as Lu's *xinxue* in terms of academic status. Affected by the regional culture and thinking pattern during its spreading, it was transformed into an academic study with local features, making up an organic part of the scholarship of eastern Zhejiang.

Zhedong *Zhuxue* was mainly composed of two schools: one was Jinhua School, represented by He Ji, Wang Bai, Jin Lüxiang (金履祥), Xu Qian (许谦), Liu Guan (柳贯), Huang Jin (黄溍) and Song Lian; and the other was Siming School, represented by Shi Mengqing and Huang Zhen. Additionally, scholars of the Ming dynasty such as Fang Xiaoru and Zhu Shunshui, could also be regarded as the representatives of *Zhuxue*.

I. Shi Mengqing and Huang Zhen

The Siming School consisted of two major branches: Jingqing Branch (静清支派) and Dongfa Branch (东发支派), respectively represented by "The Records of Jingqing Scholars" (《静清学案》) and "The Records of Dongfa Scholars" (《东发学案》), both of which were compiled into the *Scholarly Annals of the Song and Yuan Dynasties*. Both of the branches originated from *Zhuxue*, but neither stuck to its ideas conservatively. Instead, they either "creatively developed some of its propositions" in a detailed way with "deeper thinking" or criticized/opposed some of those over their paradoxes. By doing so, they showed a scholar's authentic critical thinking and the pursuit of "mind peace", which echoed Wang Yangming's idea that "*liangzhi* is the moral principle of an individual", and reflected the inner spirit of Zhedong scholarship. Therefore, the studies of both branches are viewed as the "rectification" or "dissimilation" of Zhu Xi's thought.

Jingqing Branch was named after Jingqing *Chushi* (处士)[1], the self-addressed literary name of Shi Mengqing. Shi Mengqing (1247–1306), courtesy name Jingzheng, literary name Guozhai or Jingqing *Chushi*, was a native of Yinxian County. As one of Shi Dushan (史独善)'s grandchildren, he was a member of the distinguished Shi family in the Siming area during the Song and Yuan dynasties. In the family, there were three members[2] who once served the Song imperial court as prime minister, including Shi Hao. Besides, the family had also made great achievements in culture. At the age of 12, Shi Mengqing was admitted into *Guozixue* (国子学)[3], doing well in the learning of books like *The Spring and Autumn Annals* and *The Rites of Zhou* 《周官》[4]. In the first year of the Xianchun period (1265), he was awarded the degree of *jinshi*, thereby appointed as *zhubu* of Jingling, and then as *jiaoshou* (教授)[5], in charge of educational affairs of Jiangyin and Pingjiang. He was a disciple of Yang Jie (阳吕), a scholar of Baling, Hunan Province, who was respected as "Master Xiaoyang". Most of the descendants of the Shi family were disciples of *xinxue* scholar Yang Cihu before they turned to *Zhuxue* following Shi Mengqing.

---

①   *Chushi*, literally, recluse, refers to a scholar who doesn't seek any official position.
②   Specifically, the three members of the Shi family were Shi Hao, Shi Miyuan (史弥远) and Shi Songzhi (史嵩之).
③   *Guozixue*, the Imperial Academy, the highest-level education institution in some Chinese feudal dynasties (*cf. Taixue*, in the preface).
④   *The Rites of Zhou* (《周官》 , aka. 《周礼》) records the official system of the Zhou dynasty (1046 BCE–256 BCE) and the national systems of the Warring States Period.
⑤   *Jiaoshou*, an official title, in charge of educational affairs of a certain region.

Shi Mengqing's academic turn was associated with the trend of the era during the reign of Emperor Lizong of the Song dynasty when *Zhuxue* was treated as the authentic study. However, the study of Jingqing School was not merely the replication of the ideas in *Zhuxue* but the development and rectification of them. The most prominent academic characteristic of Shi Mengqing was "to apply the Confucian principles into practical service".

In the process of spreading *Zhuxue*, Jingqing fostered numerous Confucian talents in Siming area, among whom were the two considerably well-known brothers, Cheng Duanli and Cheng Duanxue.

Cheng Duanli (1271–1345), courtesy name Jingshu, literary name Weizhai, was respected as Master Weizhai. Cheng's family originally lived in Poyang, Jiangxi, and later they moved to Yinxian County, where Cheng received education as a disciple of Shi Mengqing's. Cheng wrote three volumes of *Graded Learning Schedule* and six volumes of *Weizhai Collection*. He devoted his whole life to the education career, successively working as *jiaoyu* (教谕)[1] in Jianping and Jiande counties, as the head of Jiaxuan Academy and Jiangdong Academy, and then as *jiaoshou* in Taizhou Prefecture and Quzhou Prefecture. In terms of educational theory and methodology, Cheng inherited and formulized Zhu Xi's educational ideas. Zhu Xi's disciples summarized what Zhu Xi taught and talked about in his daily classes and compiled "Six Principles of Reading", namely, concentration and determination, sequential learning, thinking profoundly based on close reading, reading carefully with modesty, experiencing what has been read, and reading with a great effort. It was just based on the "Six Principles of Reading" that Cheng compiled his *Graded Learning Schedule (Dushu Fennian Richeng)* under the guidance of Shi Mengqing. Specifically, *fennian* means to divide the adolescent education into three phases: basic learning; lesser learning and learning of adulthood; and *richeng* means the temporal periods of reading plans, in detail: four days as a period for classics reading; five days, for history reading; six days, for

---

①   *Jiaoyu*, director of education.

Confucian articles; ten days, for assignments (including reading, reviewing and writing). Time allocation for new lessons and reviews is arranged respectively and orderly. Each book, scheduled with a notebook, is registered and checked according to the time span for the task: unit; day; period. In terms of the reading order of books, Cheng's schedule suggests to read firstly *The Lesser Learning* (《小学》) and *The Great Learning* (《大学》), to read secondly *The Analects of Confucius* (《论语》), *The Mencius* (《孟子》), and *The Doctrine of the Mean* (《中庸》), and to read finally other classics. Cheng's *Graded Learning Schedule* actually built a complete Neo-Confucian educational system with clear teaching contents and teaching planning. It exerted great influences upon the education of the Song and Yuan dynasties, and it was still regarded as study guide even in the beginning years of the Ming dynasty.

The founder of Dongfa School is Huang Zhen.

Huang Zhen (1213–1281), courtesy name Dongfa, was called Master Yuyue by his disciples. He was born in Guyao, Minghe Township (now Huangjia Village, Yangshan Township), Cixi County, Qingyuan Prefecture of the Southern Song dynasty. He was a famous scholar and thinker of late Southern Song, and also an important representative figure in the spreading and researching of *Zhuxue* in Siming area.

It was from Yueqing of Wenzhou that Huang Zhen's ancestral family moved to Cixi, and they had lived there around 200 years by the time of Huang Zhen as the seventh-generation descendant of the family.

Born into poverty, Huang Zhen applied himself diligently to his studies. Taught by his father, he perused the "Four Books"[1] as a young boy. In the first year of the Duanping period (1234) under the reign of Emperor Lizong, he entered the Yuyao County School. In the spring of the third year of the

---

[1] The Four Books, including *The Great Learning*, *The Doctrine of the Mean*, *The Analects of Confucius* and *The Mencius*, are Chinese classic texts illustrating the core value and belief system of Confucianism. They were selected by Zhu Xi of the Song dynasty to serve as a general introduction to Confucian thought, and they were, in the Ming and Qing dynasties, made the core of the official curriculum for the imperial civil service examinations.

Duanping period (1236), he continued his study at the County School of Yinxian County, learning from Wang Wenguan (王文贯), one of the third-generation disciples of Zhu Xi's. A year later, Huang Zhen began to make a living by teaching, and meanwhile engaged in some agricultural work. In the fourth year of the Baoyou period under the reign of Emperor Lizong, he was finally enrolled as *jinshi* at the age of 44 after his times of failures in the provincial-level imperial examination. Just as a saying goes, "Heaven helps those who help themselves."

In his early years, Huang Zhen tasted the hardships of life as one of the lower-class people. Therefore, when he later worked as an official, he issued many practical measures to save the people out of trouble based on his investigation of the real civil situation. In the first year of the Kaiqing period under the reign of Emperor Lizong, Huang Zhen was awarded the title of *digonglang* (迪功郎)[1] after a three-year vacancy of duty, and started his official career as *xianwei* (县尉)[2] of Wuxian County, Pingjiang Prefecture. What he did in his positions "all earned reputation" due to his diligence in administration and his exclusion of malpractices.

After the Yuan dynasty annihilated the Song dynasty, Huang Zhen started his secluded life in a forest, vowing not to serve the Yuan dynasty as an official. About his seclusion, Quan Zuwang made a detailed depiction, "In his later years, Huang Zhen returned from his official residence to the Zeshan Mountain in Lingxu Township, Dinghai County, where he named his house Zeshan Xingguan[3] and his room Guilai Zhilu[4]. Soon, he moved to the Nanhu Lake of Yinxian County, and then moved to Huanxi, where he called himself Zhangxishan Jushi (a resident of Zhangxi Mountain). Not long after, he started his hermit life at Tonggu (now Tong'ao Village, Ningbo)." During such an unstable period, Huang moved around here and there so as to avoid the pursuit

---

[1]   *Digonglang*, a ninth-grade official rank.
[2]   *Xianwei*, subordinate of the magistrate, in charge of public security.
[3]   Xingguan refers to a temporary dwelling place for a guest.
[4]   Guilai Zhilu refers to a residence for one who comes back home after his resign.

of the Yuan soldiers. Finally, he led a secluded life in Baozhuang Mountain to the east of the city of Ningbo until he died of worry and anger 5 years later.

As an official, Huang Zhen cared much about the people's hardship, scorned fame and wealth, harbored integrity and honesty, and kept his noble character. After the fall of the Song dynasty, he was determined to live a hermit life, thereby showing his high dignity as a scholar-bureaucrat. He was highly praised as "a famous Jiangnan official for his proficiency in the Confucian classics, noble character and effective administrative practice". In commemoration of his great achievements, his disciples built an academy near Zeshan Mountain after his death.

Although Huang Zhen was a follower of *Zhuxue*, his study covered a larger and broader area. Proficient in Confucian classics and history, he made great contributions to the study of Confucian classics, Neo-Confucianism and history. Among his works, four kinds of masterpieces can still be seen today: ninety-seven volumes of *Huang Zhen's Daily Records*, nineteen volumes of *Brief Chronicles of Ancient and Contemporary Dynasties*, one volume of *A Sequal to the Brief Chronicles of Anciert and Contemporary Dynasties* (《古今纪要逸编》), and one volume of *Records of History Compiling in Wuchen Year*.

Huang Zhen's academic inheritance mainly came from Zhu Xi, and partly from the studies of Lü Zuqian and Zhang Shi (张栻)[1]. Quan Zuwang claimed that Huang Zhen, as a disciple in the fourth generation of Zhu Xi's Neo-Confucianism, had made a great contribution to the spread and development of *Zhuxue* in Siming area. Quan also argued that Huang's inheritance of *Zhuxue*, on the one hand, rectified the exegetic inclination of Zhu Xi's followers, pursuing the deeper exploration of the essence of *Zhuxue*, and on the other hand, focused on the expression of his own viewpoints through the critical thinking based on the pursuit of "mind peace", thereby "revitalizing the spirit

---

① Zhu Xi, Lü Zuqian and Zhang Shi were together called "Three Confucian Sages of Southeastern China".

of Master Zhu Xi".

Huang Zhen was an authentic Neo-Confucian, and he put forward some positive proposals to reform maladministration and revitalize national power in the vulnerable Southern Song society.

The ethical code was treated as the foundation of a country. In Huang Zhen's social and political thoughts, maintaining the code of ethics was the first issue in ruling a country. He believed that the code of ethics was the basic value of a society, laying the foundation for the existence of everything including that of a state or an imperial court. According to the code, loyalty and filial piety were the foundation of a country, and must be observed generations after generations. He believed that filial piety was a fundamental value, and it laid the ground for all such things as people's compassion, sympathy and kindness, their behavior of universal love for people and animals, and even the great achievements in governing a country and building a peaceful world.

Huang Zhen believed that a monarch, on the premise of safeguarding the monarchy, should keep sincerity in mind, harbor modesty for advice with modesty, take the safety of his country as his own responsibility, and have self-discipline, so as to guide his subjects with his own integrity. He also claimed that a monarch should maintain the code of ethics and rule the state together with the scholar-bureaucrats. In addition, a sovereign should take benevolence as the foundation of his governance, ruling the state with virtues; meanwhile a minister should serve his lord according to the reasonable principles while respecting and loving him. Huang's statements on the monarch-minister relationship derived from the ideas of Confucius and Mencius, though they were totally different from the imperial autocracy represented by the idea that "a minister has to die when required to do so by his monarch".

Huang Zhen suggested simplifying administration and fulfilling redundancies so as to save the people's labor. As long as Confucian scholars were involved in the theory of politics and state governance, they all regarded whether to be supported by the people as the fundamental factor to decide the rise and fall of a country, and they all took supporting and benefiting the people as the core of their political proposition. Huang Zhen argued that if an imperial court was obsessed with benefits, then the lower-rank officials would choose to please their lords with benefits so that the harms to the people were just caused by those who valued their own gains. Thereby, he clearly stated that it was only the simplified administration that could bring convenience to the people, i.e., an imperial court should reduce its official staff so as to reduce the possibilities for officials to exploit the people. Huang was quite clear about the root cause of the people's poverty, which, however, could only be relieved by a fundamental adjustment of the systematic oppression and exploitation in the whole feudal society. This idea meant that the imperial court should give up exploitation, which was impossible for both himself and the emperor.

In terms of the Neo-Confucian thought, Huang Zhen inherited some basic views of Zhu Xi's. For example, he said, "$li^{①}$ remains unchanged no matter how many ages it goes through." He also said, "All things equally reflect the function of the heavenly principle, be it a very tiny thing or a fairly short movement of action." However, Huang Zhen rectified Cheng Yi and Zhu Xi's concept of "*dao*", arguing that the "*dao*" doesn't go beyond things, and *dao* is *li*, by which people do everything, just as by a road/way people walk. Furthermore, Huang Zhen claimed that *dao* doesn't go beyond the things in the universe, nor is it illusionary or mysterious. Instead, *dao* exists in what people see and do in everyday life. Thereby, he drew the conclusion that "*dao* is in the things and affairs". This thought, to some extent, deviated from Zhu Xi's Neo-Confucianism and went closer to the view of Chen Liang who believed "*dao* is conveyed in the daily practice".

Huang Zhen criticized Buddhism and Taoism as well as their diffusion into Neo-Confucianism. He especially upbraided Lu Jiuyuan over his *xinxue*, denouncing his "preaching Zen by way of Confucianism". As for Yang Shi

---

① The term *li* (理) is the core concept of Zhu Xi's Neo-Confucianism, also known as "the heavenly principle", "the principle of universe", or "the cosmic principle".

(杨时)[①] and Xie Liangzuo (谢良佐), two disciples of Cheng Yi and Cheng Hao, Huang argued that Yang's scholarship was mixed with Buddhism and that Xie's learning was even worse, and it had more disadvantages, although Xie himself was a very talented scholar. He also criticized scholars like Zhang Jiucheng (张九成), Lu Jiuyuan and Yang Jian, believing that their "preaching Zen by the way of Confucianism" was influenced by Xie Liangzuo. In his eyes, Confucianism, if impacted by Zen, would lead to "the worst of the disasters for Confucians". From above, it can be surely asserted that Huang was an authentic Neo-Confucian, actively defending the purity of Confucianism.

About Huang Zhen's Neo-Confucian thought, Quan Zuwang, in his *Scholarly Annals of the Song and Yuan Dynasties*, had a discussion in a single character titled "The Records of Dongfa Scholars", in which Quan named Huang as a representative of "Dongfa School", which showed Huang's high status in the academic history. As to the knowledge inheritance in Huang's family, his three sons, namely Huang Menggan (黄梦干), Huang Shuya (黄叔雅) and Huang Shuying (黄叔英), all stuck to Huang's scholarship, in which all the three made certain academic achievements. Huang's studies were then spread by his disciples Yang Weizhen and Cheng Jing.

[①]   Yang Shi (杨时, 1053–1135), courtesy name Zhongli, literary name Guishan, was a great philosopher of the Song dynasty. Yang Shi, Xie Liangzuo, You Zuo (游酢) and Lü Dalin (吕大临) were together called "Four Great Disciples of the Cheng Brothers".

II. Fang Xiaoru

Siming *Zhuxue* witnessed an earth-shaking event in the Ming dynasty, namely, the execution of Fang Xiaoru and his "ten familial exterminations"[①]. Less than five kilometers west to the Dajiahe Township, Ninghai, Ningbo, there is a stream. To its south is the Gaicang Mountain (aka. Cha Mountain) with winding ridges, and to its north is the Xiangshan Port with blue waves. In further distance are villages like Xue'ao and Xiashan. Along the stream, which flows down the northern foot of the Gaicang Mountain, there are many peach trees, hence the name Peach Flower Stream (Taohua Xi). On the east of the stream is Xixiawang Village where most villagers are surnamed Wang, while on the west of the stream is Xishangfang Village where most residents have Fang as their family name.

Now, the former village is still populated while the latter has become a farmland. It's hard for a stranger to believe that there was once a village here on such a farmland full of all kinds of green crops. It's true that a big family had lived here in this village for about 300 years, generations after generations, along with the nature's gifts. Like villagers of other places, they had led a peaceful life, the elderly enjoying their rest, women cooking with smoke rising from the kitchen chimneys and young children reading aloud before the whole family suddenly vanished completely in a hot summer day around 600 years ago. Such a large village has become deserted since then. All these changes were caused by Zhu Di, Emperor Chengzu of the Ming dynasty, who massacred all the people here.

The village was home to Fang Xiaoru. It was just due to him that the

---

① Usually, the death penalty was "nine familial exterminations", which means to execute all of a criminal's relatives by nine clans/groups. But in the case of Fang Xiaoru, apart from his relatives of nine groups, all his disciples were also executed as the tenth group.

tragedy happened, and the aftermath is still there even more than 600 years has passed.

As a follower of the Jinhua School of Zhu Xi's Neo-Confucianism, Fang Xiaoru was a favorite disciple of Song Lian. For his great ambition, authentic Confucian scholarship, excellence of writing and loyalty before his death, Fang was honored as the "Scholarly Model of Eastern Zhejiang and Western Zhejiang"[1], "Latter-day Cheng-Zhu"[2] and "Father of the Scholarship of Ming" by Liu Zongzhou and Huang Zongxi, two great representatives of *Zhexue* (Zhejiang scholarship).

Fang Xiaoru (1357–1402), courtesy name Xizhi, was "bright and excellent in nature" in his very young age. He started to write poems at the age of 6, and developed his favorite habit of learning at around 10 years old, "reading ten lines at one go and learning a lot every day", hence the nickname "Xiao Hanzi"[3]. As a boy, he lost his mother and when he got older, he lost his father, who was wrongly sentenced to death. His father, Fang Keqin (方 克勤), was transferred to Jining, Shandong Province in the fourth year of Emperor Hongwu's reign (1371) as the magistrate of Jining Prefecture, where he implemented policies of exploiting farmlands and developing education, and obtained a sound political reputation, so that he was commended by Zhu Yuanzhang (朱元璋), Emperor Taizu of the Ming dynasty. However, he was banished later to Jiangpu, Guangdong Province, where he worked as a drudge, because of a false accusation from a lower-ranking official called Cheng Gong (程贡). While he was to be set free at the end of the year, he was involved in

---

① In the Tang dynasty, Zhejiang was divided along Qiantang River into eastern Zhejiang and western Zhejiang. The area of the two divisions was much larger than today's Zhejiang Province, also covering the partial regions of present-day Jiangxi and Anhui provinces.

② Cheng-Zhu, short for Cheng Yi, Cheng Hao and Zhu Xi, the founders of Cheng-Zhu Neo-Confucianism.

③ Xiao Hanzi, literally, little Han Yu. An honorary nickname, it indicated that young Fang Xiaoru was a latter-day Han Yu, who was a master of prose and outstanding poet of the Tang dynasty, as well as the first proponent of what later came to be known as Neo-Confucianism.

a case of corruption named "Kong Yin Case"[①] and was eventually sentenced to death in the ninth year of Emperor Hongwu's reign (1376).

When his father was in prison, Fang Xiaoru, advised by his father, paid a visit with his essays to Song Lian, who was an erudite scholar of Jiangnan area and a great master of literati in the early Ming dynasty and honored by Emperor Taizu as "The Leading State-founding Civil Official" for his profound learning, high morality and excellent essays. After reading his essays, Song Lian thought highly of Fang Xiaoru, and compared him to "the only phoenix among hundreds of birds", meanwhile he found Fang had an air of dignity with good looking, so he cheerily accepted Fang as one of his disciples. After 4 years of learning from Song, he became excellent in writing, and got admired heartfeltly by those well-educated scholars and Confucians. However, Fang Xiaoru was not satisfied with his being known just for his essays, because he had a bigger picture in his mind. He emphasized the cultivation of mind instead of the skills for writing. "Always taking it as his responsibility to demonstrate the kingly way of ruling so as to realize peace and harmony", he believed the aim of learning was to reach the level of sages like Yi and Zhou[②]—powerful enough to assist the ruling of a state, or Confucius and Mencius—intelligent enough to develop philosophical theories. He refused the idea to live a hermit life of self-entertainment with wines and poems even if one was confronted with obstacles. Therefore, he led a life full of self-control, disciplining all his daily behavior, which showed his readiness for his great ambition.

In the fifteenth year of Emperor Hongwu's reign (1382), due to the recommendation of the Grand academicians Wu Chen (吴沉) and Jie Shu (揭枢), Fang Xiaoru was called to the capital, where he was interviewed

① Kong Yin Case, literally, the Case on Pre-stamped Documents. Concerning corruption and abuse of authority, it was a well-known case of corruption in the early Ming dynasty, during which quite a lot court officials embezzled money through pre-stamped blank forms, causing a great deficit in military provisions.

② Yi and Zhou refer to Yi Yin (伊尹) of the Shang dynasty (1600 BCE–1046 BCE) and Zhou Gongdan (周公旦) of the Western Zhou dynasty (1046 BCE–771 BCE). Their names symbolize the powerful ministers in the imperial court of ancient China.

by Emperor Zhu Yuanzhang, who appreciated Fang very much for his good manners and outstanding intelligence. During the interview, Fang proposed to fulfill *renzheng* (仁政)[1] and reduce criminal punishments. But his proposal was obviously against Zhu's autocratic and repressive measures by which Zhu aimed to eliminate the threat from the high-rank officials usurping powers and to solidate his sovereignty. Therefore, although he appreciated Fang very much, Zhu remarked, "Fang is a man of integrity and dignity, but we cannot use him until he gets more experiences for his talent", and then sent him back home after awarding him a banquet, court garments and lavish gifts. In the following decade, Fang lived in countryside, reading and writing, building his complete thought system—"taking it as his responsibility to spread Ming Neo-Confucianism, to strengthen the code of ethics, to pass on knowledge and to promote the virtues of the king meanwhile sympathizing people's hardship". During this period, his ability in writing essays was acknowledged as the best. In the twenty-fifth year of Emperor Hongwu's reign (1392), in view of the repeated recommendations of the court officials, Zhu Yuanzhang met Fang again and assigned to him a position of *jiaoshou* at Hanzhong Prefecture School (i.e., the principal of the Public High School of Hanzhong Prefecture). Thereafter, Zhu Chun (朱椿), the eleventh son of Zhu Yuanzhang and Prince of Shu, invited Fang to Chengdu, where he taught Zhu's sons, including Zhu Yuelian (朱悦燫), Zhu Chun's first-born son. During his stay at the mansion of the Prince of Shu, Fang got on well with the host Zhu Chun, who then granted a new name *zhengxue* (正学)[2] to Fang's study, which was originally named as "Xunzhi Zhai", to praise highly Fang's upright character and authentic Confucian learning. Therefore, he was later respected as "Master Zhengxue", and his self-collected works were posthumously named *Xunzhizhai Collection*.

In the thirty-first year of Emperor Hongwu's reign (1398), Emperor Taizu died and Emperor Hui (also known as Emperor Jianwen) ascended the

---

[1]   *Renzheng*, benevolent governance.
[2]   *Zhengxue*, literally, upright learning.

throne. In this year, Fang Xiaoru was called to Beijing to serve as *shijiang* (侍讲)① at Hanlin Academy② (翰林). In the next year, he was promoted to Hanlin academician, working at Wenyuan Pavilion (the Imperial Library). Treated by Emperor Hui as a teacher, Fang served the emperor every day as his consultant and would make an explanation whenever the emperor had questions in reading. Later, along with their further communication, Fang was often summoned to reply the emperor's questions about the state affairs. Besides, Fang was appointed the general director in charge of the compilation of historical books like *Veritable Records of Emperor Taizu* (《太祖实录》) and *Encyclopedia of Important Issues* (《类要》). Later, Fang was granted the title *wenxue boshi* (文学博士)③, presiding over the imperial metropolitan examination together with Dong Lun (董伦) and Gao Xunzhi (高逊志) to enroll *gongshi* (贡士)④ scholars from all over the country.

When Zhu Yunwen (朱允炆), Emperor Hui, came to power, instigated by his teacher Huang Zicheng (黄子澄), the Minister of the Office of Imperial Sacrifices (*taichang si*, 太常寺), and Qi Tai (齐泰), the Minister of War, who was recommended to the position by Huang, he successively imprisoned four of his uncles after deposing them as vassal kings. Additionally, Zhu Bo (朱柏), the Prince of Xiang, was forced to commit suicide in fear. Thus, Zhu Di, the Prince of Yan, was plagued by doubts and fear, and then gathered military troops from different sides and controlled Beijing. Subsequently, Zhu Di, quoting ancestral injunctions as a pretext, launched the campaign of Pacification of National Calamity (*jingnan*, 靖难) in the name of "Ridding the Emperor of Evil Ministers" (*qingjunce*, 清君侧) so as to get rid of Qi Tai and Huang Zicheng. In the fourth lunar month of the fourth year of Emperor

---

① *Shijiang*, imperial tutor, in charge of interpreting the Confucian classics for the emperor.
② Hanlin Academy, an elite scholarly institution to perform secretarial, archival, and literary tasks for the imperial court and to establish the official interpretation of the Confucian Classics.
③ *Wenxue boshi*, a post in Hanlin Academy, literally means an erudite scholar of Confucian classics and history.
④ *Gongshi*, candidates who passed the imperial metropolitan examination, the national-level imperial civil service examination.

Jianwen's reign (1402), Zhu Di's Northern Force defeated Emperor Jianwen's Southern Force at Lingbi, Anhui Province, after they fought battles against each other along the Huaihe River. In the sixth lunar month, the Northern Force crossed the Yangtze River before besieging Nanjing, the imperial capital.

As Zhu Di's troops entered Nanjing, the imperial palace went up in flames and Emperor Jianwen was never seen again. More than fifty officials, including Qi Tai, Huang Zicheng and Fang Xiaoru, were arrested and denounced treacherous court officials. As the Prince of Yan started the uprising, his trusted follower Yao Guangxiao (姚广孝) said to him at the farewell ceremony, "Fang Xiaoru is the seed of learning of the country. Leave him alive, otherwise there would be no hope of scholarship." Knowing Fang's fame completely, Zhu Di then invited Fang into imperial palace from prison, where Fang was listed as a treacherous court official together with Huang Zicheng and Qi Tai, and requested him to draft an imperial edict of inaugural address, although Zhu Di strongly hated Fang, who had proposed strategies, drafted imperial edicts and even composed declaration of war against him. However, Fang came into the palace in mourning apparel, crying aloud. Zhu Di then comforted him with a forced smile, "Sir, why are you so sad? My aim of launching the army to Nanjing was to 'pacify the national calamity'. It was just like what Duke of Zhou[①] had done to King Cheng of the Zhou dynasty." Fang Xiaoru stopped crying and shouted, "Where is King Cheng (referring to Emperor Jianwen)?" Zhu Di replied, "He burned himself." Fang then asked, "Then why not enthrone his son?" Zhu Di faltered and said, "A country needs an emperor coming of age." Fang asked again, "Why not his brother?" Zhu Di was speechless. And then, he suppressed his anger and said, "This is a domestic matter of my family. Why do you take so much care? What matters is to draft an imperial edict on

---

① Duke of Zhou, or Zhou Gong (周公), given name Ji Dan (姬旦), was the fourth son of King Wen (周文王) who was the founder of the Zhou dynasty. When King Cheng (周成王), the grandson of King Wen, ascended to the throne at 12 years old, Duke of Zhou acted as the regent to rule the country. Here in this conversation, Zhu Di compared himself to the Duke of Zhou, and Emperor Jianwen to King Cheng.

my accession to the throne. I think only you are in the right position to do so, since I have heard of your talents for a long time." Fang picked the brush and paper and wrote down eight Chinese characters on the paper in anger, which were to the effect that "in the fourth year under the reign of Emperor Jianwen, the bandit of Yan usurped the throne". Then he threw the brush unto the ground. Zhu Di was furious and shouted, "Aren't you afraid of the nine familial exterminations?" Fang Xiaoru replied sternly, "So what if you massacre my family by ten groups?" Although Zhu Di was very angry, he imprisoned Fang instead of killing him, because he thought of Yao Guangxiao's request and what's more, he wanted to force Fang to obey his order one day. After that, Zhu Di threatened Fang by arresting his relatives, but Fang Xiaoru still cried and scolded him as before. Zhu Di then ordered the guards to "cut off his lips and tongue". But Fang still "offended the emperor by spiting blood upon him". Zhu Di was finally outraged and ordered Fang Xiaoru to be dismembered to death on the 25th day of the seventh lunar month. Fang faced death bravely. Prior to his execution, he wrote a song: "Who knows the reason of my nation's chaotic separation? The treacherous officials usurped the throne with conspiracy. The loyal officials are in wrath with blood and tears. What is it other than loyalty to die for my lord? Alas, what an abomination!" He was only 46 years old then. Pitifully, at the same time, his younger brother Fang Xiaoyou (方孝友) was also executed. Later, his wife, surnamed Zheng, and his two sons committed suicide at home, so did his two daughters, by throwing themselves into the river.

Zhu Di executed Fang Xiaoru and his relatives by "nine familial exterminations", and then expanded to "ten familial exterminations", killing Fang's disciples. In total, 873 persons were exterminated. Besides, many of Fang's other familial members were banished to the frontiers. This is a well-known massacre in Chinese history. But such a terrible thing was just the first step of Zhu Di's revenge after he came to power. In the following years, he continued his ferocity and slaughtered approximately 3,000 persons, leaving a cruel and bloody memory in the early years of the Ming dynasty.

Among Fang Xiaoru's works, only *Xunzhizhai Collection* can be seen today. According to *History of Ming* (《明史》), "Fang was good at writing essays featured with profoundness and power. Each of his articles would be widely read once it was finished... However, in the middle years of Emperor Yongle's reign, death penalty would be given to those who kept Fang's writings." Consequently, most of his works were lost such as *Important Issues in the History of the Song Dynasty* (《宋史要言》), *Records of Emperor's Ascending to Throne* (《帝王基命录》), *Civil Administration* (《文统》), *Florid Language in the Book of Changes* (《周易枝辞》), *Contents of the Rites of Zhou* (《周礼考次目录》), and *Annotations to the Self-guarding Words of King Wu of the Zhou Dynasty* (《武王戒书注》). Fortunately, thanks to Fang's disciple Wang Mo (王莫), who, at the risk of being killed, seized Fang's manuscripts and covertly complied them into *Houcheng Collection* (《缑城集》) at his own home. It was not until the Xuande period of the Ming dynasty that "the prohibition on Fang's works was cancelled, and the public was eventually allowed to read them". Then the book was renamed as *Xunzhizhai Collection*. "Xunzhi" (逊志) means a humble mind. As it goes in "Charge to Yue III" of *The Book of History* (《尚书·说命下》): "In learning there should be a humble mind and the maintenance of a constant earnestness; in such a case (the learner's) improvement will surely come." That's why Fang took Xunzhi Zhai (room) as the name of his study, and why his book was named so. Now, the 24-volume book is named as *Xunzhizhai Collection of Master Fang Zhengxue* (《方正学先生逊志斋集》), edited as one of the *First Volume of the Four-branch Book Series* (《四部丛刊初编》). Besides, both *History of Ming* and *The Records of Ming Scholars* recorded Fang Xiaoru's biography.

In terms of Fang's academic thoughts, the most prominent characteristic lies in the political ideas and the pursuit of virtues conveyed in Confucian idealism.

Fang Xiaoru was committed to seeking *"dao"* all his life, which was regarded as the Confucian idealism or the Confucian ideal of values that was repeatedly affirmed by Confucius, Mencius, the Cheng Brothers and Zhu Xi. Specifically speaking, in politics, *dao* was embodied as the way to assist a monarch to rule his country and to regulate his morality, so it was with *dao* that Fang assisted Emperor Jianwen and thereby realized his own political pursuit. That was why Fang was valued highly by the emperor. Besides, Fang refused to take severe punishments as a way to rule a country. Instead, he suggested to take *dao* of Confucian sages to restore the harmonious social atmosphere of the "three ancient dynasties"[1] and thereby to realize peace and stability for both people and their country.

Fang Xiaoru analyzed two essential factors in the evaluation of history: "*shi*" (势)[2] and "*yi*" (义)[3]. The former was the realistic power prevailing in the process of history, to which people should pay much attention, while the latter was a subtle eternal value underneath the historical course, but not limited to a certain moment or thing. *Yi* was respected as a measure and conception for both Fang's era and its following ages. For Mencius, it was the "kingly way", for Zhu Xi, it was the "heavenly principle", while for Fang Xiaoru, it was the "impartial way", which was an eternal norm for the criticism on history. Fang also explored an issue on the orthodox reign of a dynasty, claiming that only those who won people's hearts could be valued as an orthodox one. He argued that winning people's hearts meant winning the heart of heaven, which was a standard for a legitimate orthodox dynasty. Otherwise, it would be an unorthodox one. Orthodox reign was just, and unorthodox one was unjust, by which people could make a judgment in the historical evaluation and thereby to realize the commentary functions of praising, criticizing or persuading.

How to comment on Fang Xiaoru himself and the tragedy of his "ten familial exterminations"?

As for what Fang had done, historians have mainly given positive commentaries. For example, some argue that Fang's response was related to

---

[1] The three ancient dynasties refer to the Xia, Shang and Zhou dynasties.
[2] *Shi*, tendency.
[3] *Yi*, righteousness.

the imperial sovereignty and the welfare of people. His death was not just for a single family, nor out of blind loyalty to the monarch, but for the maintenance of legitimacy of the sovereign. However, opponents have second thoughts on his performance. Qian Shisheng (钱士升) of the Ming dynasty, in his *Memorial Records of Loyal Ministers of the Ming Dynasty* (《皇明表忠纪》), blamed him for the "ten familial exterminations", and believed that it was Fang's goading that led to his own death of torture, the massacre of his whole family and even the ruin of his ancestral temple and tombs. What Qian indicated was that Zhu Di's cruel slaughter was probed by Fang himself.

Fang's case is still a controversial issue nowadays. Some think Fang's penalty of "ten familial exterminations was for the legitimacy of the imperial sovereign". Some assert that Fang's death was out of worthless "blind loyalty". Scholar Zi Zhongyun (资中筠), comparing Fang's death with Bruno's, argues that "As far as the abstract personal morality is concerned, both of them were brave men who would rather die than surrender in order to defend their own 'stubborn principle'. But they had extreme difference between their respective '*dao*' and 'principle'. For Copernicus, Bruno and Galileo, the earth revolves around the sun, which was a fact they had discovered and firmly believed. That could not be changed even by a king or a Pope, unless such a conclusion was overturned by convincing arguments from more intelligent scientists. That was a scientific issue. The question is what did Fang Xiaoru defend? Was there any irrefutable truth beneath the difference of whether a grandson or a son of Zhu Yuanzhang to be an emperor? What was the difference for the country and the people?"

Zi Zhongyun's argument is the same as Zhu Di's over the issue about scholar-bureaucrats caring about the emperor's family affairs. However, in Fang's time, the emperor's family affairs were also the ones of the country and the world. It would be obviously inconsistent with the reality and would put the spiritual pursuit of scholar-bureaucrats in an underestimated situation to think what the scholar-bureaucrats cared about was just the emperor's family affairs. That fact is, Fang's death was for "seeking the rightness". Liu

Zongzhou, a scholar of the Ming dynasty, put forward the same view: "So many deaths just for the rightness". In fact, this statement was from Fang himself. According to *Fang Zhengxue's Chronicle*(《方正学年谱》), when Zhu Di asked Fang's disciples Liao Yong (廖镛) and Liao Ming (廖铭) to persuade Fang to surrender, Fang scolded them and said: "You even haven't learnt the word 'rightness' in spite of your learning for so many years!" Obviously, it was "rightness" that was what Fang stuck to during his trouble time. It was what directly determined his life or death. Then what is the connotation of the word "rightness"? Definitely, it cannot be simply interpreted as "right or wrong to the righteousness". Only by combining it with Fang's Confucian learning can it be interpreted convincingly. Actually, Fang's choice was a continuation of the spirit of Confucius's "dying for supreme virtue" and Mencius's "sacrificing for righteousness".

When the word "rightness" is considered through the combination of its original meaning by Confucius and Mencius, its connotative development by the Cheng Brothers and Zhu Xi, and the fact of Fang Xiaoru's death, it can be interpreted from four aspects: firstly, it is about the judgment on the reality. How to judge what Zhu Di had done before he ascended to throne, loyal or treacherous? Secondly, it is about the assessment on good or evil, and on benevolence or cruelty. Who was good and who was evil, the imperial court or Zhu Di? Thirdly, it is about the evaluation on the maintenance or destruction of sovereign legitimacy. Whether to maintain the existing system? Was it legitimate to usurp the throne through forceful violence? Therein good and evil were to be distinguished from each other. Fourthly, should a scholar-bureaucrat give up his learning, virtues, value and belief from Confucianism? Specifically speaking, should Fang tell lies, draft Zhu Di's inaugural address, and then be a high-ranking official, or adhere to the justice and the right way, and then be executed by ten familial exterminations? Only by this way, can the connotation of the word "rightness" be completely interpreted.

Fang Xiaoru's choice was not made on a whim but with a long-term consideration. He made the decision just to "adhere to his belief through his death". On Fang's death, Liu Zongzhou remarked, "Fang achieved one 'rightness' through numerous deaths, bearing the responsibility for generations after generations under heaven. In defending the orthodox Confucianism, he was worthy of the title of the authentic Confucian scholar of thousand years." To all autocratic monarchs even with super violent force, this means that they couldn't do brazenly whatever they want because there are still martyrs who maintain justice with their blood. The righteousness of heaven and earth would not be weakened by a tyrannical power. That is an eternal enlightenment given to the future generations by Fang Xiaoru's death!

III. Zhu Shunshui

Ascending the steps at the south gate of Longquan Mountain Park in Yuyao, you'll see four stele pavilions after walking through a moon gate engraved with four Chinese characters "*Jianxian Siqi*" (见贤思齐)[1]. They were built to honorarily mark the hometown of four ancient Confucian sages in Yuyao: Yan Ziling (严子陵) of the Han dynasty, Wang Yangming of the Ming dynasty, Zhu Shunshui and Huang Zongxi of the transitional period between the Ming and Qing dynasties. Yan Ziling's and Wang Yangming's steles were built in the nineteenth year under the reign of Emperor Qianlong of the Qing dynasty (1754), and Zhu Shunshui's and Huang Zongxi's steles were both built in the late Qing dynasty. Zhu Shunshui's stele pavilion is inscribed with "*Shengguo Binshi*" (胜国宾师)[2], eulogizing Zhu's virtues for which he, as an old adherent of the former Ming dynasty, was respected by the foreign (Japanese) monarch and his ministers. On the pavilion pillars are Chinese couplets, to the effect that he resolutely crossed the sea to Japan, willing to lead a wandering life in a foreign country, and although poor and humble there, he still held onto his aspiration and shouldered the important task of preserving Chinese culture just as what Confucius had done; he was like a pillar of the Southern Ming regime, his heart for maintaining integrity was as clear as water, and his noble character was like rivers running forever. Zhu Shunshui deserved this high evaluation.

Zhu Shunshui was a contemporary thinker and educator with Huang Zongxi and Shen Guangwen (沈光文), but his life experience and academic achievements were mainly in Japan. Therefore, in his hometown Yuyao, there were not so many historical sites about him, nor were people much aware

---

[1] *Jianxian Siqi*, literally, thinking to learn from the talented and virtuous people when seeing them.
[2] Shengguo, literally, a lost country, refers to the Ming dynasty defeated by the Qing dynasty, while *Binshi* means a person who has no official title/position but is respected by a sovereign.

of him. However, since the 1980s, Zhu's reputation has gradually risen and he has been noticed and studied by many researchers in China; in particular, some people in Japan have great respect for him, which has, to a certain extent, promoted the "craze for Shunshui Studies" in China. In 1982, in order to commemorate the 300th anniversary of Zhu Shunshui's death, the Japan Memorial Association of Zhu Shunshui and the Japan-China Cultural Exchange Association built a monument to Zhu Shunshui in Longquan Mountain, Yuyao, his hometown. On May 20th that year, a Japanese delegation headed by senator Takeshi Toba (户叶武) made a special trip to Yuyao to participate in the opening ceremony of the monument. On the front of the monument, there are eight characters in calligraphic style of running script, saying "Monument to Zhu Shunshui", inscribed by the famous calligrapher Sha Menghai (沙孟海); the back of the monument is engraved with "Commemorating the 300th anniversary of the death of Zhu Shunshui, the pioneer of China-Japan cultural exchange", with the signatures of the above-mentioned associations. Behind the monument are two pine trees, while in front of the monument are two cypress trees planted by Japanese friends, symbolizing the everlasting friendship between China and Japan.

In October 2009, a group of Japanese scholars came again to Yuyao, Zhejiang, to attend the "Sino-Japanese Seminar on 'Shunshui Studies'", during which more than 130 scholars discussed under topics like the modern significance of "Shunshui Studies", its spread and influence in Japan, Zhu Shunshui's thought on good neighborhood and friendship, the relationship between "Shunshui Studies", Japan's "Zhuxue" and "Yangming Studies", Zhu Shunshui and the loyalists of the former Ming dynasty, and the study of Zhu Shunshui's historical relics. In terms of research style, Japanese scholars focused on investigation, empirical study, case analysis and detail research, while Chinese scholars on analysis, comparison and inference. At the seminar, the scholars from both countries fully expressed their views, and had heated discussions in a strong academic atmosphere, which reflected the deep admiration of these Japanese friends for Zhu Shunshui, the "Japanese

Confucius".

Zhu Shunshui was both a great cultural messenger between China and Japan and an important representative in the history of Zhedong scholarship. In Japan, Zhu Shunshui's theory on the governance of country and the management of social affairs promoted the change of Japanese cultural course; while in China, it improved the innovation of Chinese society. Today, it still has extremely important value and inspiration to research Zhu Shunshui's academic thought.

Zhu Shunshui (1600–1682), given name Zhiyu, courtesy name Chuyu, was born in Yuyao. Shunshui was his literary name used in Japan, named after a river in the city where he was born. By this name he cherished the memory of his hometown.

Zhu Zhiyu was born into a scholar-bureaucrat family. At the age of 8, he lost his father and then his family was in decline, getting so poor that even his study was affected. As a child, Zhu studied under the guidance of Zhu Qixuan (朱契玄). Later, he was sent to Songjiang Prefecture with his eldest brother, where he became a Confucian student (*ruxuesheng*, 儒学生). With the help of Songjiang scholars such as Zhu Yongyou (朱永佑), Zhang Kentang (张肯堂) and Wu zhongluan (吴钟峦), Zhu Zhiyu studied the Six Classics intensively, especially Mao's version of *The Book of Songs* (《毛诗》)[1]. Afterwards, because of his talent and intelligence, he was admitted to the Imperial Academy (*Guozijian*) as a student titled *en gongsheng* (恩贡生)[2], and highly appreciated by examiner Wu Zhongluan. In the eleventh year of Emperor Chongzhen's reign (1638), he was recommended to the Ministry of Rites as "top one intellectual and martial talent". However, he found that "the

---

① During the early Han dynasty there were four different versions of *The Book of Songs* available: the Qi (齐), Lu (鲁), Han (韩), and Mao (毛) versions. Mao's version, called *Maoshi* (《毛诗》), was compiled and annotated by Mao Heng (毛亨) and Mao Chang (毛苌) in the Western Han dynasty (202 BCE–25 CE).

② In the Ming and Qing dynasties, in the year when an imperial edict of kindness was issued for a new emperor ascending the throne or other great celebrations, an additional batch of *gongsheng* would be selected, and this group of students was called *en gongsheng* (cf. *sui gongsheng*, 岁贡生).

manners and morals of the time were getting worse, and the national affairs deviated from the right way", and that "official positions were often given for money, while business was often fulfilled through bribe". Unable to join the disordered officialdom, he decided resolutely to give up his official career and to devote himself into academic research instead. Thereafter, he rejected several times of invitations to serve the imperial court from the last years of Emperor Chongzhen (1644) to the last years of Emperor Yongli of the Southern Ming regime.

When Li Zicheng (李自成) and his peasant army captured Beijing in the third lunar month of the seventeenth year of Emperor Chongzhen's reign (1644), the emperor hanged himself on Meishan Hill (now Jingshan in Beijing), marking the end of the Ming dynasty. This year Zhu Zhiyu was 45 years old. Shortly thereafter, Zhu Yousong (朱由崧), the Prince of Fu (*Fu Wang*, 福王), was enthroned in Nanjing as the emperor of the Southern Ming regime with the reign title Hongguang. Then, upon the recommendation of the ministers like Fang Guo'an (方国安), the Jiangnan General-in-chief, Zhu Zhiyu was summoned three times to serve the Southern Ming court, but he declined to do so. Due to his refusal of three times just in one year, he was resented by the treacherous minister Ma Shiying (马士英), and then he was pursued in the next year by the court for the crime of "disobeying the court orders and no etiquette of courtiers". Zhu Zhiyu fled to Zhoushan on a starry night to avoid disaster, where he disguised himself as a businessman. In less than one year, the Southern Ming court was broken by the Qing troops. Then, the rulers of the Qing dynasty took over the Central Plains, and carried out cruel policies of national conquest and oppression, slaughtering people, seizing lands, and making the whole country into a bloodbath. All these aroused people to rise up and resist here and there. Zhu Zhiyu participated in the campaigns of Siming people led by Wang Yi (王翊) to rebel against the Qing and re-establish the Ming. During this period, Zhu Zhiyu went to Annam (now Vietnam) twice and Japan several times to raise military funds, and also attempted to fight against the Qing troops by resorting to Japanese forces, but all failed.

In the thirteenth year of Emperor Shunzhi's reign (1656), Zhu Zhiyu was invited by Zheng Chenggong (郑成功) and Zhang Huangyan (张煌言) to return to China from Japan to resist the Qing dynasty. The next summer, Zheng Chenggong and Zhang Huangyan joined forces with each other for the Northern Expedition, recovering Guazhou (now in Yangzhou) and Zhenjiang. During the period, Zhu Zhiyu personally experienced all the battles. In the sixteenth year of Emperor Shunzhi's reign (1659), Zheng and Zhang's troops were defeated outside Nanjing. Then, Zheng Chenggong and his troops retreated to the coast of Fujian, and later went to the sea until they reached Taiwan. On the other hand, Zhang Huangyan was arrested and killed a few years later. Although giving up all his hopes on the restoration of the Ming dynasty, Zhu Zhiyu vowed never to shave his hair to be an obedient subject of the Qing monarch, so he had to cross the sea again to Japan, and never returned to his hometown. At that time, Japan implemented a closed-door policy and did not allow foreigners to stay. Fortunately, some Japanese students, including Ando Seian (安东省庵), made great efforts for his stay. One year later, they got the approval of the Japanese authority, who made an exception to allowe Zhu and other anti-Qing fighters to stay in Japan. Ando Seian and others admired Zhu so much for his profound knowledge and noble morality that they earnestly requested him to stay in Japan for a long time. Moved by their sincerity, Zhu Zhiyu decided to sojourn in Japan so as to realize his wish to "harbor his ambition and keep his Ming style of clothes". This year, Zhu Zhiyu was 60 years old.

Since Zhu Zhiyu settled in Japan, he had opened the most glorious page of his whole life. In the fourth year of Emperor Kangxi's reign (1665), Zhu was planning to purchase a piece of land in Nagasaki to earn his own living when Oyake Shosai (小宅生顺), a Confucian representative of Tokugawa Mitsukuni

(德川光国)[1], came to invite him to give lectures in Edo (now Tokyo), where Tokugawa Mitsukuni, the vice shogun of Japan and daimyo of Mito, was going to establish schools for education. With humility, Zhu arrived in Edo in the sixth month of the following year where he was greeted by Tokugawa Mitsukuni with sincere and respectful disciple rites. Tokugawa Mitsukuni thought that elderly Zhu Zhiyu was of high virtues and that it was impolite to call his name directly, so he advised him to take a literary name for himself. Zhu Zhiyu then named himself after a river called Shunshui of his hometown, hence the title "Master Shunshui". Under the influence of Tokugawa Mitsukuni, some Japanese scholars and upper-class dignitaries flocked to Zhu's residence, either as disciples or as audience of his lectures. Since then, Zhu shuttled between Edo and Mito, giving lectures in public. Thereafter, the study atmosphere of Edo flourished, which promoted the development of Japanese Confucianism. In addition to Confucianism, Zhu Shunshui also spread Chinese culture and various advanced practical scientific knowledge and skills to Japan, teaching the Japanese people such technologies as agriculture, medicine, architecture and crafts. Many of his Japanese students later became famous scholars in Chinese culture studies. The "Edo school" featured with "Shunshui Studies" exerted great impact on the later "Meiji Restoration", playing a significant role in promoting the progress of Japanese society. With a sincere hope on the lasting friendship between China and Japan, Zhu Shunshui made outstanding contributions to the friendly exchanges between the two nations, and thereby became another famous figure in the history of Sino-Japanese cultural exchanges after Master Jianzhen[2].

In the twentieth year of Emperor Kangxi's reign (1681), Zhu Shunshui fell ill and was bedridden with scabies all over his body due to his failed

---

[1]   Tokugawa Mitsukuni (德川光国, 1628–1701) was the second lord of the Mito Domain and the head of the Mito Tokugawa family, one of the three branches of the Tokugawa clan. He started to compile the *The History of Great Japan* (《大日本史》, *Dai Nihonshi*) during the Edo period (1603–1867) as an enterprise of the Mito Domain, and it was completed during the Meiji period (1868–1912).

[2]   Jianzhen (鉴真), a great Chinese monk of the Tang dynasty who propagated Buddhism in Japan.

acclimatization to the local environment. In the fourth lunar month of the following year, he died in Osaka, Japan, at the age of 83, and was buried in Zuiryusan Mountain (now in Hotachiota, Ibaraki, Japan), the cemetery of the lords of Mito Domain. In memory of his identity as a loyal Ming Confucian, his tomb was built in a pattern of the Ming dynasty, with the inscription "The Tomb of Master Zhengjun of Ming, Zhu Shunshui"[①]. Zhu got his posthumous title as "Master Wengong". Tokugawa Mitsukuni and many other officials attended his funeral.

Zhu Shunshui had few works known to the public in China, while in Japan, he wrote *Chronicle of Services in Annam* (《安南供役纪事》) and *A Brief Account of Unfortunate State Destiny* (《阳九述略》), which mainly summarized the painful lessons for the demise of the Ming dynasty and recorded what he experienced in Annam. He had been engaged in educational activities in Japan for up to 23 years, during which his academic exchanges with Japanese scholars constituted the main parts of his works. In terms of stylistic genre, his works included poetry, *fu* (赋 , prose), *shu* (疏 , annotation), *jie* (揭 , public letter), *shu* (书 , letter), *qi* (启 , document), *yi* (议 , commentary), *xu* (序 , preface), *ji* (记 , account), *ba* (跋 , postscript), *lun* (论 , essay), *bian* (辩 , debate), *zan* (赞 , paean), *zhen* (箴 , proverb), *ming* (铭 , aphorism), *cewen* (策问 , questions and answers on politics), *zatie* (杂帖 , a type of letter), *dawen* (答问, conversation), *zashuo* (杂说, miscellaneous essays), *beiming* (碑铭, inscriptions), *jiwen* (祭文, oration), *zishuo* (字说, interpretation of names), *zhaji* (札记, notes), *zaping* (杂评, miscellaneous comments), *zazhu* (杂著 , miscellaneous works), etc. The 22-volume *Collected Works of Master Zhu Shunshui* compiled by Zhu Qianzhi (朱谦之) is so far a relatively complete version of Zhu Shunshui's works.

The main part of Zhu Shunshui's academic thought was based on the

---

① The inscription was carved in Chinese characters "明徵君子朱子墓" , in which "徵君" (*zhengjun*, literally, a summoned man of noble character) was a honorific title for him. Zhu Shunshui was summoned to serve the imperial court of Ming from time to time in spite of his repeated refusals, hence the title.

reflection on the disastrous social situations of his country when the Ming was defeated by the Qing dynasty. It was also closely related to his experiences in the arduous struggle against the Qing dynasty, as well as his summary on what he did in spreading Confucianism during his long stay in Japan. Zhu's academic thought had a considerable homogeneity with that of Huang Zongxi, Wang Fuzhi, Gu Yanwu and Yan Yuan (颜元) at his time, but it had its own unique characteristics. The basic features of his academic thought lay in the emphasis on practical truth, performance and utility, advocating "the way of learning is in practice"and the idea that "the learning of sages all depends on practical fulfillment". He believed that the function and goal of scholarship was to "use proper methods to do things successfully according to their intrinsic relations and rules, and rule a country through preaching virtues". Therefore, Zhu's scholarship was based on the theory of learning for practical use.

Advocating the practical use of scholarship in reality, Zhun Shunshui firmly opposed the academic atmosphere of the Song Confucianism, which mainly focused on the nature of life instead of the practical reality. He compared this atmosphere to carving a monkey at the end of a thorn, thinking this kind of knowledge just led to the output as worthless as gravel. His severe criticism on the Song Confucianism did not mean that he completely denied the Cheng brothers and Zhu Xi's academic achievements. On the contrary, his attitude towards them was based on a rational analysis and realistic pursuit. According to his works, Zhu Shunshui had great respect for the Cheng brothers and Zhu Xi, often citing their corresponding statements in his own works or speeches. He affirmed that Master Mingdao (Cheng Hao) was generous and broad-minded, while Master Yichuan (Cheng Yi) and Master Hui'an (Zhu Xi) were inevitably picky in pursuing the realization of their own will. All that mentioned above demonstrated Zhu's attitude of seeking truth and reality.

Wang Yangming's scholarship had a great influence in the Ming dynasty, but Zhu repeatedly criticized Wang's nationally prevailing scholarship, although their hometowns were so close to each other that even the lights could be seen and the crow of chickens could be heard from one another. Obviously,

Zhu abandoned his regional contacts with Wang. He thought Wang's lectures were blended with Buddhist expressions. Nevertheless, in his letters and conversations with others, he also praised Wang for his contribution to solving various practical contradictions, calming civil strife and consolidating the order of the Ming dynasty. He also affirmed the reasonable factors in Wang's philosophy about the efforts and contributions for practical utility. This implied that Zhu adopted a very valuable attitude of rational analysis towards Wang's scholarship.

Zhu Shunshui cared about both national governance and the people's livelihood, and he believed that the core of scholarship lay in "governing the country through cultivation, and offering generous help to those in hard situations" so as to solve the urgent practical problems of the times; he argued that the practical learning beneficial to the people and society was in the "plain and ordinary" ways, without anything mysterious; the ultimate goal of scholarship was to achieve practical effects through real practice.

Zhu Shunshui was a great pacifist and also a patriot beyond national boundaries. As Liang Qichao (梁启超) remarked, "Shunshui was not only a great benefactor of Japanese spiritual civilization, but also a generous supporter of their material development." That is to say, Zhu Shunshui spread Chinese culture in Japan in both spiritual and material aspects, and the greatest contribution he made to Japan was that he educated and cultivated a group of disciples, who later became quite famous in Japanese academic and political circles. In the process of establishing Shokokan[①] and compiling *The History of Great Japan*, the far-reaching Mito School (Mitogaku[②]) and Kaisei Neo-

---

① Shokokan (彰考馆), a historical research institute. The Mito School (Mitogaku) was an influential school of Japanese thought which advocated isolationism, nativism, and reverence for the emperor. The origins of this Neo-Confucian movement dated to Mitsukuni's decision to establish a historiographical organization known as the Shokokan in 1657.
② Mitogaku, with Mitsukuni as its founding father. It was one of the most important schools of thought in Edo period.

Confucianism School (Shushigaku)[①] formed. All these exerted an important impact on Japan's academic, social, political and cultural development. The reason why his disciple Tokugawa Mitsukuni was able to create the unique Mito School of history with great achievements also lay in Zhu Shunshui's years of education and edification upon him.

Zhu Shunshui viewed Japan with an equal and friendly perspective. "I regard Japan the same as my own country. I never think it is any different from China." He saw the strengths of the Japanese people and once clearly pointed out, "It is always said that the ancients are higher than the modern people, and that China is better than the foreign country (Japan). But I think this is a remark from some short-sighted and isolated people." Zhu Shunshui had an extraordinary insight beyond national and regional prejudice. Similarly, the Japanese people also gave him a highly respectful courtesy. "Up to the kings of various domains (of Japan) and down to the educated scholars, they were all eager to treat him as a distinguished scholar."

---

① In today's Kyushu, Japan. The representatives of the school includes Ando Seian, Kaibara Ekiken (贝原益轩), etc.

Chapter Three

As Noble as the Mind:
The Glory of the Philosophy of
the Mind in Eastern Zhejiang

Zhedong was the stronghold of ancient Chinese *xinxue*. As an important branch of Song-Ming Neo-Confucianism[①], *xinxue* was established by Lu Jiuyuan, a scholar of Jinxi, Jiangxi Province. Interestingly, Zhejiang people or scholars have a special competence for the comprehension of *xinxue*. Therefore, it was instantly echoed as soon as it was disseminated in Zhedong area, where it witnessed its creative development and the rise of Siming School represented by Yang Jian. Teaching in Siming for more than 20 years, Yang Jian cultivated a large number of talents, and made great contributions to *xinxue*'s taking root in eastern Zhejiang. In the Ming dynasty, Wang Yangming, a great *xinxue* master, hit the world with his "Yangming *xinxue*" which was fast disseminated domestically and then internationally. In terms of academic achievements, Yang Jian's *xinxue* achievements surpassed Lu Jiuyuan's. Wang Yangming's learning reached the highest level, becoming the greatest one among all *xinxue* theories. Thereafter, both the later scholars of eastern Zhejiang, and the common people of entire Zhejiang were deeply impacted by *xinxue* in their studies or life.

At that time, Yang Jian gave lectures at the house of the Shi family[②] in the north of the Moon Lake, while Shen Huan and his brother Shen Bing as well as Lü Zujian on the Bamboo Islet or at Shi Shouzhi's "Bizhi" Pavilion on the lake. Therefore, the Moon Lake became the national center of *Luxue*. But the pity is that when a visitor walks along the Moon Lake today, he cannot find any signs

---

[①] Song-Ming Neo-Confucianism refers to the Neo-Confucianism in the Song and Ming dynasties. Its major representatives include Zhou Dunyi, Shao Yong, Zhang Zai, Cheng Hao, Cheng Yi, Lu Xiangshan, Zhu Xi, Wang Yangming and Wang Fuzhi.

[②] The Shi family was a distinguished family in Siming area, especially during the Song and Yuan dynasties. It had three members who once served the Song imperial court as prime minister (*cf.* Chapter Two).

related to the lectures by those elderly Confucian masters, not even a memorial, or a stone tablet carved with inscriptions like "Master Yang Wenyuan's Lecture Hall".

Fortunately, the relics of Wang Yangming are well protected in Yuyao, such a respectable place honored as "Wenxian Mingbang" (文献名邦)[1].

Wang's relics are mainly seen in the area of Longquan Mountain in the town of Yuyao.

Longquan Mountain, alias, Lingxu Mountain, is located at the center of Yuyao, with Yaojiang River running along its southern foot. It has beautiful scenery of mountain and water with "Longshan and Shunshui" (Scene of Longquan Mountain and Shunshui River) as a great view in Yuyao tour. The mountain is associated with many famous scholars in history. For example, about the mountain, Northern Song scholar Wang Anshi once composed a poem titled "Mooring on Yaojiang River" (《泊姚江》) to the effect that:

> Green the mountain is, the leaves on it swaying like waves rolling,
> Blue the water is, it reflecting the sky into the eyes, dazzling.
> Let's invite the immortals to settle in here as abode.
> Lest it be laborious for them to go up the fairyland.

Famous for its natural landscape and rich in history and culture, Longquan Mountain is the epitome of Yuyao, a provincial-level famous city of history and culture.

In Longquan Mountain, there are many scenic spots and historic sites, where numerous famous ancient figures left their footprints. One of them is Zhongtian Pavilion which was built in the Five Dynasties as a part of Longquan Temple. Another one is Longquan Well, which is said to be a rock-crevice spring flowing out of the underground rock crevices of Siming Mountain. Its water, as green as cat's eyes, runs all year round. There is still a place called Jizhong Tai (a sacrificial altar to commemorate loyal martyrs). It is said that

---

[1] Wenxian Mingbang, a famous place with valuable literature and outstanding scholarly talents.

during the Zhengtong period (1436–1449) of the Ming dynasty, Liu Qiu (刘球), a loyal official as *shijiang* at Hanlin Academy, was killed after being framed by a notorious eunuch named Wang Zhen (王振). Afterwards, to commemorate Liu Qiu, a common person of Yaojiang named Cheng Qi (成器), getting together with his likeminded fellows on the top of Longquan Mountain, made a tearful ceremony with sacrificial offerings on the top rock as the sacrificial altar, hence the name Jizhong Tai. There are also other sites worth mentioning, such as Ziling Pavilion, Yangming Pavilion, Shunshui Pavilion, Lizhou Pavilion, Zhiyang Pavilion, Zhile Pond, Wenchang Pavilion, and a few of ancestral temples and memorial halls (monuments). Besides, over the Yaojiang River at the foot of Longquan Mountain, Tongji Bridge and Shunjiang Tower form a view of "rainbow over the waves and tower on the river". The former was built in the Northern Song dynasty, and the latter in the Yuan dynasty.

Wang Yangming was born in the "Ruiyun Building" at the northern foot of Longquan Mountain. To him, the mountain was not only a site for his birth and childhood education, but also an important place where he placed his emotions and feelings, where he disseminated his *xinxue* thought, and displayed his poetic talents. Twice, he gave lectures in Zhongtian Pavilion which was then full of scholars from near and far. Wang had deep affections for his hometown. In the eighteenth year under the reign of Emperor Hongzhi of Ming (1505), when he was reappointed as an official in *wuxuan qingli si* (武选清吏司, a department mainly in charge of the affairs of military officers) of the Ministry of War, he wrote down the poem "Longquan Mountain Recalled" 《忆龙泉山》 on the memory of the natural landscape of his homeland:

> I love Longquan Temple,
> The monks have no trammel,
> All day sitting by the well fence,
> Otherwise lying under the pine trees.
> Since I bade farewell to the mountain and clouds,
> It's been three years that I am engaged in business.

I miss that spring flowing out of rock crevices,

Which, clean and smooth, all year round runs.

As seen, the word "love" is the direct outflow of his feelings, sentimentally expressing his passions and affections to his homeland.

I. Four Masters of Yongshang

In the Song and Ming dynasties, *xinxue* referred to the learning with *xin* as its *benti*, opposite to *lixue* which takes "*li*" as its *benti*. As a branch of *daoxue*, *xinxue* still based itself on the "Four Books" of Confucianism, but its major foundation was *The Mencius*. In fact, the core concepts like "*xin*" and "*liangzhi*" of the *xinxue* theory were originally the main propositions of *The Mencius*. Mencius claimed that "*ren* is man's *xin*"; and that "the feeling of commiseration belongs to all men, so does that of shame and dislike; and that of reverence and respect; and that of approving and disapproving"[①]. He believed that *ren* (仁), *yi* (义), *li* (礼) and *zhi* (智)[②] are not infused into us from the outside. We are innately furnished with them. Therefore, *xinxue* school's interpretation of the "Four Books" was centered around *The Mencius*. Meanwhile, *xinxue* appeared as the opposite of *lixue*, the former being a reaction against the latter. While *lixue*, especially Zhu Xi's *Collected Commentaries to the Four Books* (《四书章句集注》), once served as the criteria of the official ideology of the feudal ruling class and was regarded as the standard answers to the imperial civil service examination, *xinxue* did not ever enjoy such an honor. That is to say, *lixue* was official, but *xinxue* was "a party out of power", which, as a folk scholarship, was inferior to the former in terms of social status.

---

① The corresponding English version is from *The Mencius* translated by James Legge.
② *Ren*, benevolence; *yi*, righteousness; *li*, propriety; *zhi*, knowledge.

Zhang Xuecheng once said, "The Confucianism in the Song dynasty was divided into Zhu Xi's *lixue* (literally, learning of principle) and Lu Jiuyuan's *xinxue* (literally, learning of the mind). They would be forever irreconcilable with each other, and their differences would be forever inevitable." ("Zhu Xi and Lu Jiuyuan", Vol. 3 of *General Interpretation of Historiography*). Accordingly, "irreconcilable" was to describe their theoretical differences, and "inevitable" to describe the possibility of their differences. It was just by the above statement that Zhang Xuecheng seriously pointed out the academic inevitability of the difference between Zhu and Lu, and the distinction between *lixue* and *xinxue*. Lu Jiuyuan was a follower of Cheng Hao and Cheng Yi, so was Zhu Xi. Here the question is, why did Lu's learning not agree with Zhu's? By the middle of the Ming dynasty, *lixue* had occupied an absolutely dominant position in the official institutional arrangements. Then why did Wang Yangming still oppose the "fragmentation" and "rigidity" of *lixue* and advocate the theory of "*zhiliangzhi*"? It can be seen that the reason why *xinxue* scholars criticized the *lixue* theory lay not only in the fact that *lixue* system had its own problems and its theoretical incompatibility, but also in the truth that the rigidity, oppression and dogmatism of *lixue* theory inevitably led to the reflection and criticism from those scholars with independent thinking, especially when *lixue* theory was forcefully infused into the minds of the learners after it was announced as the authentic ideology of feudal rulers. Therefore, the above expression "their differences would be forever inevitable" inevitably resulted from the development tendencies of different schools as well as their consequent social impacts.

In the Southern Song dynasty, Zhedong academic culture enjoyed its independent development along with the rise of different academic schools. Among them was Siming School in Mingzhou, which mainly preached and spread Lu Jiuyuan's *xinxue* theory. The school was represented by Shu Lin, Shen Huan, Yuan Xie and Yang Jian, who were together called "Four Masters of Yongshang".

Xinxue was the core of Zhedong scholarship, and it took root deeply in eastern Zhejiang through the academic activities of the "Four Masters of Yongshang", who, therefore, were viewed as the founders of Zhedong *xinxue*.

The "Four Masters" carried out their educational and academic activities during the Qiandao, Chunxi and Qingyuan periods, under the reigns of Emperor Xiaozong and Emperor Ningzong of the Southern Song dynasty. At the time, Zhu Xi's learning rose in Fujian, so did Zhang Shi's learning in Hunan, and Lu Jiuyuan's leaning in Jiangxi, while in eastern Zhejiang, active scholars included Lü Zuqian and his brother Lü Zujian from Jinhua, Chen Liang in Yongkang, Chen Fuliang and Ye Shi from Yongjia. It was Lu Jiuyuan's *xinxue* theory that the "Four Masters" mainly disseminated in Siming area.

The following are the life experiences of the "Four Masters".

Shu Lin (1136–1199), courtesy name Fuzhi, a native of Fenghua, was respected as Master Guangping. In the eighth year of the Qiandao period (1172) of the Song dynasty, he was enrolled as *jinshi*, and then started his official career in posts like *jiaoshou* in Xinzhou and Huizhou, and *tongpan* (通判)[①] in Pingyang. For his learning, he once consulted with Lu Jiuyuan and Zhang Shi and attended the lectures of Zhu Xi and Lü Zuqian in Wuzhou (now Jinhua). Subsequently, he studied under the supervision of Lu Jiuyuan, together with his older brother Shu Hu (舒琥) and younger brother Shu Qi (舒琪). He was hardworking and sincere in learning and had pleasure in teaching, and was thereby honored as "the best teacher under heaven". Besides, he cared about national affairs, "taking the rise and fall of the state as his own responsibility, and always keeping in mind the affairs in reality, in spite of his lesser official position". "He paid special attention to the reasons of administrative chaos." His works included *Explorations of Poetics* (《诗学发微》), *Interpretation of The Book of Songs and The Book of Rites* (《诗礼讲解》) and *Classified Essays of Guangping* (《广平类稿》). But his works have been lost except the last one.

Shen Huan (1139–1191), courtesy name Shuhui, respected as Master Dingchuan, was a native of Chongqiu Town, Dinghai (now in Beilun District,

---

① *Tongpan*, a subordinate of county magistrate, is in charge of administering lawsuits.

Ningbo). In the fifth year of the Qiandao period (1169), he was registered as *jinshi*. His official posts included *xianwei* of Shangyu County, *jiaoshou* in Yangzhou and the magistrate of Wuyuan County. In the Imperial Academy (*Taixue*), he made friends with Lu Jiuling and "treated him as a teacher". There he also communicated with Xue Jixuan (薛季宣), a scholar of Yongjia School. Most of his works have been lost. The existing *Dingchuan Posthumous Works* (《定川遗书》) is a book compiled by later scholars on the records of his words and deeds.

Yuan Xie (1144–1224), courtesy name Heshu, respected as Master Jiezhai, was born in Yinxian County. After he was enrolled as *jinshi* in the eighth year of the Chunxi period (1181), he worked successively as *xianwei* of Jiangyin County, the subordinate of the head of *changping si* (常平属官)[1] of Fujian, and the prefect of Jiangzhou Prefecture. In the early years of the Qiandao period (1165–1173), he entered the Imperial Academy (*Taixue*), where he met and showed his admiration for Lu Jiuling. Later, he socialized frequently with the scholars of Jinhua and Yongjia. Proficient in ancient and present learning, he never stopped writing all his life. His works that still exist today include *Jiezhai's Notes of Lectures in the Imperial Palace on Mao's Version of The Book of Songs* (《絜斋毛诗经筵讲义》), *Yuan Zhengxian's Posthumous Works* (《袁正献公遗文钞》)[2], etc.

Yang Jian (1141–1226), courtesy name Jingzhong, respected as Master Cihu, was a native of Cixi. After he was granted the degree of *jinshi* in the fifth year of the Qiandao period, he successively served as the official registrar of Fuyang County, the magistrate of Shengxian County, and the prefect of Wenzhou. Among the "Four Masters", Yang Jian was a *xinxue* scholar with the most systematical thought. His existing works of 15 kinds, more than 90 volumes in total, are collected in *Posthumous Works of Yang Cihu* (《慈湖遗

---

[1]   Subordinate of the head of *changping si*, a department in charge of grain storage, welfare, water conservancy, etc.

[2]   Yuan Zhengxian, the posthumous title of Yuan Xie. *Yuan Zhengxian's Posthumous Works* was compiled by Yuan Shijie (袁士杰).

书》). His other 13 kinds of works have been lost.

The scholarship of the "Four Masters", first, derived from their family inheritance. For example, Yang Jian was deeply influenced by his father who himself was a scholar; Shen Huan was taught by his father Shen Zhu (沈铢); Shu Lin was deeply impacted by his father-in-law Tong Dading (童大定); and Yuan Xie learned from his father Yuan Wen (袁文) who was also a scholar. Second, their scholarship developed through their associations with other scholars. For example, Yang Jian always communicated with scholars from Yongjia and Jinhua, discussing through letters with Xu Yi (徐谊) and Xue Jixuan, two representatives of Yongjia School; Shu Lin consulted with Zhang Shi and attended the lectures of Zhu Xi and Lü Zuqian; Shen Huan had a close relationship with Lü Zujian (Lü Zuqian's brother), "therefore Shen Huan's learning was actually in line with Mingzhao scholarship (Lü Zuqian's learning)"[①]; Yuan Xie followed the learning of Lü Zuqian, and meanwhile socialized with Chen Fuliang from Yongjia. Third, the "Four Masters" were all students of Lu brothers. The common source of their learning was Lu's *xinxue*. Specifically, Shu Lin, Yuan Xie and Yang Jian were disciples of Lu Jiuyuan, while Shen Huan was a student of Lu Jiuling. Their devotion to *xinxue* theories was actually the result of active choice after their understanding of different academic movements.

Relatively comprehensive and systematic, Yang Jian's *xinxue* thought was viewed as the representative of the philosophic thoughts of the "Four Masters".

Yang Jian inherited the *xinxue* thought of the Lu brothers, and meanwhile offered his own theoretical originality. It was said that when he studied in Xunli Zhai[②] of the Imperial Academy, he realized that "the myriad things between heaven and earth are connected into one, and all of them are not outside my

---

① Mingzhao refers to Mingzhao Mountain, where Lü Zuqian gave lectures and disseminated his teachings for about 5 years, hence the name "Mingzhao scholarship".

② In the late Southern Song dynasty, the students of the Imperial Academy (*Taixue*) were divided into 20 classes under different names such as Zhengxin (rectifying mind/heart) Zhai and Chengyi (making thought sincere) Zhai, and Xunli (following principle) Zhai was one of them.

xin". He was a complete monist of "*xin*", believing that "my *xin* is *dao*" is the orthodox thought of Confucius and Mencius. In his opinion, the Confucian theories of "unity of heaven and man" and "unity of myriad things" are the theoretical basis of "*xin* is *dao*". "Unity of heaven and man" and "unity of myriad things" all mean the unity in "*xin*". "*Xin*" is a clear and self-sufficient *benti*. "The *xin* of man is clear itself, and bright itself... All men have the nature of spiritual wisdom of supreme clearness and brightness, which is not acquired from without, but is rooted in 'xin' by itself, and becomes clear and bright by itself." "*Xin*" is also the universal *benti*, i.e., "all men share the same *xin*". Now that the "*xin*" does not change with the changes of movement, day and night, life and death, and meanwhile it becomes good and bright by itself, without any imperfection, then the "*xin*" is a "shared *xin*". Yang Jian said, "Scholars are supposed to know that all men under heaven, whether they be men in the past or at present, have the same '*xin*', so did Confucius, Lu Jiuling and Lu Jiuyuan, so does Wang Youda (王有大) of Jinxi County, and so do all the people throughout the whole county."[1] This "shared *xin*" "contains heaven and earth, and conceives myriad things". Things like heaven and earth, myriad things, four seasons and all kinds of weather phenomena are all in "*xin*". In this way, the "*xin*" that Yang Jian realized through abstraction is actually the "shared *xin*" by all men, although he based "*xin*" on his subjective self-experience. In this sense, he actually drew an equal sign between the "*xin*" of an individual and that of a sage.

According to Yang Jian, man's original *xin* of supreme good is called *liangzhi liangneng* (良知良能)[2]. Everyone has it, but some people cannot introspect it by themselves due to their "self-doubt". However, this kind of

---

[1] These words are cited from Yang Jian's *An Account of the Memorial Temple of Masters Lu Jiuling and Lu Jiuyuan* (《二陆先生祠记》), which was written in 1193 at the invitation of Wang Youda, the magistrate of Jinxi County, to commemorate the completion of the temple.

[2] *Liangneng*, innate ability. This concept is derived from *The Mencius*: Mencius said, "When people who have not studied have abilities, these are inherent abilities. When people who have not deliberated have knowledge, this is inherent knowledge." (孟子曰："人之所不学而能者,其良能也;所不虑而知者,其良知也。")

human nature of supreme good and *"liangzhi liangneng"* could be inevitably obstructed by *"qibing"* (气禀)[①] and *"siyi"* (私意)[②]. Therefore, if one wants to correct errors so as to reach the supreme good, he is supposed to improve his moral consciousness. In terms of moral cultivation, Yang Jian advocated self-introspection and self-consciousness, and opposed any external coercion from without. Harboring the idea that "learning is not acquired from outside *"xin"* which is good in itself, Yang Jian denied "investigating things to extend knowledge" and "exhaustively seeking myriad principles" advocated by Cheng-Zhu Neo-Confucianism.

In terms of social and political thought, the "Four Masters" had many merits in their views.

Shu Lin's thought was characterized by concern for the people's suffering and worry for the situation that the state and the people were confronted with. Deeply worried about the social crisis of the Southern Song dynasty, he opposed the tendency of the ruling group to retreat due to its weakness in the face of the national crisis, and praised the spirit of "deliberate sacrificing". He sincerely sympathized with people's plights of poverty and sickness under the pressure of war and heavy taxes and he repeatedly mentioned, "the people today are in extreme anxiety" and "the people almost have no ways of making a living". In order to alleviate people's suffering, he put forward a series of political propositions and suggestions, including the "measures on grain storage", "measures on the business of tea and salt", "measures on taxation", and "measures on local administration". Besides, he paid attention to the rights and interests of merchants and advocated reasonable taxation to "ensure merchants' willingness to do their business".

Yuan Xie believed that the imperial court should "follow the will of people" in its administration, which was the starting point of his political thought. "Fundamentally, both the virtues of the monarch and the fame of

---

[①] *Qibing*, vital life energy in man.
[②] *Siyi*, selfish intention.

his officials depend on the conformance to the will of people". These words demonstrated the prominent feature of Yuan's political theory. He put forth that "the hearts of the people should be perceived as my own heart, and mine cannot be ignored, nor can theirs." Whatever a sovereign does should conform to both "the heart of heaven" (heavenly principle) and "the mind of people" (people's will).

Yang Jian took *xinxue* theory as the guide to conduct governance and handle administrative affairs. In his opinion, if the governance is conducted and the administrative business is handled in accordance with the mind of the people (the interest of the public), then the governance is successful and the business works. But if not so, there would be an opposite effect. This is what Yang Jian inherited and developed upon the Confucian "people-oriented" and "human-mind-oriented" ideas. Additionally, Yang Jian suggested that governance should be based on "keeping faith with people" and "cutting expenses" to show care for the people. He pointed out that "for the governance of a country, what is the most important is reference and faith", and "without respect, there must be disadvantages". Furthermore, he claimed, when the court is conducting administration, the expense must be cut down, so as to subsidize the people with the budget surplus. Otherwise, there would be higher taxation upon the people. A country opposed by its people would collapse, and its sovereign would be overthrown consequently. "Only with love to the people, can a sovereign use their labor appropriately without obstructing their work on farm, and when only a monarch loves himself and his state, can he love the people." Yang Jian inherited the traditional Confucian proposition of "governing by virtue", believing that "if the governance is not based on virtue, it is not called governing by virtue, and there would be chaotic situations". If the education of rites and music (traditional Confucian education for social order and harmony) is not based on virtue, the rules of rites and music would arouse the hypocrisy of the people; if the selection and appointment of an official are not based on virtue, "an honest and upright official would be viewed as an unworthy one and vice versa"; if reward and punishment are not based on virtue, then "the reward would be just for one's personal happiness, while the punishment would just cause one's personal anger". Additionally, Yang Jian also demonstrated the importance of administration according to law, believing that "if a decree is not carried out according to law", it would result in the evil of the people, and "would do harm to the law-abiding people".

From above, it can be seen that the political thoughts of the "Four Masters" contained a very valuable factor: affinity to the people.

The scholars in eastern Zhejiang had a preference for *xinxue*, and also had their special creative spirit. During the development of *xinxue*, from Mencius to Lu Jiuyuan and then to Wang Yangming who epitomized the theory, Siming School played an indispensable role in its dissemination and made great contributions, especially Cihu *xinxue* (represented by Yang Jian whose literary name is Yang Cihu), which produced a profound effect and influence. The scholars of this school were the main inheritors who made *xinxue* take root in eastern Zhejiang.

II. Wang Yangming

If it can be claimed that the Siming School in the Southern Song dynasty laid the foundation for the later development of *xinxue* in eastern Zhejiang, then it can be argued that Yangming *xinxue* reached the peak of this theory more than 300 years later.

Wang Yangming's life can be said to be full of legend.

Master Yangming, courtesy name Bo'an, was a native of Yuyao. He once built his study in a cave and named it Yangming Grotto (*Yangmingdong*, 阳明洞), and therefore, he was respected as "Master Yangming".

According to *Wang Yangming's Chronicle* (《王阳明年谱》), on the eve of Wang Yangming's birth, his grandmother dreamed that an infant was sent to her house from the cloud and when she woke up, Wang Yangming was just born. Hence, his grandfather named him Wang Yun ("Yun" means cloud). Thereafter, the local people called the building where he was born as "Ruiyun Building" (literally, a building with auspicious cloud). Unfortunately, he had not been able to speak by the age of 5. One day, an eminent Buddhist monk dropped by. He touched Wang's head and said, "What a lovely boy, but the pity is that the secret of heaven was laid bare." What he meant was that Wang Yangming's given name "Yun" revealed the secret of his birth. All of sudden, his grandfather awakened to it, and then changed his name into Shouren (literally, keeping benevolent). Consequently, he began to speak. This story is somewhat mythical, but it can be seen from it that he did not show any special intelligence and talent at a young age.

Wang Yangming was granted the degree of *jinshi* at the age of 28. Subsequently, he was assigned to be *zhushi* (主事)[1] in the Ministry of War,

---

[1] *Zhushi*, administrative director.

and thereby, he embarked his official career. In the first year of Emperor Zhengde's reign (1506), Wang was relegated to the head of the Post House at Longchang, in Guizhou, after he was punished with 40 floggings, because he offended Liu Jin (刘瑾), a treacherous eunuch official, when writing directly to the emperor to save loyal officials. Wang led a hard life in a dangerous environment at Longchang which was located among remote mountains. More terribly, he could not communicate in local language with the people of ethnic minorities living around, nor could he conduct research because of the lack of books and documents. Therefore, he was very lonely. In this case, the only thing that Wang Yangming could do was to meditate all day in Yangming Grotto. There he thought over and over again the theory of "investigating things to extend knowledge" until one deep night when he got his thorough and clear understanding. When he was asked what he had comprehended, he said, "[About] the way (*dao*) of the sage, my nature is self-sufficient, and it is wrong to seek the principle (*li*) from things." This is Wang Yangming's "Longchang Enlightenment" (*Longchang Wudao*, 龙场悟道), which marked a breakthrough in his *xinxue* theory and his "theory of *liangzhi*" appeared in its embryonic form. Soon after, eunuch Liu Jin was executed, and Wang Yangming was promoted to the magistrate of Luling County, Ji'an Prefecture (now in Jiangxi Province). He governed the county in an orderly manner, making outstanding achievements in administration.

Wang Yangming showed his outstanding military talent in suppressing the long-conspired rebellion of Zhu Chenhao (朱宸濠), Prince of Ning. At the beginning, Zhu Chenhao was politically ambitious, and he strengthened his military power, communicated with dignitaries, and made painstaking efforts in preparing for the rebellion. He was said to have 100,000 soldiers when he staged the battles against the court. Just in several days, his troops occupied the prefectures like Nankang and Jiujiang with the least effort, which panicked the people and shocked the society. At this time, Wang Yangming hurried to Ji'an from Fengcheng where his troops were stationed, but there what he saw was just soldiers in weak force with low morale. Faced with such circumstances,

Wang Yangming, on the one hand, applied the tactic of deception, fabricating the messages of the Ministry of War to deceptively claim that the troops from different places were on their way to conduct a converging attack against Nanchang (the base of Zhu Chenhao); on the other hand, Wang Yangming adopted the stratagem of "sowing discord among the enemy", spreading the forged secret surrender certificates of Zhu's trusted follower. Thus, Zhu Chenhao was puzzled and stayed in Nanchang for more than ten days, not daring to immediately attack Nanjing along the Yangtze River. This won very valuable time for the assembly of official troops. After the assembly was done, Wang Yangming, overriding the opinions of all other officials, first attacked Nanchang, Zhu's stronghold, and soon captured the city through internal and external cooperation, forcing Zhu Chenhao, who was on his way to attack Nanjing, to turn around to rescue Nanchang. In this way, the situation of panic and turmoil at that time was stabilized. Soon after that, the main forces of the two parties had a battle against each other at the Poyang Lake. Wang Yangming, basing his strategy on the state of tiredness of Zhu's returning troops, first attacked the enemy camp at night and won the first battle, which destroyed the morale of the enemy. Then, Wang launched a tactic to demoralize the enemy. Finally, he set fire to the enemy's camp, where the boats of the rebellious troops were linked together with iron ropes, and captured Zhu Chenhao alive. It marked the decisive victory in the war against the rebellion. Thus, in only 35 days, Wang Yangming defeated Zhu's army which was claimed to have 100,000 soldiers. However, after the rebellion, Wang Yangming did not get the reward he deserved. Instead, he was framed by the treacherous officials in the court due to their jealousy, and was nearly killed. In order to avoid trouble, he went to Jiuhua Mountain where he sat meditating on the learning of *dao* in a thatched house, so as to dispel the suspicion of Emperor Wuzong of the Ming dynasty.

When Emperor Shizong ascended to the throne of the Ming dynasty, he affirmed Wang Yangming's contribution to suppressing the rebellion, appointed him the Minister of War (Nanjing)[1], and conferred on him the noble title of Count of Xinjian (*Xinjian Bo*, 新建伯)[2]. After all these difficulties and dangers, his theory of *liangzhi* reached its mature stage. In the first year of Emperor Jiajing's reign, his "Mansion of the Count" (*Bo Fu Di*, 伯府第) was built in Dongguang Fang (now in the north of Shaoxing City). Wang Yangming stayed at home holding the ritual of filial piety after the death of Wang Hua (王华), his father. During the 8 years when Wang Yangming was home, his theory of *liangzhi* increasingly grew fully developed and caused a sensation, attracting more and more followers from near and far. In the fourth year of Emperor Jianjing's reign (1525), Yangming Academy was built in the City of Yuecheng (Shaoxing). However, as the number of Wang's disciples was getting much larger, it was said that his mansion and academy could not accommodate them at all. Therefore Wang had to rent places in and near the city, such as Tianfei Palace, Large Nengren Temple, Small Nengren Temple, Dajiao Temple, Guangxiang Temple. It can be imagined that in those days the City of Yuecheng was crowded with people, here and there, hustling and bustling. The scene entirely reflected the prosperity of Yangming *xinxue* at that time. In the sixth year of Emperor Jiajing's reign (1527), Wang Yangming was ordered by the Ming imperial court to suppress the turmoil in Guangxi where the ethnic rulers (*Tusi*) of Si'en and Tianzhou prefectures rose in rebellion[3]. As the Minister of War (Nanjing) and Censor-in-Chief of the Censorate, he commanded the troops from Guangdong, Guangxi, Hunan and Jiangxi, and quelled the revolt of the local ethnical minorities in Guangxi. In the eleventh lunar month of the seventh

---

[1] When Emperor Yongle (Zhu Di) moved the Ming capital from Nanjing to Beijing, he kept the original six ministries operating in Nanjing, and established their counterparts in Beijing.

[2] Count of Xinjian is actually the Count of Xinjian County. It was just in this county that Wang Yangming captured the head of a rebellion against emperor's sovereignty. That's why he was granted the rank of nobility with "Xinjian" in the title when he was awarded for his great military contributions to the country.

[3] The rebellion took place in Si'en (now Wuming County, Guangxi Zhuang Autonomous Region) and Tianzhou (now Tianyang County, Guangxi Zhuang Autonomous Region). Hence, it was named as "Si-Tian Rebellion" .

year of Emperor Jiajing's reign (1528)[1], Wang Yangming died of illness in Qinglongpu, Dageng County, Jiangxi Province. On his deathbed, he said, "[Now that] My heart is full of brightness, so what else need I say?" Hearing the news, his disciples, including Qian Dehong and Wang Ji, gave up the chance of taking the Imperial Examination, and went to Jiangxi and transported his coffin to Yuecheng. Then he was buried according to his will in a mountain at Hongxi (now Xianxia Mountain), Huajie Village, Lanting Town, in the southwest of Shaoxing.

The theory of *liangzhi* created by Wang Yangming is a great academic innovation. It enhanced *xinxue* to a new theoretical level, and epitomized the development of *xinxue*. He never stopped lecturing all his life, even in the time of wars, and his works were collected in the *Complete Works of Master Wang Wencheng* (《王文成公全集》). With perfect performance in both civil service and military affairs, he not only made great achievements in governance, but also suppressed domestic rebellions, and made great contributions to maintain the sovereignty of the Ming Court. Based on his meritorious deeds in "*lide* (立德), *ligong* (立功) and *liyan* (立言)"[2], he was given the posthumous title "Wencheng", and was granted a memorial tablet in the eastern wing-room of the Confucius Temple, as the 58th great Confucian scholar of that room worshiped by later generations.

The formation, development and maturity of Yang Ming's *xinxue* thought went through a tortuous and complicated process. As he himself remarked, his *xinxue* achievements came out of "serious difficulties and setbacks of thousand times".

In the process of Wang Yangming's pursuit of knowledge, there is a famous story of "Investigating Bamboo". As he was investigating bamboo, he expected to find out the way of the sages by investigating such specific

---

[1]   Specifically, Wang Yangming died on the 29th day of the eleventh lunar month in the seventh year of the Jiajing reign, which was January 9th, 1529, according to the conversion between the Chinese ancient calendar and the international Gregorian calendar.

[2]   *Lide*, establishing virtues; *ligong*, establishing accomplishments; *liyan*, establishing words.

things like bamboo. Facing the bamboo, he closed his eyes and sat quietly for seven days, but he learned nothing. What's worse, he fell ill due to such a hard mental labor and his health was also harmed. By that moment, he hadn't suspected the disadvantages of Zhu Xi's learning, but only regretted that he had no gift to become a wise sage. He wondered, "Given that things under heaven are countless, how can a man investigate them exhaustively? And how can a man attain the principles through investigating grass or trees? If he can, then how can he convert the principle of grass and trees into human moral consciousness?" This inspired him to think deeply about various issues in Zhu Xi's theory.

The core propositions of Wang Yangming's *xinxue* system include: "*xin* is *li*", "unity of knowledge and action" and "*zhiliangzhi*".

"*Xin* is *li*" means that the "heavenly principle" is in the mind of human beings rather than outside their mind. But Zhu Xi argued that the fundamental criterion for all the social moralities is the "heavenly principle" out of the mind and that if one wants to be a wise man or a sage, he should "investigate things to extend knowledge" and "seek the principle by investigating things", and only by "exhaustive research on things" can a man reach the principle of everything before finally getting the "heavenly principle". That is to say, Wang Yangming's theory is entirely on the opposite side. It argues that the mind is the "dominator" of myriad things, determining people's morals and behaviors.

"*Xin*" is the original mind, and "the mind of clear awareness". Once, Wang Yangming was taking an expedition to Nanshan Mountain with his friends and disciples when a friend took the opportunity to ask him, "Since the flowers in the mountain blossom and fall all by themselves, what do they have to do with my mind?" To this question, Yang Ming replied, "When you haven't seen the flowers, they and your mind are 'both in silence'. But when you're looking at them, they present themselves to you, in bright colors and swaying postures. They are clear and true, so you know that they are not out of your mind. Similarly, none of the phenomena like the height of the sky, the thickness of the earth, and the auspiciousness and misfortune of human beings can be reasonably judged without the cognitive activities of people with spiritual awareness." Therefore, Wang Yangming believes that the understanding of the world is closely related to people's active cognitive and practical activities.

According to the theory of psychological cognition, everything out of the mind seems "nonexistent" to the cognitive subject. If one does not "pay attention" to it "with the mind", it is "meaningless/senseless" to both the subject and the object itself—that's what Wang Yangming means by "both in silence". Thus, in cognitive activities, the "attention" of the subject is of decisive significance to the object. Meanwhile, the "attention" of subject comes out of the "mind". Therefore, Wang Yangming claims "no things outside the mind" and "no principles outside the mind".

Wang Yangming's concept of "unity of knowledge and action" emphasizes the practical characteristics of *xinxue* theory. He opposes Zhu Xi's claim that "knowledge goes before action", considering it untenable. He believes that "knowledge" itself is accompanied by action, while "action" itself with knowledge, and they are inseparable with each other. Wang puts forward three key points when discussing the relationship between knowledge and action. First, knowledge and action are treated as one united *gongfu*, and they are inseparable. The term "*gongfu*" refers to the process of knowing and practicing. Second, the relationship between knowledge and action is a dialectical unity. Knowledge is the starting point and the guide of action, while action is the result and realization of knowledge. Third, the fundamental purpose of "action" in the process of knowing and practice is to achieve the ultimate good by eliminating "unkind ideas". In essence, it is a process of cultivation and practice of moralities.

"*Zhiliangzhi*" is the academic purpose put forward by Wang Yangming in his later years. It summarizes the main characteristics of his philosophical thought and is the "key essence" of his academic final conclusion in his whole life. Wang Yangming believes that *liangzhi* is the origin of the universe and contains infinite possibilities; everyone has *liangzhi*, whether they be rich or poor, noble or humble, inferior or influential, wise or foolish; *liangzhi* itself is perfect, flawless and universally effective. Therefore, whoever is willing to be a good man can become a man of morality and nobility as long as he strives to be self-reliant and self-improved, no matter what ability he has or what fate he experiences. That is to say, everyone is equal, and everyone is able to be a sage through learning. By the statement "the street is full of sages", Wang Yangming actually means that everyone has the possibility of becoming a sage.

Wang Yangming believes that "Your *liangzhi* is your own moral principle", which indicates that *liangzhi* is the moral criterion of an individual. Everyone has "*liangzhi*". Therefore, when one observes things and analyzes problems, he has his own independent thinking and judgment, knowing right and wrong, good and evil, and he "is not supposed to deceive it [*liangzhi*]". In this sense, for any authority outside your mind, whether you obey or resist them can merely be determined by your own "*liangzhi*". You should have your own independent thinking or judgment, rather than following blindly, even if they are the words of Master Zhu Xi or Confucius. Therefore, Wang Yangming's *xinxue* theory contains strong subjectivity, including both the subjectivity of knowledge and the subjectivity of values. It establishes the spirit of self-confidence, self-esteem and self-reliance, and respects the development of individual personality and the exertion of subjective initiative, which is totally different from the practice of belittling individuals and strengthening hierarchy in traditional Chinese society. In fact, Wang's theory contains a kind of revolution of thought.

III. Scholarship of Wang Yangming's Disciples

After Wang Yangming's death, *Wangxue* was divided into different schools.

There were many kinds of views on the differentiation of *Wangxue* schools represented by Wang Yangming's disciples. For example, Wang Ji, believing some of them mistakenly interpreted Wang Yangming's learning, divided them into four schools, namely, Yanxi, Dangxia, Guiji and Mingjue[①]; while Huang Zongxi, according to human geography, divided them into seven main schools: Zhezhong *Wangxue* (in central Zhejiang), Jiangyou *Wangxue* (in Jiangxi), Nanzhong *Wangxue* (in the area nearby Nanjing), Chuzhong *Wangxue* (now in Hubei and Hunan), Beifang *Wangxue* (in northern China), Min-Yue *Wangxue* (in Fujian and Guangdong) and Taizhou *Wangxue* (in Jiangsu).

Among them, the *Wangxue* scholars from Zhezhong *Wangxue* School or Zhedong region constituted a branch with a large number of followers and extraordinary ideas. The early representatives of this school were Wang Ji, Qian Dehong, Huang Wan, Zhang Yuanbian, etc.

Wang Ji (1498–1583), courtesy name Ruzhong, literary name Longxi, was a native of Shanyin. In 1521, Wang Ji "went to study [under the supervision of Wang Yangming] for the first time", when Wang Yangming returned from Jiangxi to Yuecheng (Shaoxing). Wang Ji became a disciple of Wang Yangming later than others but he was highly valued by his teacher. Academically, Wang Ji advocated innovation and self-awareness, not sticking to the teacher's

---

① The division of these four schools was originally based on Wang Ji's criticism on other *Wangxue* scholars for their unorthodox interpretations of "*liangzhi*" theory. To be specific, Wang Ji thought of himself as the orthodox successor of Wang Yangming's leaning, and divided others' misunderstandings on the extension of "*liangzhi*" into four schools, namely, Yanxi (following), Dangxia (being at present), Guiji (returning to silence) and Mingjue (clear awareness).

theory, which was quite different from Qian Dehong's relatively conservative attitude. The internal contradiction and the academic differentiation in *Wangxue* stemmed from the different views of Wang Yangming's disciples on his "Four-sentence Teaching":

> There is no distinction of good or evil in the original substance of the mind,
>
> But there is distinction of good and evil in the activation of intention,
>
> Knowing the good and evil is "*liangzhi*",
>
> And doing good and eliminating evil is investigating things.

The above teaching was established by Wang Yangming as the "orthodox idea" in the spread of his learning. However, as for the understanding of the relationship between *benti* and *gongfu* in Wang's theory of "extension of *liangzhi*", his disciples had different interpretations. For example, Wang Ji emphasized that one should start from *xinti* (心体)[1] and replace *gongfu* with *benti* as dominator. He believed that the *xinti* has "no good or evil", nor do "intention" (*yi*, 意), "*liangzhi*" and "thing" (*wu*, 物) that *xin* applies. That is what is known as "Fourfold Nothingness" (*siwushuo*, 四无说)[2]. On the contrary, Qian Dehong, another disciple of Wang Yangming's, advocated that one should start from *gongfu*, which includes investigating things, extending knowledge[3], making sincere intention, rectifying the mind and self-cultivation, so as to realize the nature of no good or evil of the *benti*. Towards the opposite opinions, Wang Yangming harbored an inclusive attitude. He said, "The viewpoints of you two gentlemen are just for the use of each other. You'd better not take into account only one side." This debate took place on Tianquan Bridge on the evening of the eighth day of the ninth lunar month in the sixth

---

① *Xinti*, the original substance of the mind.

② Fourfold Nothingness, put forward by Wang Ji, is a term related to Wang Yangming's Four-Sentence Teachings (*cf.* the previous statement in this chapter). It means, in a transcendental sense, that the key concepts in the Four-Sentence Teachings, including the original substance of the mind, intention, *liangzhi* and thing, are all freed from attachments.

③ In *xinxue* theory, "*liangzhi*" is occasionally substituted by "*zhi*" (knowledge).

year of Emperor Jiajing's reign, hence the historical term "Tianquan Zhengdao" (天泉证道)[1].

Wang Ji put forward the theory of "*liangzhi xiancheng*" (良知现成)[2], which was criticized by scholars like Qian Dehong and Huang Wan. Qian Dehong (1496–1574), given name Kuan, courtesy name Hongfu, was a native of Yuyao. He was respected as Master Xushan by scholars who named him after Lingxushan (Lingxu Mountain). As the first and cherished disciple of Wang Yangming, he advocated self-cultivation through *gongfu* of "doing good and eliminating evil". Wang Ji's and Qian Dezhong's studies are different in the following aspects. In terms of the relationship between *benti* and *gongfu*, one is for *benti* while the other for *gongfu*; in terms of the relationship between nature and human, one is for nature while the other for human; in terms of the approaches of extension of *liangzhi*, one is for the readiness of *liangzhi* while the other for the extension of *liangzhi* through the practice of *gongfu*. According to Qian Dehong, *liangzhi*, as the original substance, is "supremely good" and "pure" in iteslf, but man has *xixin* (习心)[3], and thereby, his intention would produce the distinction of good and evil if he is influenced by the outside factors like "restraints of individual temperament or obstruction of things". So it is necessary that "effort in the extension of *liangzhi*" should be put into each link of the process. This is the indispensable *gongfu* of "doing good and eliminating evil" in moral practice. On the theory of moral cultivation, Qian emphasizes "practice of *gongfu* through things", which has its positive significance, compared with Wang Ji's empty interpretations. But in the mastery of the inner spirit of Yangming *xinxue* like "self-dominance" and "personal norms", Qian is interior to Wang Ji, and more conservative than him.

Huang Wan is another scholar who criticized Wang Ji.

---

[1]   Tianquan Zhengdao, Debate on *Dao* on Tianquan Bridge.
[2]   *Liangzhi xiancheng* literally means the "innate knowledge of the good" is in a constant state of readiness and fullness.
[3]   *Xixin*, idea/knowledge learned from what is seen and heard. It is a Confucian term opposite to *liangzhi*.

Huang Wan (1480–1554), courtesy name Shuxian, was a native of Huangyan, Taizhou. He was appointed as Minister of Rites in Nanjing and was a Hanlin Academician. At the age of 34, Huang Wan had academic talks with Wang Yangming and Zhan Ganquan (湛甘泉)[1] in the capital. Later, in Yuyao, he took on Wang Yangming's "teaching on the extension of *liangzhi*" and named it concise and straightforward "study of Confucianism", and meanwhile called himself a "disciple" of Wang Yangming's. With his learning covering both Cheng-Zhu Neo-Confucianism and Yangming *xinxue*, Huang wrote many works, and many kinds of books still exist today, more than 50 volumes in total, including *Shilong Collection* (《石龙集》). Huang Wan befriended Wang Ji, but had different academic views from the latter. In the twenty-first year of Emperor Jiajing's reign (1542), they had times of "deep debates" on their travels. Huang Wan interpreted Wang Yangming's *benti* of "*liangzhi*" according to the "theory of *genzhi*" (艮止之旨)[2], believing the contact of man's *liangzhi* with the things outside the mind should be in the same way as what is shown by the hexagram "*gen*" in *The Book of Changes*. That is to say, "Resting when it is the time to rest, and acting when it is the time to act. When one's movements and pauses all take place at the proper time for them, his way (of proceeding) is brilliant and intelligent". He criticized Wang Ji's idea that "Nothingness is the orthodox idea of Confucianism", claiming that Wang's thought that views *xinti* as "nothingness" not only "falls into emptiness" in moral cultivation, but also blends with Taoist idea that "the nameless is the beginning of heaven and earth" and Buddhist idea that "formlessness is infinite stillness", so that it cannot be categorized into Confucianism.

Zhang Yuanbian (1538–1588), courtesy name Zijin, literary name Yanghe, was a native of Shaoxing. His academic thought derived from the theory of Wang Ji, but he disagreed with the argument that "Wang Ji only focuses on

---

[1] Ganquan is the literary name of Zhan Ruoshui (湛若水), a famous thinker, philosopher, politician, educator, calligraphist and great Confucian scholar of the Ming dynasty.

[2] Literally, *genzhi* means that the hexagram "*gen*" in Eight Diagram denotes immobility or stillness. The theory of *genzhi* was put forth by Huang Wan based on his study on *The Book of Changes*.

benti but evades *gongfu*". Therefore, he stood out and openly "criticized Wang Ji". Like Qian Dehong, he opposed the idea that "there is no distinction of good and evil for *liangzhi*" and denied Wang Ji's theory of "Fourfold Nothingness". In the practice of moral cultivation, Zhang advocated "perception goes side by side with cultivation". "Perception" refers to the understanding of the original substance of *liangzhi*, while "cultivation" refers to the adherence in moral practice. He said, "Cultivation with perception is authentic cultivation; and perception based on cultivation is authentic perception... perception goes side by side with cultivation."

In addition, Ji Ben (季本), another disciple of Wang Yangming, also raised dissent against Wang Ji's theory "full of emptiness". Ji Ben (1485–1563), courtesy name Mingde, literary name Pengshan, was a native of Kuaiji. In his more than 20 years of work as an official, wherever he went he always gathered disciples and lectured *Wangxue*, diligently and tirelessly. Opposite to Wang Ji's theory viewing the nature as dominator, Ji Ben "valued *li* (principle), rather than the nature, as dominator". He disagreed with the empty talk on *miaowu* (妙悟)[1] mentioned in Buddhism, but advocated starting with the study of Confucian classics in learning and putting the learning into practical use. Ji Ben's learning had a distinct practical characteristic.

Following Wang Ji, the leading figure of *Wangxue* School in central Zhejiang was Zhou Rudeng (周汝登, 1547–1629), a native of Shengxian County of Yue Prefecture (now in Shaoxing). His courtesy name is Jiyuan and literary name Haimen. A disciple of Wang Ji, Zhou was born nearly 50 years later than his teacher. Zhou firmly trusted Wang Ji's theory of "Fourfold Nothingness" and developed it in his own way. He introduced the ideas of Buddhism and Taoism into the theory of "*liangzhi*", therefore his learning was full of strong color of Zen.

In the Tianqi and Chongzhen periods (1621–1644) of the Ming dynasty, Zhezhong *Wangxue* was mainly composed of three schools, namely Liu

---

[1] *Miaowu*, spiritual perception.

Zongzhou School, Tao Shiliang School and Shen Guomo School.

Tao Shiliang (1571–1640) was a disciple of Zhou Rudeng's, and therefore he inherited the thought of Zhou Rudeng, fond of introducing ideas of Buddhism into Confucianism. He attached importance to Wang Ji's research approach of replacing *gongfu* with *benti*, believing that "if *benti* is known, then *gongfu* is seen in it". Besides, he also followed the Buddhist belief of "karma" (retribution for sin), which represented a trend of social thought in the late Ming dynasty, namely, confluence of *xinxue* and Buddhism.

Shen Guomo was another disciple of Zhou Rudeng's. His academic activities were mainly in Yuyao, where he gave lectures on *Wangxue* at Yaojiang Academy. On the relationship between "extending (the innate) knowledge" (*zhizhi*, 致知) and "seeking sincerity in the mind" (*chengyi*, 诚意), Shen advocated that *zhizhi* should be given priority, believing that "if learning does not start with the extension of innate knowledge, then there would be the disadvantage of 'no authentic sincerity'". On the relationship between learning and its practical use, Shen argued, "the reason why human mind is not rectified lies in the misunderstanding of learning". Learning is above everything else. Both Tao Shiliang School and Shen Guomo School had academic disputes with Jishan School (Liu Zongzhou School) which was on behalf of those *Wangxue* schools that advocated rectifying *Wangxue* theory.

IV. Jishan School

In eastern Zhejiang, Liu Zongzhou and Huang Zongxi can be viewed as two key figures in the development of Zhedong scholarship.

Liu Zongzhou (1578–1645), courtesy name Qidong, literary name Niantai, was a native of Shanyin. Because he lectured in Jishan Mountain in the north of Shanyin, he was respected as "Master Jishan". In the twenty-ninth year of Emperor Wanli's reign (1601), he was granted the degree of *jinshi*. Thereafter, he served as *zhushi* in the Ministry of Rites, the prefect of Shuntian Prefecture (Beijing), the censor-in-chief of the Censorate, etc. An upright man in nature, he always spoke frankly in front of the emperor, but was dismissed several times. Striving for the rights of survival for the people in the late Ming dynasty, he wrote to the emperor many times to denounce the maladministration of the government. He insisted on the anti-Qing stance, opposed national oppression, and participated in the planning of anti-Qing affairs. In the second year of Emperor Shunzhi's reign (1645), the Qing army went southward and occupied Yangzhou, Nanjing and then Hangzhou. Witnessing the failure of anti-Qing campaigns, Liu Zongzhou was full of anger and agony, and finally died of hunger strike. Liu Zongzhou had 376 disciples in total, including Huang Zongxi and Chen Que. His works were compiled into the 40-volume *Complete Works of Master Liu Zongzhou* (《刘子全书》) by Dong Ruisheng (董瑞生) and the 24-volume *Supplementary Compilation of Complete Works of Master Liu Zongzhou* (《刘子全书遗编》) by Shen Fucan (沈复粲).

In terms of Liu Zongzhou's academic source and lineage, at the age of 26, he was formally acknowledged as a disciple of Xu Fuyuan (许孚远), a Neo-Confucian of Deqing (in Huzhou, Zhejiang Province). Xu was a disciple of Tang Shu (唐枢) who was a student of Zhan Ganquan, a Ming-dynasty Neo-

Confucian, and Zhan's academic thought was close to that of Wang Yangming. Liu Zongzhou was the last great *xinxue* scholar of the Song and Ming dynasties. Although his academic thought took *xinxue* as its core, it meanwhile included and integrated the essence of Zhu Xi's *lixue* and Lu Jiuyuan's *xinxue*. Based on the differentiation, explanation and rectification of the doctrines of Cheng-Zhu Neo-Confucianism and Lu-Wang *xinxue*, Liu Zongzhou put forward the concept of "*shendu*" which was of great practical significance.

Liu Zongzhou, in his learning, elevated the status of "*renxin*" (人心, human mind), combined "*renxin*" with "*daoxin*", individual temperament with heavenly principle, and *gongfu* with *benti*, emphasized "*gongfu*" for "*shendu*" in practice, and also denied the rigid theory of dualism developed by the Confucian scholars of Song, namely, the division of "human mind" and "the mind of *dao*", as well as the separation of "heavenly principle" and "man's desire". Besides, Liu Zongzhou developed the theme of "sincere intention" in *The Great Learning*, and thereby put forward the "theory of sincere intention" which takes "intention" of the mind as original substance". Also called by some scholars as the "theory of subjective intention", it was an important rectification on Wang Yangming's theory of "*liangzhi*".

Liu Zongzhou's disciples inherited and developed his academic thought and formed their own theories. Their studies were together called "Jishan School" in history. The scholars who spread the thought of the school were divided into three groups: First, Zhedong scholars who inherited Liu Zongzhou's theory. They further developed Liu's theory and created their own more complete and newer thoughts, continuing rectifying Wang Yangming's *xinxue* theory, and gradually realizing the historical turn from Yangming *xinxue* to Zhedong historical studies. Huang Zongxi was one of the representatives of this group. Second, non-Zhedong scholars represented by Cheng Que and Zhu Yuan (祝渊), who demonstrated their academic creativity when disseminating Liu's theory. Third, those who deviated from Liu's learning and shifted their scholarship from *xinxue* to *lixue*. They include Zhang Yangyuan (张杨园), Wu

Fanchang (吴蕃昌) and Shen Yun (沈昀), etc. Among them, Zhedong scholars, including Huang Zongxi, established Zhedong historical studies, forming the mainstream in the evolution and development of Liu Zongzhou's thought and theories.

Huang Zongxi is an authentic successor of Liu Zongzhou's learning. When following Liu's theory, he demonstrated his great creativity in extending new possible academic space. From the perspective of philosophy, Huang's thought could still be categorized into Wang Yangming's *xinxue* system, but he rectified Wang's system when inheriting Liu Zongzhou's *xinxue* theory, therefore, Huang's learning belongs to rectified *Wangxue*. During the process, Huang developed Wang Yangming's theory of "unity of knowledge and action" into the theory of "*gongfu* is *benti*", which is of more practical significance.

The theory that "*gongfu* is *benti*" is an important proposition with epochal significance. It marks the shift from the ontology of traditional Neo-Confucianism (*xinxue*) to the theory of practice and methodology, which is a major change in the theme of philosophical research. Cheng-Zhu Neo-Confucianism discusses the original substance of myriad things in the universe without taking into account the human subjectivity. This abstract discussion actually has no direct relationship with the shaping of ideal sages required in essence by Confucianism. Therefore, the so-called theory of "investigating things for extension of knowledge" is bound to be fragmented; Lu Jiuyuan's *xinxue* draws the discussion of external "heavenly principle" back to the subjectivity itself, and establishes the priority of the subject's mind and nature in making sages. However, Lu's *xin* in his theory that "universe is my heart-mind" is still an abstract *benti*; although Wang Yangming's theory of "extension of *liangzhi*" is based on the theory of *xinxue*, he actually emphasizes the unity of internal original substance of *liangzhi* and the external heavenly principle in the dialectical interaction, and establishes the inseparable integrity of *benti* and *gongfu*. His propositions such as so-called "unity of knowledge and action", "understanding *benti* is *gongfu*", and "understanding *benti* through *gongfu*" actually view the *benti* (i.e., truth) as the realization process closely related to *gongfu*. Liu Zongzhou made a further development and put forward theory of "*shendu*", integrating *benti* and *gongfu*, and correcting the one-sided empty idea of "replacing *gongfu* with *benti*". Liu believed "the more meticulous the *gongfu* is, the clearer the *benti* is", by which he realized the turn from the learning of mind and nature of the Song and Ming scholard to the learning of practice. Huang Zongxi, when inheriting the theory of Liu Zongzhou, put forward a new proposition that "the mind has no *benti* and where *gongfu* reaches is *benti*", and thoroughly cracked the transcendental idealism of Confucian epistemology and moral cultivation theory, realizing the shift from traditional philosophical ontology to epistemology and theory of practice. Besides, Huang Zongxi's theory also has internal similarities with the concept that "human nature is a possibility" by Ernst Cassirer (1874–1945, a German Jewish philosopher) in modern Western philosophy and the concept of "practice first"[1] in Marxist philosophy. It was just under the guidance of these advanced philosophic thoughts that Zhedong scholarship made such unprecedented achievements.

Huang Zongxi's progressive philosophical thought had an important impact on his historical research and the establishment of Zhedong School of historical studies, which will be further elaborated in the following chapter.

Chen Que was another important disciple of Liu Zongzhou's.

Chen Que (1604–1677), courtesy name Qianchu, was a native of Haining, Zhejiang Province. His given name was Daoyong, and original courtesy name Feixuan. His wrote works of up to hundreds of thousands of Chinese characters in total, including "Criticism on The Great Learning", "Zen Barriers" (《禅障》), "Interpretation of Nature" (《性解》), "Notes on Learning" (《学谱》), "On Books of Burials", "Customs of Burial Rites" (《丧俗》) and "Conventions on Burials" (《葬约》), as well as some poems. It was in his middle age that Chen became Liu Zongzhou's disciple, but he won great

---

[1] Marxists hold that man's social practice alone is the criterion of the truth of his knowledge of the external world.

achievements in his academic thought through developing and expanding Liu's theory. Qian Mu (钱穆) wrote in his book *Academic History of China in Recent 300 Years* (《中国近三百年学术史》), "Qianchu (Chen Que)'s learning is derived from the theory of Liu Zongzhou, and can be traced back to the teachings of Wang Yangming, and even to the ideas of Mencius." His most innovative achievements lie in his work of developing the idea of "Good of Nature". His academic achievements were not as good as Huang Zongxi's in general, and some of his views even contradicted Huang's. Nevertheless, he formed his own academic characteristics. That is to say, Chen and Huang both had their own merits. On the outlook of human nature and the relationship between principle and desire, he affirmed the idea that the good or evil in human nature depends on what is acquired instead of what is innate. He advocated that "*qi*" (气), "*cai*" (才) and "*xing*" (性)[①] cannot be separated. He disagreed with the Song scholars on their teachings of the opposition between "nature of heaven and earth" and "nature of individual temperament" or the contradiction between "heavenly principle" and "human desire". He said, "The heavenly principle is seen from human desires. The proper human desire is what is thought to be the heavenly principle. If there is no human desire, then there is no heavenly principle." On the outlook of knowledge and action, he advocated the unity of "rectifying heart/mind" and "practical pursuit" and the unity of knowledge and action. He claimed, "A heart/mind rectified leads to right investigation of things and right extension of knowledge, while a heart/mind not rectified leads to wrong investigation of things and wrong extension of knowledge." Meanwhile, "rectifying heart/mind" should be combined with "practical action". Besides, he advocated "learning of *suwei*[②]", i.e., "learning of practice". Believing that one needs to make practical efforts, because "learning is endless" and it is impossible to have a sudden awareness

---

① *Qi*, vital force; *cai*, gift; *xing*, nature.

② *Suwei* (素位) literally means to be satisfied with the current state/position. The learning of *suwei* emphasizes practical principle, practical action, practical effect and practical learning.

or to achieve it overnight, Chen opposed Zhu Xi's view of "getting a thorough understanding all of sudden". On the viewpoint about *The Great Learning*, Chen disagreed on listing the book in to "Confucian classics" as was done by Cheng-Zhu Neo-Confucians, pointing out that "today has today's supreme good, and tomorrow has tomorrow's one", and therefore, there is no absolutely unchanged standard of "supreme good for the pursuit of knowledge". In response to various superstitions at that time, he expressed his atheistic view that neither heaven nor earth has their will, nor could they bring disasters or blessings to people, that is to say, "Whether man is good or not, his disaster or blessing depends on himself, instead of being given by heaven and earth." Also, he drastically attacked Buddhism, pointing out that the so-called "releasing all living creatures from the sea of misery actually means the extinction of them".

As a folk thinker, Pan Pingge was a maverick, much more rebellious than Chen Que. But his academic thought can also be categorized into the system of *xinxue* theory.

Pan Pingge (1610–1677), courtesy name Yongwei, was a native of Wenxi, Cixi County, Zhejiang Province (now in Zhenhai District, Ningbo). As a folk thinker during the Ming and Qing dynasties, he had never been a high-ranking official in his life and received little attention, and therefore, the records of his life and experiences were seldom archived. It was Mao Wenqiang (毛文强), a disciple of Huang Zongxi's, who paid early attention to and introduced Pan's academic thought, and compiled Pan's remaining drafts into *Edition of Master Pan's Records of Pursuing Benevolence* (《潘子求仁录辑要》), meanwhile writing "Biography of Master Pan Pingge" (《潘先生传》) at the beginning of the book. According to Mao Wenqiang, Pan was born into an ordinary family. His parents died early, so he was brought up by his grandparents. His learning was mainly from his self-study. At the age of 15 or 16, viewing himself as an extraordinary person with traditional Chinese virtues, he was determined to make great achievements in his life. At the age of 18, he aspired to become a sage and believed that he could become a man like Confucius or Mencius.

From the age of 21 to 27 or 28, he studied Cheng-Zhu Neo-Confucianism, Wang Yangming *xinxue* and the learning of Luo Hongxian (罗洪先)[1]. In addition, he learned the ideas of Buddhism and Taoism. At the age of 38, he devoted himself to the Confucian learning, and established his own unique philosophical system of *"qiuren"* (求仁)[2] featured with subjective practice, based on the propositions like "loyalty and forgiveness" put forth by Confucius and Zengzi (曾子), "benevolence and righteousness" by Mencius, and "the benevolent views himself in unity with the myriad things between heaven and earth" by Wang Yangming and other Confucian scholars. Meanwhile, Pan denied the learning of morality, mind and nature of Neo-Confucianism since the Song and Ming dynasties, giving a direct comment that "Zhu Xi is associated with Taoism, while Lu Jiuyuan with Buddhism", which reflected the aversion of civilians and citizens to official philosophy. During the formation of his unique academic thought, Pan Pingge wrote many works, including 10-volume *Records of Pursuing Benevolence* (《求仁录》), 10-volume *Records on the Teachings of Confucius and Mencius* (《著道录》), 6-volume *Interpretation of the Four Books* (《四书发明》), 6-volume *Interpretation of The Classic of Filial Piety* (《孝经发明》), 2-volume *Commentaries on Buddhism and Taoism* (《辨二氏之学》), and 5-volume *Records of Word Corresponding to Sage's Thought* (《契圣录》)[3].

Pan Pingge denied the viewpoints on universe and human nature of *lixue* and *xinxue*, aiming at putting forward his own philosophical concepts of *"ren"* and *"qiuren"* featuring subjective practice ethics. He clearly wrote at the outset, "The learning of Confucius is based on the pursuit of benevolence. Benevolence is human nature. Pursuing benevolence is to restore the original

---

[1]   Luo Hongxian (罗洪先, 1504–1564), courtesy name Dafu, literary name Nian'an, was a native of Jishui, Jiangxi Province. He was a scholar in the Ming dynasty and an outstanding geographical cartographer.

[2]   *Qiuren*, pursuing benevolence.

[3]   According to Chen Xiaohong's study, among all Pan's works, only the *Records of Pursuing Benevolence* has been kept today, and all the others have been lost. (*cf.* Chen Xiaohong. *A Study on Pan Pingge's Thought*. Shanghai: Shanghai Normal University, 2012.)

nature." He summed up the whole significance of the learning of Confucius as "pursuing benevolence", which was viewed as a proposition of subjective practicality. "Pursuing" is based on the subject's activeness and conscious initiative, while "pursuing benevolence" is both a practical philosophy and a practical ethics. "Benevolence" is the origin of human nature which is actually in line with the origin of the myriad things between heaven and earth. Meanwhile, human beings and the myriad things are originally united as one. Therefore, Pan's philosophy of "pursuing benevolence" actually involves many philosophical thoughts, such as viewpoints on human nature, cosmology and practical ethics.

During Ming-Qing transition when Pan Pingge lived, there were three major academic schools in eastern Zhejiang. First, the early one was Jishan School represented by Liu Zongzhou. It had many a large number of followers with high academic level; shortly after that, Huang Zongxi became more and more influential with his academic achievements. His gave lectures and ran his Zhengren Academy successfully in Ningbo, boasting a large group of excellent disciples including Wang Sitong, Wang Sida, etc. Second, the Yaojiang Academy represented by Shen Guomo and Guan Zongsheng also had its large scale and influence. Pan Pingge's thought was full of unique characteristics, but his academic influence was not great at that time. That is because, on the one hand, he had no academic lineage with famous great scholars, and on the other hand, in the places like Shaoxing and Kunshan, where he lived for a long time, his teaching activities didn't cause much response and thereby won little attention at that time. Interestingly, his thought aroused great echoes among Huang Zongxi's disciples. For example, after his argument with Chen Chizhong (陈赤衷)[①], even Wan Sitong, Mao Wenqiang and other Huang Zongxi's disciples accepted his thought. That caused Lizhou's vigilance

---

① Chen Chizhong (1627–1687), courtesy name Kuixian, literary name Huangcun. In 1667, he went to Yuyao, where he became a disciple of Huang Zongxi's. Then, he established Yongshang Seminar for Confucian Classics with Chen Xigu and Zheng Liang (郑梁).

and antipathy, which was really regrettable. But fortunately, Mao Wenqiang acknowledged Pan's thought, and edited his works into the *Edition of Master Pan's Records of Pursuing Benevolence*. Mao's work won the approval of book collector Zheng Xing, who then printed the book. That's why Pan's learning can be seen today.

Chapter Four

Collection of Various Thoughts:
The Achievements of Zhedong School of Philology

Ancient Chinese philology mainly focused on literature sorting, including literature collection, identification of authenticity, classification and cataloging, circulation and utilization, as well as combing of the history of literature development, revision of words or characters, identification of distinctive editions, evaluation of the pros and cons of contents, compilation of catalogues, etc. It was as followed what Zhang Xuecheng defined, "distinguishing different academic schools and tracing their respective origins".

The leading scholars of Zhedong School were mainly Wang Yinglin, Quan Zuwang, Zhang Xuecheng, etc. Additionally, what Shao Jinhan, Huang Shisan and Huang Yizhou did in literature sorting also belonged to philology, but their work could also be categorized into the learning of Confucian classics, because the main part of their efforts lay in the annotation and interpretation of Confucian classics.

I. Wang Yinglin

In China, there are three well-known children's enlightenment books, namely, *Three-Character Classic* (《三字经》), *Hundred Family Names* (《百家姓》) and *Thousand-Character Text* (《千字文》), which are together called "San Bai Qian" ("三百千")[①]. Among them, the *Three-Character Classic* was

---

① San Bai Qian, abbreviation of the *Pinyin* names of the above-mentioned three books.

first finished by Wang Yinglin, a scholar in the Southern Song dynasty. Later, it was revised and supplemented by scholars of the following dynasties, and then became the text we see today. Because of its stylistic conciseness and appropriateness, its rhythmic verse and its richness in encyclopedic knowledge, including history, astronomy, geography and morality, for more than 700 years, it has always been an excellent reading for Chinese children to accept the enlightenment of traditional Chinese culture until today when it has even become a book for children worldwide. Its precious value could be seen in the ancient saying: "By fluently reciting *Three-Character Classic*, one can learn all the affairs under heaven and know well the sage's rites and rituals."

Wang Yinglin, the original compiler of the *Three-Character Classic*, was a great Ningbo scholar in the late Southern Song dynasty. It was in a place called Nianshu Xiang[1] in today's urban area of Ningbo where Wang read books in those days. Hence the place got its honorable name "Wang Shangshu Di Xiang"[2]. In his early fifties, Wang resigned and returned to his hometown, where he led a secluded life for around 20 years. During this period, he wrote books while supervising the study of his sons, and finished many writings. Wang Yinglin's tomb is in Tong'ao Village, Wuxiang Town in Yinzhou District, Ningbo. On a hill covered with wild grass, visitors can still vaguely see the tomb path of the past. On both sides of the path are two conspicuous stone figures of a civil official and a military general. The head of the general is broken, while the official still stands upright in awe, with a special expression on his thin face. The great scholar [Wang Yinglin] is long gone, but his spirit is still there! His quiet cemetery is the best place for nostalgia.

Wang Yinglin, courtesy name Bohou, literary name Shenning Jushi, was respected as Master Houzhai. Wang Yinglin's ancestral home was Xunyi County (now Kaifeng), Henan Province. In the first year of the Jianyan period (1127), Wang Andao (王安道), Wang Yinglin's great-grandfather, escorted

---

[1] Nianshu Xiang, literally, a lane where someone reads or studies.
[2] Wang Shangshu Di Xiang, literally, the lane where Minister Wang Yinglin's Mansion was.

Emperor Zhao Gou to the south, and then he, with his family, settled down in Siming.

Wang Hui (王㧑), Wang Yinglin's father, learned in his childhood from Lou Fang (楼昉), a scholar teaching in his hometown. Lou Fang was a disciple of Lü Zuqian. Therefore, Wang Hui's learning was in line with the theory of Lü Zuqian. In the sixteenth year of the Jiading period (1223) under the reign of Emperor Ningzong of the Song dynasty, Wang Hui was enrolled as *jinshi jidi* (进士及第)[1]. Coincidentally, his twin sons were born in the same year, so he named them Wang Yinglin and Wang Yingfeng (王应凤) for good luck[2]. Honest and frank, Wang Hui covered a large and broad area in his learning. He once worked as the historiographer in the Academy of National History and the reviser of the Academy of Records. Wang Yinglin and his brother Wang Yingfeng were intelligent and diligent in their childhood, especially Wang Yinglin, who had read through the Six Classics by the age of 9 and was thereby called a prodigy. Wang Hui, with high hopes for his twins, was extremely strict in their study. After each lecture, he would sit in the classroom to supervise their review and then ask them to answer questions within limited time. The two brothers would be immediately scolded as soon as they were a little slow to answer. As a result, the two brothers worked harder and harder, together made progress in their study and developed their agile thinking.

In the first year of the Chunyou period (1241), Wang Yinglin was enrolled as *jinshi* at the age of 19. But he was not satisfied with that achievement, for he thought what the scholars then were pursuing through imperial examination was not authentic learning but fames and wealth. So he was determined to further his study. Later, he was arranged by his father to study under the supervision of Wang Ye (王埜) at Wuzhou where he and his father worked. In the third year of the Chunyou period (1243), he was transferred to the position of official registrar of Xi'an County, Quzhou. In the ninth year of the Chunyou

---

[1] *Jinshi jidi*, among the top three in the highest imperial examination.

[2] "Lin" in the name "Yinglin" refers to *qilin* (麒麟) or kylin, while "feng" in the name "Yingfeng" refers to phoenix. Both mythical animals stand for good luck in Chinese culture.

period (1249), his official rank was promoted to *congshilang* (从事郎)[1].

In the third year of the Baoyou period (1255), he was transferred to Yangzhou Prefecture School where he worked as *jiaoshou*. In the next year (1266), Wang Yinglin passed the examination of *boxue hongci ke* (博学鸿词科)[2], an examination above the level of *jinshi* in the Song dynasty held every three years. The examination was hosted by the emperor himself and only the first three candidates were to be enrolled. Usually, those who passed the examination were directly assigned to the offices in the imperial court, where they would be highly valued. In the fifth month of the same year, Wang was posted as a counselor of Jiying Palace (集英殿)[3], in charge of rechecking the performance of examinees in the highest imperial examination (*dianshi*). When Emperor Lizong was hosting *dianshi* at Jiying Palace, he attempted to shift the seventh candidate to the first one after he checked all the papers recommended by the examiners. Then, he ordered Wang Yinglin to recheck. Wang, finishing the recheck, immediately turned to the emperor, "This paper is in an authentic ancient style, like a mirror to reflect one's behavior. It is full of firm loyalty to the nation. Congratulations to your majesty on getting such a talent." Then this paper was ranked first. Finally, it turned out to be the paper of great talent Wen Tianxiang (文天祥)[4] when the names of passing examinees were announced. By this event, it can be said that Wang Yinglin was a wise man knowing how to find out talents.

In the first year of the Kaiqing period, Wang Yinglin was promoted to the post of *zhubu* of the Office of Imperial Sacrifices at the age of 37, and he was very much worried about the national situation. At that time, the Jin (Jurchen)

---

[1] *Congshilang*, a sub-eighth-rank official title among the imperial official system of nine ranks.

[2] *Boxue hongci ke* (博学鸿词科), written as "博学宏词科" before the Qing Emperor Qianlong. It was a specialty for scholars who were erudite and excellent in writing.

[3] Jiying Dian, Jiying Palace, built for the highest imperial examination. Jiying, literally, gathering elites.

[4] Wen Tianxiang, a Chinese poet and politician in the Southern Song dynasty. For his resistance to Kublai Khan's invasion to the Southern Song dynasty, and for his refusal to yield to the Yuan dynasty despite being captured and tortured, he is a popular symbol of patriotism and righteousness in China.

army was deployed along the Huaihe River, threatening the security of the Song borders. On the other side, the Song dynasty was trapped in a weak and poor situation. Seeing this, Wang Yinglin wrote an official statement to request the emperor to "clarify the responsibilities of the officials according to state laws and disciplines, prevent ministers from cheating, and look for sages to assist the imperial descendants". He pointed out that the border defense along the Huaihe River was intense, although Right Prime Minister[①] Ding Daquan (丁大全) was purposely concealing border affairs. Mentioning that the local roads in Sichuan were blocked, that the taxes of the imperial court were too heavy, and that the people lived in hardship, Wang even bluntly persuaded the emperor, "Your Majesty, please don't feel comfortable just for your own peace, or feel relieved merely due to the words of honor and joy." When Ding Daquan got to know these words, he was full of anger and hatred in heart and falsely accused Wang Yinglin of making trouble on purpose. Consequently, Wang Yinglin was dismissed from his office. Soon, the Song army was defeated in the border war against the Jin dynasty. It was not until then that Wang Yinglin wasn't reappointed. He first served as *tongpan* in Taizhou and then was promoted to *taichang boshi* (太常博士)[②].

When Wang Yinglin worked as an official in Beijing, he lived next to Tang Dongjian (汤东涧), then deputy minister of the Office of Imperial Sacrifices. They often stayed with each other, talking about the similarities and differences of the schools of Confucianism studies in the Song dynasty. Besides, they discussed various other issues, such as the system of Yongjia School, the studies of Master Shasui[③] on the ancient version of *The Book of Changes*, the theoretical similarities and differences between such academic schools as

---

① Right prime minister, a relative term of left prime minister in ancient Chinese official system. "Right" means the principal, while "left times" deputy.
② *Taichang boshi*, a post of *taichang si* (Office of Imperial Sacrifices), mainly in charge of teaching Confucian classics (*cf.* the note on *boshi* in Chapter Two).
③ Shasui (沙随) is the literary name of Cheng Jiong (程迥), a scholar and poet of the Southern Song dynasty. His works included *Textual Criticism on The Ancient Book of Changes* (《古易考》).

Lianxue (濂学), *Luoxue, Guanxue* (关学), *Minxue*[1] and Jiangxi School[2], the studies of the School of Master Cai[3] on *Hetu and Luoshu* (河图洛书)[4], as well as *jingshu* and *weishu*[5], and the historical studies of western Shu[6]. Wang Yinglin had his own insight into these academic problems. He would give a thorough thought for them and analyze the profound reasons beneath. Tang Dongjian admired Wang Yinglin's knowledge so much that he often said to people, "Among so many talents that I have seen in my life, only Wang Bohou (courtesy name of Wang Yinglin) can be called an authentic scholar." And then he recommended Wang Yinglin to work for the prime minister.

During the reign of Emperor Duzong, Wang Yinglin often admonished the emperor to be industrious and thrifty, to show love to the people with diligent administration, and to resist potential temptation and maintain the loyalty from the people. These admonitions were highly valued by Emperor Duzong, but resulted in the anger of Jia Sidao (贾似道), the prime minister and Emperor Duzong's uncle-in-law. For this reason, Jia repeatedly suggested to expel Wang out of the court, but he was afraid of Wang Yinglin's great reputation and dared not act rashly. Then, he resorted to Bao Hui (包恢) and asked him to warn Wang Yinglin not to say more in front of Emperor Duzong. Hearing Bao Hui's message, Wang Yinglin smiled and said, "It's a small crime to offend the prime minister, but it's a big one to deceive the emperor".

---

[1] In detail, *Lianxue* is the learning of Lianxi, represented by Zhou Dunyi; *Luoxue*, the learning of Luoyang/Yiluo, by Cheng Hao and Cheng Yi; *Guanxue*, the learning of Guanzhong, by Zhang Zai; *Minxue*, the learning of Fujian, by Zhu Xi.

[2] Jiangxi School, a *xinxue* school represented by Lu Jiuyuan, a native of Jiangxi Province.

[3] School of Master Cai, alias, Xishan School (of Master Cai), established by Cai Yuanding (蔡元定). Its learning derived from Cheng Hao & Cheng Yi, Zhang Zai and Shao Yong, focusing on two aspects: *lixue* and *xiangshuxue* (the studies on the hexagram symbols of *The Book of Changes*).

[4] *Hetu and Luoshu*, literally, the former means "the Yellow River chart" and the latter "the inscription of Luo River" . As two cosmological or numerological diagrams, they were employed by both Daoists and Confucians to explain the correlation of the hexagrams of *The Book of Changes* with the universe and human life.

[5] The former refers to the Confucian classics; while the latter, also called "*yizhoushu*" (逸周书), refers to the rest Zhou-dynasty books which were not chosen into Confucian classics.

[6] It was an ancient southwestern area of China, covering present-day Sichuan, Chongqing, and parts of Yunnan and Shaanxi.

In the first year of the Xianchun period under the reign of Emperor Duzong, Wang Yinglin, at the age of 43, was appointed the subordinate of the Minister of Rites as a concurrent post. Later he was gradually promoted to *sheren* (舍人)[1] and *zhongshu sheren* (中书舍人)[2]. In a cold winter day, thunders burst frequently, which frightened the court officials, who then had a heated discussion. Immediately, Wang Yinglin turned to the emperor and said, "This is a sign for those ministers who disobey the orders of the emperor. It is their arrogancy and treachery that lead to the wrath of heaven." Saying so, Wang attempted to warn those treacherous officials, and to strengthen the laws and disciplines. Hearing this, Jia Sidao was very angry with Wang Yinglin and determined to expel him out of the court. In the fifth year of the Xianchun period, Wang Yinglin was transferred to Huizhou as the governor. Two years later, Wang was reassigned to be the head of Imperial Secretariat. Unwilling to see the treacherous ministers in power, Wang Yinglin repeatedly requested to resign, but his requests were not approved. Afterwards, he took the concurrent position of *shilang* (侍郎)[3] of the Ministry of Official Personnel Affairs. Although Wang Yinglin's written advice had little effect, he kept his loyalty and straightforwardness, and continuously wrote to Emperor Duzong to demonstrate his worry about the state, which annoyed the emperor very much. Seeing this, Jia Sidao attempted to drive out Wang Yinglin again. Coincidently, Wang's mother died at the time. Thus, Wang Yinglin resigned with this excuse and returned home.

In the first year of the Deyou period (1275) under the reign of Emperor Gong, Jia Sidao's troops were defeated by Kublai Khan's military force at the Yangtze River, which shocked the imperial court of the Southern Song dynasty. Before long, Wang Yinglin was assigned to be *zhongshu sheren* again, and

---

[1]   *Sheren*, imperial secretary.
[2]   *Zhongshu sheren*, mainly in charge of drafting imperial mandates.
[3]   *Shilang*, deputy minister.

meanwhile he took the post of *zhixueshiyuan* (直学士院)[①]. Then, he soon offered the emperor ten suggestions: "1) To suppress enemy immediately; 2) to confirm administrative and punitive policies; 3) to clarify the sense of honor and shame; 4) to be considerate of the people; 5) to seek high-ranking military officers; 6) to strengthen military training; 7) to prepare provisions and funds for troops; 8) to recommend talents with abilities and responsibilities; 9) to select suitable heads of local governments like governors or prefects; 10) to reinforce coastal defense." Thereafter, Wang provided another ten pieces of advice, but "none was actually applied". Later, Wang Yinglin was transferred to the Minister of Rites, and meanwhile took charge of *jishizhong* (给事中)[②]. During this period, Prime Minister Liu Mengyan (留梦炎) appointed Xu Nang (徐囊), a member of his clique, as *yushi* (御史)[③], and Huang Wanshi (黄万石)—"a rough man of no learning, who lost the city of Nanchang and did harm to the country"—as Jiangxi *zhizhishi* (制置史)[④]. Wang Yinglin angrily wrote to the emperor to prevent Liu Mengyan from appointing his partisans, usurping official positions and harming the country. But all his suggestions were neglected, without any response. Seeing the declining national power, the increasing border crisis and the disorderly imperial court, as well as the gratuitous misinterpretation of his own enthusiastic hope, Wang Yinglin felt it difficult to serve the country in spite of his high position, so he resigned and returned to his hometown Yinxian County, where he spent time in teaching his children and doing academic writing. Afterwards, for several times, he refused the invitations from the court which asked him to go back to work as Hanlin academician. He even started his secluded life, and refused any social activity, when the nation was under the reign of the Yuan dynasty. In the second year of the Zhenyuan period under the reign of Emperor Chengzong (1296) of the

---

① *Zhixueshiyuan*, literally, auxiliary Hanlin academician, a title of concurrent post for an official who worked partly for Hanlin Academy but not as a Hanlin academician.
② *Jishizhong*, in charge of giving suggestions, expostulations and supervisions.
③ *Yushi*, investigating censor.
④ *Zhizhishi*, in charge of military affairs on border defense.

Yuan dynasty, Wang Yinglin died of illness at the age of 74.

In his decades of work as an official, Wang Yinglin, out of concern about the fate of the country, called for reform to revitalize the state. Unfortunately, the Southern Song dynasty was already in decline. The upper ruling class only pursued their own pleasure in the transitory peace, without any intention of governing the country wholeheartedly. The court was dominated by some greedy and incompetent high-ranking officials. Those in power suppressed or even persecuted some positive suggestions for revitalizing the country through reforming the maladministration. In such a case, although Wang was a high-ranking official, he had no opportunity to demonstrate his ambition. However, as an outstanding scholar, Wang Yinglin inherited the fine tradition of Zhedong scholarship, and made great achievements in the field of philology with his skill of "literature sorting" through "extensive searching and exhaustive study". As a forerunner, Wang Yinglin laid the foundation for the textual research of the Qing scholars, and was called "Master of Philology".

Wang Yinglin was a knowledgeable and quick-witted scholar. In his thirties, he made many years of preparation for the examination of *boxue hongci ke*. While working, he borrowed books from various private libraries and studied very hard. He read tons of books, "ranging from Confucian classics, history, as well as commentaries and records, to the works of various pre-Qin schools of thought, from the books of Buddhism and Taoism to the literature on the development of contemporary laws and regulations, from the readings on food and clothing to the good deeds and words of ancient sages, from the records of family affairs to the anecdotes in privately compiled history". After detailed sorting and analyzing, he compiled all these materials into the well-known book *Jade Sea*, which was divided into 248 types in 21 categories: astronomy, law and calendar, geography, state-owned schools, books or articles by ancient sages, literary works, imperial mandate, rites, rules of carriage, sedan chair and clothing, appliances, sacrifice, music, academies, election, official system, military system, tributes, official buildings, economy, military success and signs of luck.

With clear structure as well as full and accurate contents, this book became a necessary reference book for intellectuals to prepare for the examination of *boxue hongci ke* at that time. It was one of Wang Yinglin's important achievements in bibliography, and the other one was his *Text-critical Commentaries on the Bibliographical Treatises of The Book of Han*. The ten-volume book, known as the first monographic achievement in the study of *Treatises of The Book of Han* (《汉志》), was famous for its "erudition". It was adopted into the compilation of the *Complete Library in the Four Branches of Literature*.

Wang Yinglin was also a famous Song-dynasty expert of *jiyixue* (辑佚学) studies[①]. The books he edited, *Textual Researches on the Three Versions of The Book of Songs* and *Zheng Kangcheng's Annotations to The Book of Changes* (《周易郑康成注》), occupied an important position in the development history of *jiyixue* studies in China. According to Zheng Qiao (郑樵)'s *jiyixue* theory, "the contents of the ancient books actually still exist in spite of their nominal loss". Wang Yinglin created an effective method of collection and amplification in editing those lost materials. This method could be summarized into two aspects: one is to search widely according to the existing records or catalogs, which is the first step of this work. When choosing the materials by which to compile lost books, one must first collect all kinds of encyclopedic books compiled by predecessors, the explanations and annotations to the Confucian classics and historical books made by former scholars. The other one is to indicate the source of the materials, collate them according to different documents, so as to make a mutual verification in a contrastive way and then to trace their origins. Afterwards, Wang developed further the method and summarized a set of effective steps for the book compilation and literature

---

① *Jiyixue*, literally, the studies on the collecting of lost literature. It involves the act of collecting and sorting out the lost literature materials recorded in other surviving documents in the form of quotation, so that the lost books and documents can be restored entirely or partially. As a discipline, it focuses on the history, methods, principles and other related issues of the edition of lost books or materials.

sorting, including annotation, collation, textual research, discrimination, etc. *Reading Notes about Difficulties in Learning* was Wang Yinglin's monograph of textual research, and it included various aspects of traditional Chinese scholarship, with emphasis on discussions of Confucian classics. Covering four categories of traditional Chinese learning, namely, *jing, shi, zi* and *ji*, the book was among the three great works of textual research of the Song dynasty, together with *Rongzhai Essays* (《容斋随笔》) by Hong Mai (洪迈) and *Dream Pool Essays* (《梦溪笔谈》) by Shen Kuo (沈括). As a masterpiece of philology, this book fully presented Wang Yinglin's methods and thought of textual research. There were both accompanying notes and in-text notes in this book—all notes were clearly explained based on wide-range quotations and exhaustive trace-searching. Wang Yinglin also expounded the deviation of words, the ambiguity of appellation and the absurdity of historical facts. The notes were also involved with the division of sentences or clauses in ancient books, the analysis on the quoted examples in historical books, the indication of material sources and the addition of historical facts. In terms of collation, Wang Yinglin advocated maintaining the original appearance of the text/characters, opposing arbitrary changes. He emphasized the careful and rigorous discrimination of related materials and the full use of practical methods like contrastive collation, contextual collation, standard-based collation, and collation of logical reasoning. These methods provided valuable experience of collation for later scholars, especially those in the Qing dynasty.

An erudite scholar, Wang Yinglin compiled a great variety of types of works all his life. Apart from the *Reading Notes about Difficulties in Learning*, a work of reading notes, *Jade Sea*, an encyclopedic book, and the *Text-critical Commentaries on the Bibliographical Treatises of The Book of Han*, a bibliographic writing, he wrote many children enlightenment readings, including *Three-character Classic* and other five monographic children books: *Satirical Ballads of the Lesser Learning* (《小学讽咏》), *Instructions on Enlightenment* (《蒙训》), *A Deep Blue Pearl for the Lesser Learning* (《小学绀珠》), *Quick Access to Surnames* (《姓氏急就篇》), and *Supplementary*

Annotations to the Quick Access to Chinese Characters (《急就篇补注》).
Unfortunately, the *Satirical Ballads of the Lesser Learning* and *Instructions on
Enlightenment* were lost. Wang Yinglin's emphasis on children's enlightenment
education, on the one hand, resulted from the popularization of children's
enlightenment education in the Song dynasty; on the other hand, it was the
embodiment of his scholarly thought of "learning for practical use" and
"learning based on historical studies". He advocated that a child be educated
not only with ethics and morals but also with natural and scientific knowledge,
so as to broaden their horizon. Therefore, basically, all the children's readings
he compiled were featured with comprehensive knowledge, lively form and
practical use. Besides *Three-character Classic*, it is also true to other books.
For example, what is told in *A Deep Blue Pearl for the Lesser Learning* focuses
on the easy-learned knowledge like "names and numbers of the things in the
world". It "starts from three elements (heaven, earth and man), and ends with
all things, vertically going through dynasties, and horizontally coving all
kinds of things and affairs". The content is arranged according to categories
and orders; in addition to the list of surnames, *Quick Access to Surnames*
covers common knowledge about things in society and nature, such as naming
of things, allusions, astronomy, geography and animals and plants. These
children's readings seem low-level, but they actually reflect the great academic
achievements of Wang Yinglin, the "Master of Philology".

II. Shao Jinhan

Following Wang Yinglin, Quan Zuwang was regarded as another master of philology of eastern Zhejiang.

Quan Zuwang dedicated his whole life to the studies of Confucian classics and history, collecting and sorting out all kinds of documents and materials, and leaving us outstanding philological works with far-reaching influence. He added supplements to *Scholarly Annals of the Song and Yuan Dynasties*, emendated *Commentary on the Water Classic* (《水经注》)[①] seven times, annotated *Reading Notes about Difficulties in Learning* three times, and compiled *Continued Collection of Ancient Yongshang Poems*. Quan Zuwang's literature sorting emphasized on synthesizing the ideas from different sources and forming them into a systematic frame. Believing "it is a shame lacking even a certain piece of knowledge", he paid much attention to the authenticity of the documents. He valued the first-hand documents obtained by himself, and even went personally to make an investigation on those questionable points. It can be said that Quan Zuwang's thought of philology was in line with the spirit of his historical studies, respected by scholars. Quan Zuwang's life experience and scholarship will be introduced in detail in the chapter on "Zhedong historical studies".

In the Qing dynasty, textual research was flourishing. Textual research, also known as textual criticism (*kaozhengxue*, 考证学) or *puxue* (朴学), was mainly about sorting out, collating and annotating ancient works as well as collecting and editing the lost ones. In fact, textual research is not a discipline in the strict sense, but a method of scholarly research. For textual research,

---

① *Commentary on the Water Classic* (《水经注》), a work on the ancient geography of China, describing the traditional understanding of the waterways and ancient canals. It was compiled by Li Daoyuan (郦道元) during the Northern Wei dynasty (386–534).

Liang Qichao claimed with a few brief words in his *Intellectual Trends in the Ch'ing Period* (《清代学术概论》)[①]: The fundamental method of textual research is "seeking truth from facts" and "no believing without evidence"; its research scope, centering on Confucian classics, covers such academic areas as traditional lesser learning (basic knowledge), phonology, historical studies, calendrical astronomy and astrology, geography, laws and regulations, epigraphy, collation, collection of lost works. Because its citations were mostly drawn from the Han dynasty, textual research was also known as "*Hanxue*" (the Han studies).

From eastern Zhejiang, Shao Jinhan was a famous scholar of Confucian classics, historian and philologist in the Qian-Jia period (1736–1820)[②]. He was regarded by Ruan Yuan as "the best scholar of both Confucian classics and historical studies, long being highly praised domestically". Textual research was flourishing in the Qian-Jia period, and therefore, Shao's academic style was influenced by the broad-viewed style of textual research of this period. Meanwhile, it was impacted by the traditional academic style of Zhedong scholars like Wang Yangming, Liu Zongzhou and Huan Zongxi. Shao Jinhan's *Semantic Annotations to Erya* (《尔雅正义》)[③], as the first one to re-annotate the Confucian classics among the works by Qing Confucians, played an important role in the history of Confucian classics in the Qing dynasty. Shao's historical research was more respected by scholars at that time. As Qian Daxin argued, the scholars of the Qian-Jia period "viewed Dai Zhen (戴震)[④] as the best in Confucian classics, while Shao Jinhan as the top one in historical studies".

---

① Publication information of the English version of this book: Liang Qichao. *Intellectual Trend in the Ch'ing Period*. Immanuel C. Y. Hsü. (trans.). cambridge, MA: Harvard University Press, 1959.

② The Qian-Jia period lasted from Emperor Qianlong's reign (1736–1796) to Emperor Jiaqing's reign (1796–1820) of the Qing dynasty.

③ It is a book based on *Erya* (《尔雅》, *Approaches to Correct Expressions*), an early Chinese lexicon.

④ Dai Zhen (戴震, 1724–1777), courtesy name Dongyuan/Shenxiu, literary name Gaoxi, a native of Xiuning (now Tunxi District, Huangshan, Anhui Province), is a philosopher and scholar of textual research and Confucian classics.

Shao Jinhan (1743–1796), courtesy name Yutong, literary name Nanjiang, was a native of Yuyao, Zhejiang Province. He was very smart in his childhood, and could memorize forever whatever he had read for three times. But unfortunately, he was always haunted by diseases all his life. Furthermore, his left eye was poor-sighted. As a young boy, he was enlightened by his grandfather Shao Xiangrong (邵向荣). By the age of 4 or 5, he had already mastered the four tones of Chinese pronunciations and the six elements[1] of *The Books of Songs.* By the age of 7, he had learnt how to write long poems with complex rhythms and rhymes. At the age 12, he attended *xianshi* (县试)[2]. When Li Hunan (李化楠), the host of the examination and the magistrate of the county, asked him to recite designated chapters of Five Classics[3], Shao Jinhan performed excellently without any word lost. In the thirtieth year of Emperor Qianlong's reign (1765), he was enrolled as *juren* (举人)[4] after he passed *xiangshi* (乡试)[5] at the age of 23. Six years later, he was granted *jinshi chushen* (进士出身)[6] degree as the top one candidate in *huishi* (会试)[7] hosted by the Ministry of Rites. Shao Jinhan's solid academic foundation resulted not only from the scholarly edification of his family, but also from the strict supervision of his family elders. He was especially influenced by the academic atmosphere of his hometown in eastern Zhejiang. He was deeply inspired when he "was learning the theories of masters like Liu Zongzhou and Huang Zongxi" in his childhood. His learning was based on three masters, namely, Wang Yangming, Liu Zongzhou and Huang Zongxi. "Whenever he talked about things, he would highly praise the three masters

---

[1] Specifically, the six elements include ballads (*feng*, 风), court hymns (*ya*, 雅), eulogies (*song*, 颂), narratives (*fu*, 赋), analogies (*bi*, 比) and associations (*xing*, 兴).

[2] *Xianshi*, the county-level imperial civil service examination.

[3] Five Classics (*wujing*, 五经), namely, *The Book of Changes, The Book of History, The Book of Songs, The Book of Rites* and *The Spring and Autumn Annals* (*cf.* Six Classics).

[4] *Juren*, literally, recommended scholar, a title granted to a scholar who passed the provincial-level imperial civil service examination (*xiangshi*).

[5] *Xiangshi*, the provincial-level imperial examination.

[6] *Jinshi chushen*, second-rate *jinshi.*

[7] *Huishi*, the metropolitan imperial examination.

talkatively. That was perhaps because Shao wanted to treat them as his models in view of his admiration to their scholarship and personality."

In the thirty-eighth year of Emperor Qianlong's reign (1773), the imperial court hosted the compilation of *Complete Library in the Four Branches of Literature*. It was an official-compiled book of the largest scale, and also a book series of the greatest influence in imperial China. In such a grand cultural activity with groundbreaking significance, Shao Jinhan, together with Zhou Yongnian (周永年), Dai Zhen, Yu Ji (余集) and Yang Changlin (杨昌霖), was recruited into the "Institution for *Complete Library in the Four Branches of Literatune*". With great reputation among the scholars, they were then honored as "Five Summoned Men of Noble Character". Working as a compilation official with the title *shujishi* (庶吉士)[1] of Hanlin Academy, Shao met his important turning point in his life. To work in the institution was a glorious honor, but Shao Jinhan, "indifferent to the fame", just treated it as an opportunity to further his study instead of regarding it as a ladder for his promotion. Soon after he entered the institution, he got thoroughly familiar with the documents there. "Whenever the general director asked him for certain information, he would accurately tell the specific source without any mistake", and thereby, he was called an omniscient man. From then on, he devoted most of his time and energy to the study of Confucian classics and the collection of old history. During this period, Shao Jinhan was in charge of compiling the category of *shi*. He not only personally collated most of the documents, but also wrote most of the abstracts of this category. Meanwhile, Shao Jinhan participated in the compiling of *Continued Compilation of Three Comprehensive Historical Works* (《续三通》)[2]. With more than 10 years of work in the above-mentioned institution and several years of experience

---

[1] *Shujishi*, literally, good man of high virtues, was a scholastic title during the Ming and Qing dynasties for those selected *jinshi* who would further their study instead of working as officials.

[2] Specifically, it includes the *Continued Compilation of General Study of the Literary Remains* (《续文献通考》), *Continued Compilation of General Treatises* (《续通志》) and *Continued Compilation of Comprehensive Statutes* (《续通典》).

in the Office for the Compilation of History, he made great and glorious achievements.

From the perspective of the positions of civil service, Shao Jinhan was the only one working in Hanlin Academy among the scholars of Zhedong School. However, he was an upright and honest official, unwilling to socialize. It was said that during his tenure in the capital, "he supported himself by teaching students and never paid a visit to the families of high-ranking officials". Therefore, his official rank was never higher than fourth grade in spite of his diligent work of more than 20 years.

Shao Jinhan made many friends all his life, up to 48 "friends", according to a survey by some scholar, but only Zhang Xuecheng of Kuaiji was regarded as the one who had close relationship with him. As followers of Zhedong School, both of them were scholastically influenced by Wang Yangming, Liu Zongzhou and Huang Zongxi. In the thirty-sixth year under the reign of Emperor Qianlong (1771), they got acquainted with each other in the capital. Later, they met again in Taiping[1] *Shiyuan*[2] of Anhui Province. In the following two decades, they wrote to each other, discussing academic issues and sharing common interests, and became intimate friends. However, compared with Zhang Xuecheng, Shao was more influenced by Qian-Jia School[3] which was well known for textual research.

Shao Jinhan was an erudite scholar with a very good memory. He read a large number of books and especially liked to trace the origin of knowledge, aiming at seeking truth from facts. Throughout his life, he was engaged in the collation and research of classic literature, no matter when he worked as an official in court or as a teacher at home. According to the existing materials, he wrote a lot of works all his life, and all his achievements in literature sorting

---

[1]   Taiping, Taiping County (now Huangshan District of Huangshan, Anhui Province).

[2]   *Shiyuan*, the office of local military governor's agents.

[3]   Also called the School of Han Studies (*Hanxue*), it is a philosophical school that interpreted the Confucian texts mainly with philological methods and relied exclusively on the originals of the Confucian classics created during the Han dynasty.

can be categorized into the following types: 1) Annotated books, including *Semantic Annotations to Erya, Interpretation of The Mencius* (《孟子述义》), *Semantic Annotations to Guliangzhuan* (《谷梁正义》)[1], *Ancient Annotations to Guliangzhuan* (《谷梁古注》) and *Annotations to Etiquette and Rites* (《仪礼笺》). 2) Collection of lost works, including *The Old History of the Five Dynasties* (《旧五代史》), *Oral Records of the Great Norm* (《洪范口义》), *General Instruction to the Great Norm* (《洪范统一》), *Chronicles of Emperor Gaozong and Emperor Xiaozong of the Song Dynasty* (《两朝纲目备要》), *Collection on Nature and Emotions* (《性情集》), *Lin'an Collection* (《临安集》), *Annals of Nine States* (《九国志》) and *Records of Southeast* (《东南纪闻》). Among the above writings, *The Old History of the Five Dynasties* was the most influential one, which was followed by all later historians. 3) Bibliographic works, including *Abstracts of the Historical Records in Complete Library in the Four Branches of Literature* (《四库史部提要》). 4) Epigraphic writings, including "Chapters on Epigraphy" of *Continued Compilation of General Treatises* (《续通志·金石略》) and *Bibliography of Geography and Epigraph* (《方舆金石编目》). 5) Local chronicles, including *Annals of Hangzhou Prefecture* (《杭州府志》) and *Annals of Yuyao County* (《余姚县志》). 6) Compiled books, including *Records of the Capital of the Southern Song Dynasty* (《南都事略》) and *Treatises of the History of Song* (《宋志》). Besides, his disciples compiled his posthumous manuscripts into *Nanjiang Reading Notes* (《南江札记》), *Nanjiang Essays* (《南江文钞》) and *Nanjiang Poetry* (《南江诗钞》).Unfortunately, many of his works have been lost and only several books can be seen today.

Shao Jinhan inherited the excellent tradition of "learning for practical use" of Zhedong scholarship. Firstly, as a boy, Shao Jinhan studied under the supervision of his grandfather Shao Xiangrong, who was a younger brother and student of Shao Tingcai. Secondly, Shao Tingcai rooted his own learning

---

[1] *Guliangzhuan* (《谷梁传》, *Guliang's Commentaries on The Spring and Autumn Annals*) by Guliang Chi (谷梁赤).

in the studies of Wang Yangming and Liu Zongzhou, and meanwhile accepted the theory of Huang Zongxi, thereby making great achievements in Neo-Confucianism, historical studies and literature. That was why Shao Jinhan got access to and then inherited the learning of Zhedong scholar Huang Zongxi. More importantly, Zhedong School was featured with patriotism, focusing on learning for practical use, emphasizing comprehensive learning, preferring historical studies, pursuing integrity and uprightness, and valuing dignity. All these deeply influenced Shao Jinhan. Growing up with the inspiration of Zhedong scholarship, Shao Jinhan was apparently impacted by Zhedong academic predecessors on his purpose of historical studies.

Hong Liangji (洪亮吉), a famous scholar and contemporary of Shao Jinhan, commented on Shao's scholarship: "He learns everything and especially emphasizes tracing the origin of knowledge and seeking truth from facts." Shao's above emphasis can be regarded as his basic attitude and academic style in historical studies.

Shao Jinhan also had an excellent performance in the research and collation of Confucian classics. Seeking evidence through extensive reading and gaining an insight into details through close reading, he aimed at elaborating the essential meanings implicated in ancient books. Among the three commentaries on *The Spring and Autumn Annals*[1], he wrote two annotated books about *Guliangzhuan*, namely, *Ancient Annotations to Guliangzhuan* and *Semantic Annotations to Guliangzhuan*. Additionally, there are 125 reading notes about the *Commentaries of Zuo* in his posthumous book *Nanjiang Reading Notes*. In the same book, there are 386 reading notes on the textual research of *The Mencius*. Besides, based on his study of *The Mencius*, he wrote *Interpretation of The Mencius*. Also, he conducted researches on other Confucian classics, including *The Book of Songs*, *The Book of History* 《尚书》 and *Etiquette and Rites* (《仪礼》). However, it was his research on *Semantic*

---

[1] Specifically, the three commentaries on *The Spring and Autumn Annals* are *Commentaries of Gongyang* (《公羊传》), *Commentaries of Zuo* (《左传》), and *Commentaries of Guliang* (《谷梁传》).

Annotations to Erya that covered his greatest effort, the longest time span and the biggest influence.

Shao Jinhan based his research on *Erya* on its version of stone inscription in the Tang dynasty, its block-printed version of the Song dynasty and the citations about it from various printed books. "Checking the text of *Erya*, collating and adding notes to Guo Pu (郭璞)'s annotations to the book", he made great brain effort to the compilation of *Semantic Annotations to Erya*, revised the book three times, and finally finished it after 10 years. With originality and creativity, it was the first one among the new-annotated Thirteen Classics by Qing scholars. A milestone in the research of *Erya*, this book laid out a basic frame of annotating *Erya* for the Qing scholars, and was viewed as the precedent of the Qing dynasty to re-annotate the Confucian classics.

In the academic career all his life, Shao Jinhan spent most of his time in researching Confucian classics and historical works, annotating them, collecting the lost ones of them and making textual research on them, so that he gained a good grasp of academic skills. Faced with the fact that "all those who discussed *The History of the Song Dynasty* (《宋史》) would ridicule its disorder and messiness but few of them would revise it", Shao Jinhan started his work of collation and textual criticism on the book. According to the existing 40 or more notes of textual research on *The History of the Song Dynasty* in *Nanjiang Reading Notes*, he demonstrated his outstanding capability in rectification and amendment.

Shao Jinhan's textual research on *The History of the Song Dynasty* covered a wide range of contents, including time span, official position, geography, names of people, numbers, genealogy, products and names of things and places, systems, and historical facts. Following the research achievements of Shen Shibo (沈世泊) on his *Corrections to The History of the Song Dynasty* (《宋史就正编》), Shao pointed out the distortion in writing and the mistakes in exemplification in the book, in addition to his textual research on historical events. Besides, he also rectified the errors in *A New History of the Song Dynasty* (《宋史新编》) by Ke Weiqi (柯维骐).

In terms of the evaluation of Shao Jinhan's academic thought, although Zhang Xuecheng spoke highly of his academic morality and Lamented that Shao's death marked "the end of philology of eastern Zhejiang". Zhang was actually not satisfied with Shao's "orthodox ideas in writing" and "views from personal acquisition". On the contrary, some scholars who were engaged in textual research in a large range had a high evaluation of Shao Jinhan. For example, about Shao's *Semantic Annotations to Erya*, Hong Liangji "highly praised it as a work with excellent viewpoints"; Qian Daxin believed that Shao's learning of Confucian classics "aimed at seeking truth from facts, and was helpful to scholars"; Ruan Yuan claimed that Shao's learning in both Confucian classics and historical studies was the most outstanding in a certain period and regretted for "just knowing Shao's achievement in Confucian classics but not knowing his wonderful performance in historical studies"; Duan Yucai (段玉裁) wrote specially to Shao Jinhan to congratulate him on the merits of his *Erya Zhengyi*, "the glorious book explores facts in an entire and detailed way based on rich and accurate materials, needless to say that it is actually much better than the work of Xing Bing (邢昺)"[①]. Besides, Jiang Fan (江藩) listed Shao Jinhan as a *Hanxue* scholar in the *Origin and Development of the Han Studies in the Qing Dynasty* (《国朝汉学师承记》).

---

① Xing Bing (邢昺, 932–1010), courtesy name Shuming, a scholar and educator of the Northern Song dynasty. He authored *Commentaries on Erya* based on the *Annotations to Erya* by Guo Pu of the Jin dynasty (265–420).

III. Huang Shisan and Huang Yizhou

Quan Zuwang and Shao Jinhan were the representatives of Zhedong scholarship in the 18th century, while Huang Shisan and his son Huang Yizhou were the representatives of Siming scholars in the 19th century. The father and his son were originally natives of Zhoushan and later they settled in Zhenhai. Both Zhoushan and Zhenhai were governed by Ningbo Prefecture of eastern Zhejiang. Nevertheless, their scholarship was not in close association with the tradition of eastern Zhejiang represented by Wang Yangming, Liu Zongzhou and Huang Zongxi. Instead, their learning focused on the research of Confucian classics and ancient rites, in line with the scholarship of Zheng Xuan (郑 玄) of the Han dynasty and Zhu Xi of the Song dynasty. Their academic efforts mainly centered on the textual research, interpretation and collation of Confucian classic texts, and thereby integrated the related knowledge. Actually, their scholarship held a similar approach to the learning of Dai Zhen and Duan Yucai, belonging to the category of philology.

Huang Shisan (1789–1862), courtesy name Weixiang, was a native of Ziwei Town, Dinghai (now in Zhoushan). In the twelfth year of Emperor Daoguang's reign (1832), he was selected as *sui gongsheng*[①], and then attended the provincial-level imperial examination two years later. Unfortunately, he had to withdraw midway after hearing that his mother had died of illness. In the following years, he didn't attend the examination any more but engaged himself in academic studies. In his study, he didn't restrict himself into a certain academic school or movement. Instead, he read through all kinds of

---

① *Sui gongsheng*, literally, annually selected *gongsheng*. In the Ming and Qing dynasties, every year or every two or three years, students were selected from the official public schools of various levels into *Guozijian/Guozixue* (the Imperial Academy) for further study. Those selected were called *sui gong* or *sui gongsheng* (*cf. en gongsheng*).

Confucian classics, historical books and philosophical works with thorough consideration on the past and present, and therefore, he gained a wide range of knowledge. He studied *The Analects of Confucius* in his thirties, the laws and regulations of different dynasties in his forties and *The Book of History* in his fifties, while he became interested in rites in his late years, believing "rites are for delight, for good nature and for destiny". Thereby, he composed three works, namely, *On Obeying the Rules of Rites* (《复礼说》), *On Exalting the Rules of Rites* (《崇礼说》) and *On Self-restraining by Rites* (《约礼说》). All his life, Huang Shisan was indulged in writing books. He finished 110 volumes of books in total, including *Commentaries on The Analects of Confucius*, *Commentaries on The Book of Songs*, *Comprehensive Interpretation of the Preface and Introductions in The Book of Songs* (《诗序通说》), *Interpretation of The Spring and Autumn Annals*, *A Brief Chronicle of the Late Zhou Dynasty*, *Commentaries on the Confucian Classics* in *Jingju Collection* (《儆居集经说》), *Commentaries on History* (《史说》), *Basic Knowledge of The Book of History* and *Huang Zhen's Instructions on Learning* (《黄氏塾课》). In the twentieth year of Emperor Daoguang's reign (1840), after the British army invaded Dinghai, Huang Shisan moved to Huangjiaqiao Village, Haiyan Town, Zhenhai County (now in Chaiqiao Subdistrict, Beilun District, Ningbo), where he wrote *Five Admonitions* (《五箴》) by imitating a work of the same name by Han Yu of the Tang dynasty, reminding the authorities to be vigilant against the ambitions of foreign invaders.

Huang Yizhou (1828–1899), given name Yuantong, was the fourth son of Huang Shisan. He was enrolled as *juren* after passing the provincial-level imperial examination in the ninth year of Emperor Tongzhi's reign (1870). In terms of official positions, he successively served as *xundao* (训导)[1] in Suichang and Haiyan counties, and as *jiaoshou* in Chuzhou (now Lishui) Prefecture School. Later, he was granted the post of *zhongshu* (中书)[2] of

---

[1] *Xundao*, assistant director of education.
[2] *Zhongshu*, secretary, in charge of drafting, recording, translating and hand-copying official documents.

the Grand Secretariat through a special recommendation. At the invitation of Huang Tifang (黄体芳), the educational inspector of Jiangsu, Huang Yizhou worked as a lecturer in Nanjing Academy for up to 15 years, where he taught students to broaden their academic horizon, obey the rules of rites and seek truth from facts instead of being trapped by sectarianism. Many outstanding intellectuals of Jiangnan area were his students. In the fifth year of Emperor Guangxu's reign, when Ningbo prefect Zong Yuanhan established Bianzhi Academy on the Bamboo Islet of the Moon Lake, Huang Yizhou was invited to set up teaching rules and regulations for the school, where he was specialized in the teaching of Confucian classics. During this period, more than 1,000 students were registered in his lectures. Apart from his academic achievements, Huang was a man of filial piety, supporting and taking after his parents for more than three decades without leaving them. Inheriting his family learning modestly and obeying traditional rites strictly, Huang Yizhou was a pure Confucian scholar of the late Qing dynasty.

Following the academic steps of the elders of his family, Huang Yizhou often studied together with his elder brothers, Huang Jingmeng (黄儆孟) and Huang Jingzhong (黄儆仲), mutually helping and supervising. He devoted himself to the study of Confucian classics, especially proficient in "Sanli" (三 礼, Three Rites), namely, *The Rites of Zhou, Etiquette and Rites*, and *The Book of Rites* (《礼记》). Reading through the annotations, commentaries and essays related to "Sanli" from the Han and Tang dynasties to the Qing dynasty, he researched and expounded in detail the ancient ritual system, school, fief, farm taxation, musical temperament, criminal laws, naming of things and even divination. His learning boasted a large scale but exquisite thinking. Therefore, he was regarded as the most outstanding scholar in the study of "Sanli" in the late Qing dynasty.

For the perspective of the academic thought on Confucian classics, Huang Yizhou was a knowledgeable scholar without sectarianism. Although

his learning was in line with the Neo-Confucianism of Lü Liuliang (吕留良)①
and Zhu Xi, he was not just an pure follower of them. Harboring the idea of
inclusive learning, he not only accepted Zhu Xi's achievements in the *Songxue*
studies, but also followed Quan Zuwang's academic style of textual criticism
on Confucian classics. However, he held an exclusive attitude towards the
xinxue studies of Lu Jiuyuan and Wang Yangming, claiming that their studies
were excessively valued, but actually they were not orthodox. When studying
the "Four Books", Huang Yizhou argued that when Mencius followed the
learning of Confucius, he developed Confucius' statement on learning and
put forward the idea that "a scholar should be able to concisely express the
orthodox essence after a wide range of study". Nevertheless, he had not directly
learned from Confucius but through Master Zisi. That is to say, it was Master
Zisi who bridged the learning of Mencius and Confucius. Therefore, Huang
wrote *Interpretation of Collection of Master Zisi* (《子思子辑解》)②.

Huang Yizhou's works included monographs *The History of Life Rituals*
and *General Interpretation of Confucian Classics*, and compiled and edited
works like the *Textual Research of Methods of the Minister of War Concerning
Military Rituals* (《军礼司马法考征》) and *Interpretation of Collection of
Master Zisi*. Also, Huang Yizhou wrote two volumes of *Introductions and
Commentaries on Confucian Classics* (《经说略》) and four volumes of
Commentaries on Confucians Classics (《群经说》). By them, he specially
interpreted such practical things as the names, products, measuring, and
quantity. In particular, the *Commentaries on Confucians Classics*, as brilliant as
The History of Life Rituals, was included in *Jingji Miscellaneous Writings*.

Among the works by Huang Shisan and Huang Yizhou, *The History
of Life Rituals* and *Commentaries on The Analects of Confucius* were of the

---

① Lü Liuliang (吕留良 , 1629–1683), a scholar of Cheng-Zhu Neo-Confucianism at the turn of Ming
and Qing dynasties.
② The above words (of the source text) about Confucius, Mencius and Master Zisi were actually
paraphrased from the statement in the "Biography of Huang Shisan" of *Draft History of the Qing
Dynasty* (《清史稿》). For clear logic and expression, the translation is presented partially based
on the original text instead of the paraphrased one.

greatest influence.

The *Commentaries on The Analects of Confucius* was a book for the annotation and research on *The Analects of Confucius*. It recorded the words and deeds of Confucius, his disciples and their contemporaries, and was regarded by later scholars as the most reliable material for studying Confucius' theory of life as well as his social and political thought. The annotations to *The Analects of Confucius* by scholars of different dynasties were as many as stars. Among them, *Collected Interpretations of The Analects of Confucius* (《论语集解》) by He Yan (何晏) was a representative work of the textual-research-centered *Hanxue* studies, while *Collected Annotations to The Analects of Confucius* (《论语集注》) by Zhu Xi was a representative work of the creativity-focused *Songxue* studies. The value of these two works was recognized by the scholars of all dynasties. Huang Shisan's *Commentaries on The Analects of Confucius* first absorbed the main contents of these two books, and then included the research findings of the scholars in the Ming and Qing dynasties. That is to say, the *Commentaries on The Analects of Confucius* almost combed the whole history of the studies of *The Analects of Confucius*. Zhang Binglin's evaluation on this book is: "In writing *Commentaries on The Analects of Confucius*, Huang Shisan frequently presented valuable expressions, which are different from those of the former scholars but stick to the core ideas, although his words are really flowery."

The History of Life Rituals is the representative work of Huang Yizhou, who spent 30 years in completing it from age of 32 to 61. The 100-volume book is composed of 49 chapters with more than one million Chinese characters. It analyzes and examines in detail the issues of ritual system, academic system, fief, official positions and farm taxes, and summarizes the research findings on "rites" in the past 2,000 years. In the whole feudal era of China, the "rites" involved different kinds of fields like political system, laws and regulations, ethics and social customs. They played an extremely important role in traditional Chinese culture, usually compared to the structure, bricks and tiles of the palace of feudalism. Therefore, the work was of great importance to the society at that time, winning an immortal academic position for Huang Yizhou. Yu Yue, a widely-recognized master of traditional Chinese culture in the late Qing dynasty, claimed in the "Preface of The History of Life Rituals" (《礼书通故序》): "Among the learning of Confucian classics, only the study of 'rites' has been full of academic disputes since ancient times, hard to draw a final conclusion. The book adopts the ideas of different scholars from different Confucian classics instead of sticking to the learning of a certain school. It seeks truth from facts and only followed the good ones." Liang Qichao, in his *Chinese Academic History of Recent Three Hundred Years* (《中国近三百年学术史》), also mentioned the book and thought it "the greatest achievement of the study of rites in the Qing dynasty".

Hereby, it can be seen that the research of Huang Shisan and Huang Yizhou played an important role in Chinese academic history.

Chapter Five

Seeking the Origin Through History:
The Extension of Zhedong Historical Studies

It was Huang Zongxi's lecturing in Ningbo Baiyun Manor that prominently marked the formation of Zhedong School of historical studies. Therefore, the manor is well-known home and abroad as an important academic site of Zhedong School. It is where Yongshang Zhengren Academy was located and also the birth place of the Zhedong School in the Qing dynasty.

Baiyun Manor is located in Guanjiang'an (now in Baiyun Park), Baiyun Subdistrict, Haishu District, Ningbo. It originally belonged to Wan Tai, an official of the Ministry of Revenue in the late Ming dynasty. But it was named after Master Baiyun, the honorary title of Wan Tai's son Wan Sixuan (万斯选) who wrote *Baiyun Collection* (《白云集》) and was buried here after his death.

In the seventh year of Emperor Kangxi's reign (1668), in the Qing dynasty, at the invitation of Wan Tai and other scholars, Huang Zongxi, a famous thinker and the representative of "Zhedong School" at the turn of Ming and Qing dynasties, lectured at first in Wan Tai's mansion at Guangji Street and then in Yanqing Temple. In the ninth year of Emperor Kangxi's reign (1670), Huang moved to Baiyun Manor, where he established "Zhengren Academy" to give lectures to his disciples. During the reign of Emperor Qianlong, Quan Zuwang, an academic adherent of Huang Zongxi, added "Yongshang" to the name of the academy so as to distinguish it from its counterpart in Shaoxing, hence the name "Yongshang Zhengren Academy".

Huang Zongxi was a key figure in the history of the development of Zhedong scholarship. Erudite, profound in thought and rich in writings, Huang was ranked among the three great thinkers at the turn of Ming and Qing dynasties, together with Gu Yanwu and Wang Fuzhi. Also, he was good at innovation and enlightenment, thereby deserving the honor of "Great Authority on Enlightenment".

By the end of the Qing dynasty, Yongshang Zhengren Academy had been deserted. In 1934, some Ningbo natives represented by Yang Juting (杨菊庭) restored the academy and Wan's former residence with raised funds after they paid a visit there. At present, Baiyun Manor covers an area of about 4,000 square meters, composed of Yongshang Zhengren Academy, the former residence and cemetery of the Wan family. It has four buildings of flush gable roofs covering an area of 650 square meters, two facing east and two south. There is still a Ming-style gate on which are three Chinese characters "Bai Yun Zhuang" (白云庄, Baiyun Manor) inscribed by Mr. Sha Menghai, a famous contemporary calligrapher. On the porch pillars of the main hall, visitors can see Quan Zuwang's couplets:

> Brave and unrestrained, commanding the military affairs under heaven;
> Excellent and outstanding, reading the literary books of the ancient times.

Inside the buildings of the manor are exhibition rooms for "Zhejiang scholarship and culture" and "Historical relics of the Wan family". To the west of the academy are the tombs of Wang Bangfu (万邦孚), Wan Sixuan, Wan Sichang (万斯昌) and Wan Shibiao (万世标). In front of Wan Bangfu's tomb is a Ming-dynasty *paifang* (牌坊)[1] inscribed with "Ming military governor honorable Wan rest in peace". Along the path to the grave are *huabiao* (华表)[2], a pair of stone horses, and an epigraph for Wan Sixuan written by Huang Zongxi.

After the reform and opening-up in 1978, the government attached importance to construction and protection of cultural relics. Baiyun Manor was then renovated, with new-built Baiyun Park on its west, which has now

---

[1] *Paifang*, a memorial archway.
[2] *Huabiao*, an ornamental or symbolic stone column erected in front of palaces, bridges, city gates, tombs or other places.

become a place of recreation and relaxation for local folks. Entering the park, visitors first see a small winding and tranquil river, which flows quietly in the park, bringing a bit of romance and charm of a graceful water town. Stepping into the high wall of Baiyun Manor, tourists find dense bamboos and green grass, feeling a little cool in such an ancient and quiet environment even in a summer afternoon. Across a small empty land surrounded by buildings is a huge courtyard, where guests can enjoy luxuriant green bamboos and trees and even see the fruit dotted on a tall tree named medicinal citron in the harvest days of autumn. Finally, visitors can walk into the inside of the courtyard along a winding path.

Let's imagine a scenario: One day in the spring of 1668, a thin-faced gentleman walked deliberately into Baiyun Manor, with a ribbon on his head and a Confucian classic in his hand. That was Huang Zongxi, a master of Confucian classics, historian and thinker at the turn of Ming and Qing dynasties. It must have been a very lively and bustling day when all the Wan's family, together with many Ningbo scholars, respectfully greeted Huang with tea and wine, and talked with him about history, Confucian classics, worldly affairs and situations of the country. It was just by Huang Zongxi's efforts that Zhedong scholarship was led to a new world.

I. Huang Zongxi

Huang Zongxi (1610–1695), a native of Yuyao, Zhejiang, courtesy name Taichong, literary name Nanlei, was respected as Master Lizhou.

Huang Zongxi was born in a village named Huangzhupu in Tongde Town, Yuyao County, which is now called Pukou Village, belonging to Mingwei Town, Yuyao, Zhejiang Province. On the eve of Huang Zongxi's birth, his mother Lady Yao had a dream that she was cradling a *qilin*[①] in her arms, and thereby named him *lin'er* after *qilin*. His father, Huang Zunsu (黄尊素), was enrolled as *jinshi* in the Wanli period (1573–1620) and then served in positions like *tuiguan* (推官)[②] in Ningguo Prefecture (now in Anhui Province) and *yushi* of Shandong *Dao*[③]. It was in the Tianqi period (1621–1627) that Huang Zunsu was promoted to the post of *zhongguan yushi* (中官御史)[④]. At the time, the national situations were worrying to him. An honest official, Huang Zunsu kept close contact with the Donglin Faction[⑤], and wrote three times to the emperor, blaming the notorious "eunuch faction" led by Wei Zhongxian (魏忠贤) , but he was dismissed after impeaching the high-ranking eunuch Wei. In the fifth year of Emperor Tianqi's reign (1625), the eunuch faction made a massive counterattack against Donglin Faction, murdering six of its members, namely,

---

① *Qilin* or Chinese unicorn is a mythical beast that symbolizes good luck and prosperity. Legend says that *qilin* would appear during the reign of a good monarch, or shortly before the birth or death of a sage.

② *Tuiguan*, in charge of justice and evaluation of officials.

③ *Dao* (道), provincial-level division under the Censorate (*Duchayuan*). In the Ming dynasty, the Censorate divided the whole state into thirteen *Dao* according to the provincial administrative division named *buzhengshi si*.

④ *Zhongguan yushi*, investigating censor of the imperial court officials.

⑤ Donglin Faction, a Confucian group of scholar-officials in the Ming dynasty. They pushed relentlessly for the national moral rearmament under Emperor Tianqi's reign. Later, they suffered gruesome political repression by the eunuch faction led by high-ranking eunuch official Wei Zhongxian, and many of them were purged from key positions in the imperial court.

Yang Lian (杨涟), Zuo Guangdou (左光斗), Wei Dazhong (魏大中), Yuan Huazhong (袁化中), Zhou Ruichao (周瑞朝), and Gu Dazhang (顾大章). In the sixth year of Emperor Tianqi's reign (1626), they imprisoned another seven Donglin members, including Huang Zunsu, Gao Panlong (高攀龙) and Zhou Shunchang (周顺昌), who were tortured to death. Subsequently, the eunuch faction continued to make false accusations against Donglin members who were almost killed or expelled entirely at last.

At that time, Huang Zongxi was only a young man of 17 years old. He was extremely sad and angry, and determined to take revenge. Seeing the new throned Emperor Chongzhen begin to clear away the eunuch faction, Huang Zongxi went to Beijing in the first lunar month of the first year of Emperor Chongzhen's reign (1628) to recount his grievances on his father's death, which caused a sensation in the government and the public because of the braveness and filial piety of such a young man. With his efforts, the remaining partisans of the eunuch faction, including Xu Xianchun (许显纯) and Cui Yingyuan (崔 应元), were executed. Huang finally took avenge. After his father's funeral, Huang Zongxi, following his father's will, went to Shaoxing where he started his study under the guide of Liu Zongzhou.

Afterwards, Huang Zongxi made friends everywhere when he traveled to Nanjing, Suzhou, Changshu, Hangzhou, Shaoxing, Yuyao, Ningbo and other places. During this period, he got acquainted with many famous scholars of Jiangnan literary societies and poetry societies, including Zhang Pu (张 溥) and Wan Tai, and joined Fushe Society[1]. Besides, he sat for the imperial civil service examination in Nanjing but failed, and then he returned to his hometown, where he made a determined effort to the study of Confucian classics and history. Meanwhile, he read extensively, covering the pre-Qin works of the various schools of thought as well as the books on astronomy, geography, calendar, mathematics, music, Buddhism and Taoism.

---

[1]   Fushe Society, also known as the Revival Society, was the largest literary movement of the late Ming dynasty that had political intentions. Its most important representatives were scholar-bureaucrats Zhang Pu and Zhang Cai (张采).

Following Fushe Society, he participated in the political struggle against Ruan Dacheng (阮大铖), a remaining eunuch faction partisan. Meanwhile, he co-wrote the "Notice on Prevention Upheavals in the Old Capital (Nanjing)" (《留都防乱公揭》) so as to expulse Ruan. At that time, the Donglin followers were led by Gu Gao (顾杲) from Wuxi, and the Tianqi period co-victims were led by Huang Zongxi. What they had done provoked Ruan Dacheng's hatred of them. In the seventeenth year of Emperor Chongzhen's reign, Li Zicheng broke into Beijing, causing the fall of the Ming dynasty. Later, Emperor Hongguang established the Southern Ming regime in Nanjing where Ruan Dacheng was promoted to the Minister of War. Then, with great power in hand, Ruan started his revenge against the Fushe members, attempting to kill all the 140 scholars who signed their names on that "Notice", including Huang Zongxi. But soon the Qing army invaded southwards and captured Nanjing. Thereafter, Huang Zongxi fled to his hometown.

In the second year of Emperor Shunzhi's reign, the Qing army occupied Hangzhou and then advanced towards eastern Zhejiang. Then, Zhu Yihai (朱以海), the Ming Prince of Lu, was invited by an anti-Qing army to Shaoxing as State Supervisor, where they began the eight-year-long anti-Qing struggles defending eastern Zhejiang. Huang Zongxi, together with his younger brothers Huang Zongyan and Huang Zonghui (黄宗会), donated all their family properties, and organized a troop of more than 600 soldiers recruited from the locals of his hometown, Huangzhupu. Named "Shizhong Ying" (世忠营)[1], the troop participated in many anti-Qing battles led by the regime of Prince of Lu. In the second lunar month of the third year of Emperor Shunzhi's reign (1646), Huang Zongxi was appointed by the Prince of Lu as *zhushi* of *zhifang si* (兵部职方司主事)[2], and soon appointed a concurrent position of investigating censor. Defeated by the Qing force on the tenth day of the sixth lunar month of the same year, Huang Zongxi led the remnants of more than

---

[1] Shizhong Ying, loyal battalion.
[2] *Zhifang si*, a department of the Ministry of War, in charge of military fortifications.

500 soldiers into Siming Mountain, where they insisted on armed resistance against the Qing soldiers. Later, Huang Zongxi was repeatedly wanted by the Qing imperial court, so he had to take refuge in Hua'an Mountain (to the north of Siming Mountain) with his mother and children. Zhu Yihai, the Prince of Lu, fled to Zhoushan and then Fujian, where he re-established his regime, and in the seventh lunar month of the sixth year of Emperor Shunzhi's reign (1649), he went to the coastal waters of Linhai, Taizhou, Zhejiang. Hearing the news, Huang Zongxi was immediately on his way to the exiled regime. There, he met the Prince of Lu, who appointed him as the vice censor-in-chief of the Censorate. Although Huang Zongxi was a minister, he had no real power. Therefore, his daily task was to read and lecture, and to annotate such calendars as *Season-Granting Calendar* (《授时历》) and *Western Calendar* (《泰西历》)[①] in his spare time. Later, Huang was sent by the Prince of Lu to Japan as a companion of Ruan Mei (阮美) who was appointed to ask for Japanese military assistance. They arrived in Nagasaki and Tsushima (Island) in Japan, but they had to return home in disappointment due to the refusal of Japan. Soon after that, Huang Zongxi left the exiled regime and went back to his hometown to take refuge, leading a secluded life. In the tenth year under the reign of Emperor Shunzhi (1653) of Qing dynasty, the Ming Prince of Lu was forced to cancel the title of "State Supervisor", which marked the complete failure of the anti-Qing struggles in eastern Zhejiang.

In those years, Huang Zongxi led an unstable life, moving here and there, and his family suffered a lot with him. His daughter-in-law, his son and his granddaughter died one after another, and his former residence was caught in fire twice. Therefore, he wrote with grief and indignation such poetic lines as "Even a half of my family passed away in drifting, and troubled times lasted ten years without stopping", "I went through death threats for ten times, and in one year my house was caught in fire twice". In the eighteenth year of Emperor

---

① The Western Calendar was first introduced into China by Matteo Ricci (1552–1610), an Italian Jesuit missionary, in the 16th century. But it is not confirmed whether the Western Calendar used by Huang Zongxi in 1649 was the Julian Calendar or Gregorian Calendar.

Shunzhi's reign (1661), the Yongli regime of Southern Ming fell, and Zheng Chenggong, a famous anti-Qing general, crossed over to Taiwan. Confronted with such a terrible case, Huang Zongxi became hopeless, and then devoted himself to scholarly lecturing and writing.

Huang Zongxi gave lectures mainly in the period when he was from 54 to 70 years old. During the years, hundreds of people, including some Qing officials, worshipped him and became his disciples. The places of his lectures, besides his residence, were mainly in Yuxi (Tongxiang), Yuezhong (Shaoxing), Haichang (Haining) and Yongshang (Yinxian County, Ningbo), etc.

In the late autumn of the sixth year of Emperor Kangxi's reign (1667), Huang Zongxi, together with his schoolfellows like Jiang Xizhe (姜希辙) and Zhang Ying'ao (张应鳌), resumed the lectures at "Zhengren Academy" founded by his teacher Liu Zongzhou in Shaoxing. In the next two years, he gave lectures there many times, spreading Liu's scholarship and demonstrating his academic integrity. From the fifteenth to eighteenth year of Emperor Kangxi's reign (1676–1679), Huang Zongxi lectured quite a few times in Haichang, where he taught knowledge of natural sciences like astronomy and calendar of both China and the West. The magistrate of Haichang County, Xu Sanli (许三礼), gathered many officials to attend his lectures. It was in the period when he established and ran the "Yongshang Zhengren Academy" that his lectures functioned to the best effect. At the beginning of the fourth year of Emperor Kangxi's reign, more than 20 famous Ningbo scholars, including Wan Sida and Wan Sitong, went to Yuyao to visit Huang for academic guidance. Afterwards, Huang went to Ningbo to give lectures. There he made his proposal of establishing "Zhengren Academy". From the seventh year to the fourteenth year of Emperor Kangxi's reign (1668–1675), the academy lasted 8 years, during which it was estimated that there were around 100 listeners attending the lectures.

In his lectures, Huang Zongxi opposed empty talks and advocated learning for practical use, especially emphasizing on the mastery of the knowledge from Confucian classics and history. He required his students "first to have an exhaustive study on the Confucian classics" and "then to understand history by reading". When lecturing, he emphasized not only the study of Confucian classics and history, but also natural science, including Western modern scientific knowledge. His son Huang Baijia (黃百家) inherited his learning, and made high attainments in such areas as Confucian classics, historical studies, calendar and mathematics, and his books can still be seen today. Under the influence of Huang Zongxi's thought and academic style, "Zhedong School" of the Qing dynasty was formed with the disciples of the "Yongshang Zhengren Academy" as its main force. The school's academic tradition lasted through the Qian-Jia period to the end of the Qing dynasty, and its academic atmosphere impacted eastern Zhejiang and even the whole nation. The school had a wide range of academic research, including Confucian classics, historical studies, natural science, etc., among which historical studies had the highest rank.

In the eighteenth year of Emperor Kangxi's reign (1679), Huang Zongxi stopped lecturing, and spared no effort to write books. The following are his major works.

Waiting for the Dawn: A Plan for the Prince criticized the feudal autocratic monarchy system, and revealed for the first time that "it is only the monarch who is the great harm to the state". It put forward a political program with the tendency of democratic enlightenment in such aspects as politics, economy, law, the military, education and culture, and designed a blueprint of the future ideal society.

Collection of the Essays of Ming (《明文案》) was compiled into 217 volumes at first, and then expanded to 482 volumes, renamed as *Anthology of the Essays of Ming* (《明文海》); *The Records of Ming Scholars* was compiled into 62 volumes, with 1,000,000 Chinese characters approximately. With 17 separate chapters, the book took the School of Wang Yangming as the mainstream and also included various other schools. It recorded the deeds, speeches and academic thoughts of more than 200 scholars in the Ming dynasty. It is a monograph of dynastic history on academic thought, systematically summarizing the academic development and evolution of the Ming dynasty.

Scholarly Annals of the Song and Yuan Dynasties was supplemented into 100 volumes by Huang Baijia and Quan Zuwang after they completed his unfinished works, *The Records of Song Scholars* (《宋儒学案》) and *The Records of Yuan Scholars* (《元儒学案》).

In addition, he also spent a lot of energy editing *The Records of Ming History* (《明史案》), but only finished the important historical and geographical monographs such as *Records of the Exiled Regime* (《行朝录》), *Records of the Hongguang Period of Ming* (《弘光实录抄》), and *Chronicles of Siming Mountain* (《四明山志》). Besides, Huang Zongxi was good at the research on such natural sciences as astronomy, geography and mathematics, completing more than 20 kinds of works on natural science, including *Annotation to Season-Granting Calendar* (《授时历故》), *Calculation of Season-Granting Calendar* (《授时历法假如》).

On the third day of the seventh lunar month in the thirty-fourth year of Emperor Kangxi's reign (1695), Huang Zongxi died after he was bedridden for a long time. During his illness, he wrote "Lizhou in Remaining Days" (《梨洲末命》), asking his family to hold a simple funeral for him: "On the next day of my death, carry me with palm mattress to the grave, no more quilt or mattress needed", "put me onto a stone bed without coffin, and cancel all the burial rituals like Buddhist ceremony or other memorial services". Huang's ideas of changing old customs made an extraordinary difference.

Huang Zongxi was an enlightening scholar, erudite and innovative in many disciplines, such as Confucian classics (philosophy), politics, law, economics, historical studies. His scholarship was featured with the emphasis on historical studies.

Huang Zongxi absorbed the essence of Wang Yangming's and Liu Zongzhou's philosophical theories. With the idea that "Enough *gongfu* leads to *benti*", Huang made a systematic theoretical thinking on the *benti-gongfu* theory of Zhedong *xinxue* School, and laid a theoretical foundation for the turn of Zhedong scholarship from *xinxue* to the historical studies based on the orientation of "learning for practical use". Thus, from the height of the spirit of the times, through the theoretical generalization of practical activities, Huang Zongxi established the foothold of constructing a new theory, and raised the traditional category of "*gongfu*" to the category of "*benti*". Meanwhile, he absorbed the doctrines of *lixue* so as to reform, rectify and develop *xinxue*, and thereby laid a theoretical foundation for the new development of Zhedong scholarship.

In terms of political thought, Huang Zongxi put forward the view that "the people are the hosts, and the monarch is the guest". In view of his experience during the tragic fall of the Ming dynasty, his reflection not only involved the collapse of the Ming dynasty, but also extended the thinking to the political system of the whole feudal society for nearly 2,000 years. Huang Zongxi's *Waiting for the Dawn: A Plan for the Prince* and *Advice for the Future Generations* (《留书》) criticized China's feudal autocratic monarchy system, and comprehensively expounded his imagination of the future society from such aspects as politics, law, economy, the military, culture and education. The two books are still of great significance in the present context.

Huang Zongxi hated the autocratic monarchy system of "*jia tianxia*" (家天下, hereditary monarchy), considering it the biggest curse contaminating the people. In Huang's opinion, the pleasure of a monarch himself is based on the suffering of all the people, and his private benefits are beautified as the public interests. That is a cannibalistic logic of a feudal monarch, who oppresses and exploits all the people, regards the property created by the people as the private property of his royal family, and views the people as the private belongings of his own. For such a monarch, subjects naturally regard him as "the worst evildoer under heaven", and "they would resent him, view him a foe, and call him a tyrant". At the same time, the entire bureaucracy under the autocratic monarchy would be the lackeys and accomplices of the monarch, helping the monarch to exploit all the people, regardless of their troubled life. Thus, Huang Zongxi profoundly revealed the fundamental opposition between feudal autocracy and people's survival and interests.

Against the autocratic monarchy, Huang Zongxi proposed to "reform based on ancient political system" and put forward the social and political ideal that "the people are the hosts, and the monarch is the guest". Why is a monarch needed? Why is a country needed? There is not any other reason except their service for the people and the affairs under heaven. The duty of a monarch is originally supposed to promote benefits and eliminate disadvantages for the people under heaven. To be a monarch is supposed to be much more painstaking and laborious than to be the people, which is a natural relationship between the monarch and the people. Furthermore, the duty of a minister is to serve the people rather than the monarch. His relationship with the monarch should be that between students and their teacher or that between friends. The monarch and ministers have their respective duties, like "those who cut trees together", one singing the work song and the others backing. There is no reason to compare the relationship between monarch and ministers with that between father and son.

Depending on the ideal that "the people are the hosts, and the monarch is the guest", Huang Zongxi designed a systematic political reform strategy, the core of which is to restrict the "monarchical power" and prevent its abuse. Although Huang Zongxi's thought on social ideal and blueprint of political reform cannot be called "democratism", it transcended the ideas of its predecessors and demonstrated its foresight of the future, containing valuable factors of modern enlightenment.

"Both industry (handicraft) and commerce as foundations" was Huang Zongxi's important proposition on the social economic structure. As he argued, "Due to their poor understanding, some scholars usually demote industry (handicraft) and commerce and falsely proposed to restrict them. In fact, both the two sectors are what our sage monarch wants and they are equally foundational." The authentic "reign of sage monarch" lies in the fact that he does not restrain the craftsmen and merchants who are conducive to social and economic development. Instead, he manages to attract them to his country and support their operation and healthy development, treating them as essential as agriculture for the national development. Huang Zongxi's thought, reflecting the requirements of farmers and emerging citizens, conformed to the developmental trend of the sprouts of capitalism.

Huang Zongxi was an outstanding historian with unique insight, which was particularly reflected in his research on academic history, including the writing of *The Records of Ming Scholars* and *Scholarly Annals of the Song and Yuan Dynasties*. The concepts he put forth, including "personal acquisition", "orthodox idea", "diversity begotten by one origin", "learning through various approaches and considerations" and "those who study human nature and destiny must resort to history", all contained profound insights into academic history, and had extraordinary philosophical methodological significance.

"Yiben" refers to the way of the sages in Confucianism, while in a broad sense it is the totality or the whole of academic truths. *"Wanshu"* means Confucian scholars' diverse comprehensions of the way of the sages. It also refers to the various methods or approaches adopted in the pursuit of truth. According to Huang Zongxi, scholarship is a public instrument for all people, not limited to private use. Everyone is entitled to the pursuit of academic truth and every scholar can do his best to explore and understand it. With enough efforts and time, he will reach the truth. "The more the efforts, the clearer the truth." Different academic schools may have different degrees of understandings on truth, but they are all on their way to truth. Huang Zongxi advocated "learning through various approaches and considerations", and argued that scholars should pay attention to "one-sided views" and acknowledge "opposite statements". Only in this way can the learning conform to the objective development of the diversification of truth. Even Buddhism and Taoism claim that "achievements depend on the exhaustive study on the diversity of the mind", and therefore the understanding of *"dao"* is in various degrees.

Based on the outlook of academic truth embodied by *"yiben wanshu"*, Huang Zongxi proposed to break academic monopoly, get rid of academic sectarianism, and deny parroting others' doctrines. Contrary to the outlooks of "diversity begotten by one origin" and "learning through various approaches and considerations", some shabby scholars always limited the diversified academic approaches into but one truth or path, and measured all ancient and contemporary academic development with their fixed and rigid scholarly standards. For them, whatever was different from their ideas would be heresy. In their eyes, only one voice or mind was allowed and no independent thinking was needed. For them, it would be totally fine just to follow. Accordingly, it could be said that Huang's above statements actually profoundly disclosed the arbitrariness, narrowness and folly of feudal ideology and culture, which had a great significance of enlightening for the evolution towards modern democratic civilization.

Huang Zongxi was a thinker and also a great educator. A key figure in the academic lineage of eastern Zhejiang, Huang inherited the learning of Wang Yangming and Liu Zongzhou, and passed his to Wan Sitong, Quan Zuwang and Zhang Xuecheng, exerting a significant impact on the subsequent scholars and even the modern revolution.

When Huang Zongxi gave lectures in Ningbo, he was diligent and tireless in working and teaching, and cultivated a group of excellent talents proficient in a great variety of disciplines such as Confucian classics, historical studies, literature and natural science, which changed the trend of "scholarly declination" in Ningbo area following the middle of the Ming dynasty. It might as well be said that by the efforts of Huang Zongxi himself, the century-long academic tradition of Ningbo was founded.

II. Wan Sitong

About 35 kilometers west to downtown Ningbo is Chunhu Town, Fenghua. Facing Xiangshan Port, it is a good place with beautiful mountains and rivers. Two kilometers east to the town, there is a small mountain with an altitude of only 100 meters, called Wuyangguan Mountain. On the flat slope of its southern hillside, there is an unimpressive ancient tomb. However, the owner of the tomb is an extraordinary person—Wan Sitong. He is one of the main compilers of *History of Ming*, the last of the book series "The Twenty-four Histories"[1], the most important twenty-four historical books written in biographical genre.

A native of Ningbo, Wan Sitong originally lived near the Moon Lake and later moved to Baiyun Manor in the west of the city. Then why is his tomb in Chunhu Town, Fenghua? That's because Wan's second wife, Lady Fu, was from Hu'ao Village, Fenghua. After Wan Sitong was summoned to Beijing to compile the *History of Ming*, Lady Fu moved back to her hometown accompanied by Wan Shibiao, Wan Sitong's only son. Later, Wan Sitong was buried there after his death. At that time, Hu'ao folks always affectionately called Wan Sitong "Son-in-law of Hu'ao". In the fifty-eighth year of Emperor Kangxi's reign (1719), Wang Xuling (王顼龄), the grand academician of the Grand Secretariat, inscribed the epigraph: "The Tomb of Neo-Confucian Master Wan Jiye[2] of Yinxian County and His Wives Lady Zhuang and Lady Fu." Hanlin Academician Qiu Lian (裘琏) wrote the tomb couplet: "Although comparable to Ban Gu and Sima Qian in his achievements, [Wan Sitong still

---

① Also known as *Orthodox Histories*. The whole set of books contains 3,213 volumes in around 40 million words, considered one of the most important sources on Chinese history and culture.
② Wan Jiye (万季野), courtesy name of Wan Sitong.

kept] a humble identity of a common man."①

Because Wan Sitong's descendants moved to other places, his tomb had long been abandoned before it was found again by Xie Wufeng (谢午峰), a native of Ningbo, in the period of Emperor Tongzhi (1862–1875). In the twenty-fifth year of the Republican period (1936), in order to arouse the national anti-Japan awareness, the government ordered to list Wan Sitong as a model of refusing to work for the Qing dynasty into the "locals of high virtue and talent of Zhejiang". Then in the late spring of the same year, Zhedong scholars like Zhuang Songfu (庄崧甫) initiated the movement to rebuild Wan Sitong's tomb by raising funds from all over the country. Thereafter, dignitaries and well-known scholars of the National Government made donations one after another. In the middle summer of 1937, the tomb was restored with a stone archway in front of it. Inscriptions on the front and back of the archway were respectively inscribed by Chiang Kai-shek and Lin Sen (林森), chairman of the National Government. On the two pillars of the archway are the two lines of a tomb couplet by Zhuang Songfu, which reads,

With a pen of history writing as powerful as a strong troop, the master never dies;

As a common man who keeps his modesty for his whole life, he is fever admirable.

Meanwhile, a new memorial temple called "Xiangxian Temple"② was built in the town of Chunhu to the west the tomb.

During the "Cultural Revolution" (1966–1976), Wan's tomb, including its tomb path and stone archway, was destroyed into ruins except its base and stone tablets which were lying quietly in the arms of mountain and river. The tomb demonstrates forever the spirit of such a "historiographer as a common man" who cared no reputation, surrendered to nothing, and dedicated himself

---

① When Wan Sitong was summoned to Beijing to compile the *History of Ming*, he refused the offer of official position but worked as a common man instead.
② Xiangxian Temple, built to commemorate the former locals of high virtues and talents.

to the historical studies. In 1985, the local government rebuilt Wan's tomb, and in 2006, it was listed as one of the Sixth Batch of National Key Cultural Relics Protection Units.

Wan Sitong (1638–1702), courtesy name Jiye, literary name Shiyuan, was born into the Wan family, a gentry family of Yongshang featuring both intellectual and martial heritage.

Wan Sitong, the eighth son of Wan Tai and the youngest of the "Eight Dragons of the Wan family", was born in the former residence of the Wan family at Guangji Street of Ningbo in the eleventh year of Emperor Chongzhen's reign. When he was 9 years old, the Qing army crossed the Qiantang River and invaded eastern Zhejiang. The Wan family was forced to hide in the mountain near Yulin Village of Fenghua for 3 years. Since then, Wan Sitong, a noble boy, had gradually grown into a man who could support himself by his own laboring, and thereby got a deeper understanding of the hardships of the folks. That deeply influenced Wan Sitong's thought in historical studies which was featured with the affinity to the people. In his boyhood, Wan Sitong was very naughty, unwilling to read any book, which worried his father very much. Once, he was shut in his father's study, where the boy, out of boredom, started to look through the books on the history of the Ming dynasty on the bookshelf. The more he read, the more fascinated he became, and he could even clearly remember all what he read. Gradually, he developed a good habit of reading. On an autumn day of the year when Wan Sitong was 14 years old (1652, the ninth year in the reign of Emperor Shunzhi of Qing), he saw his father secretly taking out some treasured things that Emperor Taizu of Ming (Zhu Yuanzhang) gave to his ancestor Wan Bin (万斌), such as emperor's signature, certificate of appointment and wooden amulet, as well as the "Painting of Loyalty and Chastity" (四忠三节图) drawn by his ancestor Wan Quan (万全), and showing them to the "Six Poets of Jiaolin", a group of Ming loyalists, who were filled with emotions when appreciating them, and then recorded what had happened to them in their respective poem(s). This undoubtedly inspired Wan Sitong's loyalty to the former Ming dynasty and his love for the nation, and also influenced his thought of historical studies in the following years.

In the sixth year under the reign of Emperor Kangxi, Wan Sitong and other scholars invited Huang Zongxi to give lectures in Ningbo, where Huang mainly focused on the Confucian classics, including *The Book of Changes*, *The Book of History*, *The Book of Songs*, *The Book of Rites*, and *The Spring and Autumn Annals*, as well as the learning of Master Liu Zongzhou. In Yongshang Zhengren Academy, the place where Huang gave lectures, there were more than 100 disciples at most, of whom 16 were praised by Huang Zongxi. Although Wan Sitong was younger than most of these disciples, he was praised highly by his teachers and friends. Two years later, in the eighth year of Emperor Kangxi's reign (1669), in order to make a living, Wan Sitong went to the home of Jiang Xizhe, who was one of the founders of Shaoxing Zhengren Academy, to teach Confucian classics to his son Jiang Yao (姜垚). In the thirteenth year of Emperor Kangxi's reign (1674), Wan Sitong was invited to the Li family in the east of the city to teach Confucian classics to their children. With a certain salary, he eventually got rid of his long-term poverty, and started his stable life, so that the speed of his book writing was getting higher. Within 5 years, he almost completed two important works. One was *Yuefu Poetry of Ming* (《明乐府》), and the other was *Supplementary Chronological Tables of China's History* (《补历代史表》)[①] which was nearly finished. Thereafter, Wan Sitong's fame spread gradually and widely, and in the seventeenth year under the reign of Emperor Kangxi (1678), Zhejiang authority recommended him to sit for an official entrance examination called *boxue hongci ke*, strongly suggesting him to work as an official, but he refused. Coincidentally, Xu Qianxue (徐乾学), a great Kunshan scholar, who was observing rituals of filial piety at home, hired him to join the composition of *Funeral Rituals* (《丧礼》), so he hurried to Kunshan, where he went to Xu Qianxue's private library called "Chuanshi Building". For Wan Sitong, such a book-loving man, it was a great

---

① The book was finally published as *Chronological Tables of China's History* (《列代纪年》/《历史年表》).

opportunity of studying and learning in such a collection of numerous books. Besides, Ye Jiulai (叶九来) had a private library called "Banjian Garden" in Kunshan at the time, which had both a very rich collection of books and beautiful scenery. Wan Sitong also liked to go there to have a read or rest.

In the eighteenth year of Emperor Kangxi's reign, Academician Xu Yuanwen (徐元文) of the Grand Secretariat, the younger brother of Xu Qianxue , was appointed by the imperial court as *jianxiu* (监修)[1] to organize the compiling of *History of Ming*. Then he recommended Wan Sitong to join the work. Initially, the Qing court summoned Huang Zongxi to do the job, but he refused. However, Huang Zongxi thought it a great cause, which involved the judgment of loyalty and treachery and the influence on the later generations, so he encouraged Wan Sitong to take the recommendation, because he believed Wan could do it well. Later, he expressed his attitude towards Wan's work in the poetic lines:

> Whether it is loyal or treacherous,
>
> The reputation of the Ming figures is under the judgment of a common man[2].

At first, Wan Sitong, with his nephew Wan Yan (万言), went to the north (Beijing) to compile the *History of Ming*. Following Huang Zongxi's instructions, Wan Sitong stayed in Xu Yuanwen's home. Refusing official titles and salaries, Wan entered the Bureau of History as a common man. Wan's work in Beijing lasted 19 years, during which all the manuscripts of the five-hundred volumes of *History of Ming* were finished after Wan's personal examination and review. At that time, 50 or 60 compilers participated in the project, and their first draft of each part would be collected, and then sent to Wan Sitong for review. After each draft was checked, for any issue to be added or verified, Wan would point out precisely where and how to find the specific information needed, without any fault. Actually, it was Wan Sitong who genuinely worked

---

①   *Jianxiu*, compiling supervisor.
②   Wan Sitong was called "historiographer as a common man".

as the chief compiler. Following Xu Yuanwen, Grand Academician Zhang Yushu (张玉书), Grand Academician Chen Tingjing (陈廷敬), and Minister Wang Hongxu (王鸿绪) consecutively served as the general director of the program, but all of them still invited Wan Sitong to continue compiling the book.

In the twenty-ninth year of Emperor Kangxi's reign (1690), Xu Qianxue, the head of the Ministry of Justice and general director of the Institution for the History of Ming, and his brother Xu Yuanwen, the grand academician of the Grand Secretariat and compiling supervisor of *History of Ming*, were impeached one after another, and both of them returned to Kunshan, Jiangsu Province. But Wan Sitong, as the one who was recommended by the two brothers, didn't leave Beijing, because of the sincere requests of Zhang Yushu, the new compiling supervisor and Chen Tingjing, the new general director. Besides, Wan Sitong moved to Jiangnan Guild Hall from Bishan Hall. In the same year, Beijing official Qiu Zhao'ao (仇兆鳌), who was Wan's schoolmate at Yongshang Zhengren Academy, invited Wan to give lectures in Beijing, where Wan mainly lectured on Confucian classics and history. The audience, 40 or 50 persons in total and sometimes even up to 100, were those "who were interested in ancient learning or who was preparing for the imperial civil service examination", including high-ranking officials or non-official scholars. In his late years, Wan Sitong suffered from poor eyesight, beriberi and hypertension. On the eighth day of the fourth lunar month of the forty-first year of Emperor Kangxi's reign (1702), he suddenly died in Wang Hongxu's residence in Beijing. Such a great historian passed away in a desolate way.

On how many kinds of works Wan Sitong had done, people had different opinions. According to the textual research of Chen Xunci (陈训慈) and Fang Zuyou, there were 33 kinds of works attributed to Wan Sitong, mainly including 500 volumes of *The Manuscript of the History of Ming* (《明史稿》), and 64 volumes of *Supplementary Chronological Tables of China's History*. Beside, at the invitation of Xu Qianxue, he joined the compilation of *General Study of Rites* (《读礼通考》).

Wan Sitong's academic thought was mainly reflected in his research of history and Confucian classics, and he had a clear practical inclination in philosophy.

Wan Sitong learned ancient prose and poetry when he was young, mainly focusing on the literary writing; in his adulthood, Wan specialized in Confucian classics; after his middle age, Wan emphasized the historical studies which he thought to be "the learning necessary for the state", exploring the ancient and modern systems in detail. All his academic turns were closely related to his spirit of "learning for practical purpose".

Wan Sitong believed that "practical learning" was vital to a Confucian and that the basic responsibility of a Confucian intellectual was to seek benefits for all people under heaven and save all people from disasters. He thought "today's people look more 'haggard' than the previous generation, thus, it is necessary for a Confucian scholar to talk about 'practical learning' every day". Therefore, Wan Sitong vowed to serve the country with his knowledge, and aimed at writing significant articles, guiding people's life and saving the people from disasters. "To be honest, I often prefer the practical learning", he argued. The key to "practical learning" is to deeply summarize historical experience and explore the good laws of governing the country in previous dynasties, so as to serve as a teacher for emperors and to make laws for all ages. In order to seek the good measures of governing the country, Wan Sitong evaluated the gains and losses of the laws of the past dynasties. He observed the "extreme disadvantages" of the Yuan, Ming and Qing dynasties, and "cleared up their bad aspects". With the value pursuit of "obeying the will of heaven" and "saving people from disasters", Wan Sitong was looking for "a long-term strategy for all ages".

Wan Sitong's thought of historical studies based on "practical learning" was mainly reflected in the following aspects.

He paid attention to the study of modern history. Wan Sitong's historical research focused on modern history, that is, the study of Ming history. Unlike scholars who extolled "wise emperor", Wan Sitong focused on the criticism and analysis on the history of the Ming dynasty. He argued that the Ming dynasty abandoned the measures of good governance of the Han, Tang and Song dynasties. Instead, it inherited the corrupt policies of the Yuan dynasty. Wan Sitong paid special attention to the analysis and criticism on the system of the Ming dynasty.

In his writings like essays and poems, Wan Sitong, in a way of acrimony, exposed the shortcomings of the emperors of the Ming dynasty: the tyranny of Emperor Taizu, the cruelty of Emperor Chengzu, the debauchery of Emperor Wuzong, the greed of Emperor Shenzong, the dark reign of Emperor Xizong, and the hypocrisy of Emperor Sizong, vividly describing their images. Moreover, the sharp edge of Wan Sitong's criticism was not directed at a certain individual monarch, but a considerable number of monarchs, and it implied that Wan Sitong had a negative idea for the autocratic monarchy.

Wan Sitong's theory of "practical learning" was based on the Confucian people-oriented thought, but it had its own characteristics. For example, his people-oriented thought was combined with the social reality at that time. It was concerned about the suffering of the people, and paid attention to the solution of practical problems. Wan Sitong believed that the people at the turn of Ming and Qing dynasties were going through a harder time than those of previous dynasties. Their suffering was reflected in Wan Sitong's poetic lines:

No officials care about the people's pale faces in the hard days,
No people are aware of how luxurious the bureaucrats' life is.

If all those with political power are like Wang Zhi, the Minister of Justice, then no one would see a man in a road-side ditch who was starved to death.

The expressions like "people's pale faces" and "bureaucrats' luxurious life" constitute a sharp contrast and pungent satire. They reflect the opposition between the officials and the people and the cause-effect relationship between the officials' luxury and people's poor livelihood. These words express Wan Sitong's deep sympathy for the people in trouble.

In addition to his outstanding achievements in historical studies, Wan

Sitong was also good at the studies of Confucian classics, mainly including the studies of *The Book of Songs*, *The Book of Rites* and *The Book of History*. The characteristic of Wan Sitong's thought of Confucian classics was to view the Confucian classics from the perspective of history, that is, "taking Confucian classics as history". Wan Sitong's Confucian thought was full of spirit of skepticism and wisdom of innovation. On the basis of independent thinking and extensive evidence, he denied the ideas of Zheng Xuan[①], Zhu Xi and other Confucians, and even suspected that the Confucian classics were not written by sages. He sought proofs in the commentaries of the Confucian classics, attached importance to reliable evidence, and advocated statements with reason and evidence, so as to pursue the spirit of seeking truth from facts.

Wan Sitong's study of Confucian classics and history was deeply influenced by Huang Zongxi. He inherited and developed Huang's national democratic thought and the spirit of practical learning. In terms of academic research methods, Wan attached great importance to broad view, integration, reflection and textual research, which had a far-reaching impact on the later schools like Zhedong School, especially on the Qian-Jia School which basically adopted Wan's academic research methods.

Later scholars thought highly of Wan Sitong's writings, learning and morality. In the "Biography of Master Wan Zhenwen" (《万贞文先生传》), the author Quan Zuwang remarked that Wan's posthumous name, "Zhenwen", was a very appropriate evaluation for him. "Zhen" is for his character, while "wen" is for his achievement in Confucian classics and historical studies. The former means upright and determined, that is to say, Wan had a pursuit of "faithfulness to history" so that he never yielded to any high-ranking official or imperial relative who demanded him to write them positively in history; the latter means that Wan was excellent in his learning.

Liang Qichao highly praised Wan's achievement in historical studies:

---

①   Zheng Xuan (郑玄, 127–200), courtesy name Kangcheng, a native of Gaomi County of Beihai Prefecture (now Gaomi, Shandong Province), a great Confucian scholar in the end of the Eastern Han dynasty.

It has been widely acknowledged in the academic circle that among "The Twenty-four Histories", the *History of Ming* is the best compiled one except "The Early Four Histories", namely, Sima Qian's *Records of the Grand Historian of China*, Ban Gu's *The Book of Han*, Fan Ye (范晔)'s *The Book of the Later Han* (《后汉书》), and Chen Shou (陈寿)'s *Annals of the Three Kingdoms* (《三国志》). Besides, although it was also a book compiled under the official supervision, it was, in fact, completed entirely out of Wan Jiye (Wan Sitong)'s personal efforts.

From the view of today's scholars of historical studies, Liang's above words are commonly regarded as an insightful comment.

III. Quan Zuwang

Quan Zuwang was an outstanding historian in the early Qing dynasty. His personality and writing won wide praise from later generations. Some people call him "the top one after Ban Gu and Sima Qian, the two most famous historians"; some people like Hu Shi[1] claim that "Quan Zuwang is one of the cleverest persons in the world except Zhu Xi". Still, some remark that "Quan Zuwang is a mirror reflecting the soul of Chinese literati", as Quan had an infinite love for his nation and hometown, a straightforward character against evil things, and a sentiment that couldn't be corrupted by a fortune or suppressed by force. Besides, Quan had a high virtue, an insightful observation and excellent writing skills, and he also had selfless dedication to the cause of historiography.

Quan Zuwang was commented by the scholars of later generations with the remark "*yuehun shibi*" (越魂史笔)[2]. As modern historian Du Weiyun (杜维运) argued, "Scholars of Zhedong School of historical studies shared the same origin but boasted their own features. For example, Huang Zongxi's and Wan Sitong's features lay in the broadness of their range of study, Zhang Xuecheng's in insightful view, and Quan Zuwang's in the spirit of Zhedong School of historical studies." According to the above remark, "*yuehun*" (越魂)[3] refers to the spirit of Zhedong School of historical studies, while "*shibi*" (史笔)[4] refers to "a great historian" or "the most valuable historical work". However, Quan Zuwang's achievements in "historical studies" and "philology"

---

[1] Hu Shi (胡适, 1891–1962), or Hu Shih, courtesy name Shizhi, a Chinese philosopher and essayist. He is widely recognized today as a key contributor to Chinese liberalism.

[2] *Yuehun shibi*, a great historian with the spirit of Zhedong School of historical studies.

[3] *Yuehun*, literally, soul of Yue area.

[4] *Shibi*, literally, a pen for history writing.

cannot be summarized just through one aspect. As Zhang Xuecheng said, "Those who study human nature and destiny must resort to history." That is to say, Quan Zuwang's features of the above two disciplines lay in the integration of Confucian classics, Neo-Confucianism, historical studies and regional documents, and in the unity of a thinker's wisdom, a historian's acumen and a litterateur's talent. Ruan Yuan, a scholar in the Qing dynasty, once said, "Among the three disciplines, namely Confucian classics, historical studies and writing, it is enough for a scholar to master just one of them. But Quan Xieshan (Quan Zuwang) mastered all three of them."

Quan Zuwang was hailed as the most prominent biographical historian since Sima Qian. The biographies he wrote were not only historical records, but also a process of seeking truth with deepest feelings and emotions. A reader would be moved from time to time by his desolate writing of self-consciousness and emotions. In his "Records of Meihualing" (《梅花岭记》), Quan Zuwang highly praised the spirit of Shi Kefa (史可法), a famous anti-Qing minister of the Ming dynasty. This article took loyalty as the main line, unfolded in a sentimental style. Hundreds of years later, people are still moved and would burst into tears when reading this article. In "The Brief Biography of Feng Jingdi[①]" (《冯京第小传》), Quan vividly depicted anti-Qing warrior Feng Jingdi: With a thin figure, he had a spirit as bright as the clouds in the sunny sky, and a voice as shocking as the sound of dignified rhythm, sending a shudder of fear through others. Quan said, "Even if hundreds of years have passed, I can still feel like the white-haired man being in front of my teary eyes." Whenever Quan completed a story, he would read it with tears and when he finished reading the whole one, he would cry endlessly. Therefore, Quan's biographies are very vivid and moving, realizing the purpose of outflow of true feelings. Quan Zuwang searched every corner of the old literature for the lost

---

① Feng Jingdi (冯京第), courtesy name Jizhong, literary name Dianxi, respected as Master Dianxi, a native of Cixi, Ningbo. He was a scholar at the turn of Ming and Qing dynasties, and an anti-Qing warrior. Besides, he was one of the 140 scholars who signed on the "Notice on Prevention Upheavals in the Old Capital (Nanjing)" in the eleventh year of Emperor Chongzhen's reign.

records of the deeds of those anti-Qing martyrs, and collected them. Therefore, his writing of biography has become a model of Chinese biography literature, ascending an enviable peak.

Quan Zuwang was born in Baitanli (on the Mist Islet) on the west bank of the Moon Lake in the forty-fourth year in the reign of Emperor Kangxi (1705) of Qing dynasty. In his adulthood, he addressed himself "Owner of Jieqi Pavilion" and "Owner of Shuangjiu Mountain House". Therefore, his posthumous collection was named *Jieqiting Collection* by its editor Dong Bingchun (董秉纯), a disciple of Quan Zuwang's. He was respected as Master Xieshan by the scholars at the time according to his literary name Xieshan.

Quan Zuwang was born into an upright family loyal to the nation. When the Qing army invaded the south, Quan's great-grandfather Quan Dahe (全大和) and his grandfather Quan Wuqi (全吾骐) led their whole family to a deep mountain where they avoided the Qing troops. Quan Zuwang's father Quan Shu (全书, courtesy name Yinyuan) was a teacher of Confucian classics and poems in his hometown. Thus, from the age of 4 to 13, Quan Zuwang was taught by his father who "taught him in person, and instructed him to comprehend the basic knowledge about reading and writing". The personal teaching of his father to him was both strict and inspiring. When Zuwang could use brush, he was asked by his father to copy books. From the age of 14, he studied in a private school called "Sanyu Thatched Cottage" where he was taught by Dong Zhengguo (董正国). At the age of 18, Zuwang luckily met his paternal aunt-in-law, the daughter of famous anti-Qing minister Zhang Cangshui (张苍水), and then had a clearer understanding of Zhang Cangshui's heroic deeds in the "20 years of righteous resistance".

At the age of 16, he took the provincial-level imperial examination held in Hangzhou for the first time, but failed. Fortunately, there he got to know Li Fu (李绂), the chief examiner, and later they became close friends. Also, he paid a visit to Zha Shenxing (查慎行), a famous poet and prose writer, and asked for advice on the writing of ancient prose. Later, Quan Zuwang went to Hangzhou many times, where he made lots of friends, including Li E (厉鹗), Hang Shijun

(杭世骏), and Zhao Yu (赵昱).

At the age of 21, Quan began to collect local documents for the compilation of "the scattered records of the lost country[①]", and completed his first book *Cangtianji* (《沧天记》). As a teenager, Quan developed his own unique hobbies. He loved reading, especially books of history and geography, and was indulged in the collection of the documents about "the loyalists to the lost country". All these laid the foundation for his wide-ranging and profound scholarship.

From 26 to 32 years old, Quan Zuwang went through a hard time in Beijing. In his own words, it was "a poor period in the capital". But that was also an important stage of his life journey. In the first year of Emperor Qianlong's reign (1736), he was enrolled as *jinshi*, and then selected into the *shuchang guan* (庶常馆)[②] of Hanlin Academy as *shujishi*. Soon he was recommended to sit for another entrance examination for *boxue hongci ke*, but he failed to take the examination because Grand Academician Zhang Tingyu (张廷玉) offered a special suggestion to the emperor that "whoever has been recommended to be enrolled as *jinshi* should not be supposed to take the examination of *boxue hongci ke*". Disappointed, Quan felt angry with Zhang. In the second year of Emperor Qianlong's reign (1737), he was ranked in the second class after the graduation examination of Hanlin Academy. Originally, the second-class *jinshi* could stay in the academy for further study, but Zhang Tingyu ordered them to leave and wait to fill the vacant official positions like county magistrate. One thing led to another, and Quan became so wrathful with Zhang Tingyu that he refused Fang Bao (方苞)'s recommendation to work as a ritual official in Beijing, and returned home in the early winter of the same year with the anger of "relegation" and "abandoning the post".

In the winter of 1737, he got to his hometown where he began his "ten-year academic career at home". During the period, he led a peaceful, full but

① The lost country refers to the Ming dynasty.
② *Shuchang guan*, a department for newly-enrolled high-ranking *jinshi* to further their study.

poor life. But far away from the intrigues in the officialdom, he gradually shifted his energy and attention to academic research, and thereby made great achievements. For example, he added supplements to the *Scholarly Annals of the Song and Yuan Dynasties*, annotated *Reading Notes about Difficulties in Learning* three times, compiled *Continued Collection of Ancient Yongshang Poems* and finished the writing of many essays and poems later collected into *Jieqiting Collection*.

In the late autumn of the thirteenth year of Emperor Qianlong's reign (1748), at the invitation of Du Butang (杜补堂), the prefect of Shaoxing, Quan Zuwang, at the age of 43, became the head of Jishan Academy. Liu Zongzhou, a great Ming Confucian and a "loyalist to the lost country", once gave lectures in Jishan Mountain in the north of Shaoxing city, so Liu was called Master Jishan. Quan Zuwang respected Liu Zongzhou as a model in both Confucianism study and morality, and in his spare time, he often visited the places where Liu Zongzhou lived or studied, meanwhile expressing his admiration for Liu through poems or essays. In mid-winter of 1748, Quan Zuwang resigned from the post of head of Jishan Academy after only three months. The reason why he quit, according to the *Chronicle of Master Quan Xieshan* (《全谢山先生年谱》) written by Jiang Tianshu (蒋天枢), lay in his anger with Fang Guancheng (方观承), the governor of Zhejiang, who "arbitrarily deleted several martyrs". Fang died for the Ming dynasty in the Ming-Qing transition that were collected in Quan's "Inscriptions for Those Worshiped in Master Liu Zongzhou's Temple" (《子刘子祠堂配享碑》). That mattered much to Quan Zuwang, who thought it did harm to his belief, ideal and the principle of his scholarship. Therefore, despite his poverty, he resolutely quit the well-paid job as the head of Jishan Academy.

In the late spring of the seventeenth year of Emperor Qianlong's reign (1752), at the invitation of Su Chang (苏昌), the governor of Guangdong Province, Quan Zuwang traveled 5,000 *li* (2,500 kilometers) to Duanzhou, Guangdong Province, where he worked as the head of Tianzhang Academy (also known as Duanxi Academy) and his teaching was of great effects.

Unfortunately, in the third lunar month of the eighteenth year of Emperor Qianlong's reign (1753), Quan Zuwang was seriously ill and decided to resign. But the local officials sincerely persuaded him to spend more time in Duanxi Academy, so he stayed there for a few more months. At that time, the governor actually intended to made a special recommendation for him to become an official, but Quan Zuwang had decided not to be an official again, so he resolutely resigned and returned home. In the early autumn of the same year, he arrived in Yongshang, which was recorded in his poetic lines, "By the stone window of my room in my hometown, I see the azalea flowers in blossom." After several months in Ningbo, he gradually recovered from his illness. Later, he went to Hangzhou, Yangzhou and other places, meanwhile studying *Commentary on the Water Classic* and making supplements to the *Scholarly Annals of the Song and Yuan Dynasties*. In the third lunar month of the twentieth year of Emperor Qianlong's reign (1755), his son, who had just reached the age of 13, died unfortunately, which caused too much sorrow to Quan Zuwang who then became seriously ill. Thereafter, "he wrote ten poems and one epigraph to memorialize his son before he quit writing". One day, he urgently asked his disciples like Dong Bingchun and Jiang Xueyong (蒋学镛) to meet him at his bedside, where he, in finger signs, asked them to revise his manuscripts, and then left them his will. On the second day of the seventh lunar month of the same year, Quan died of illness at home.

Quan Zuwang was a famous early-Qing scholar in Confucian classics, historical studies, and literary writing and studies. "His learning was profound and wide-ranging with various points associated with each other in his books." His academic thought covered such areas as historical studies, philology, historical geography, Confucian classics, Neo-Confucianism and literature, of which historical studies and philology were of the greatest contribution.

Quan Zuwang's main works are as follows:

He made supplements to the *Scholarly Annals of the Song and Yuan Dynasties*. The compilation of this book was initiated by Huang Zongxi, who completed 59 academic cases in 67 volumes, among its 91 academic cases in

100 volumes. Then it was supplemented and extended by Huang Baijia, Huang Zongxi's son. In the eleventh year of Emperor Qianlong's reign (1746), Quan Zuwnag was commissioned to continue to compile the book, which was finally completed 9 years later. Quan's contribution to the book lay mainly in the addition of 32 academic cases in a total of 33 volumes into *Scholarly Annals of the Song and Yuan Dynasties*, accounting for one third of the whole book; he made effort in adding catalogues into *Scholarly Annals of the Song and Yuan Dynasties*; based on his newly-discovered literature documents, he revised the book with additional information and rectified the deficiencies and mistakes of Huang Zongxi's original text; more importantly, he clarified the development path of Neo-Confucianism in the Song and Yuan dynasties, and fully and fairly evaluated the ideas of various academic schools and scholars. As for the Neo-Confucianism, there were many schools and scholars in the Song and Ming dynasties, and the academic debate between different schools was very hot. It can be said that the history of the development of Neo-Confucianism in the Song and Ming dynasties is that of debates between "a hundred schools of thought". Quan Zuwang believed that everyone is equal in academia, and he had a supportive attitude towards these debates. Meanwhile, he made an objective evaluation of various schools and their representatives. He valued "great Confucian scholars", "authentic Confucian scholars" and "profound Confucian scholars" and treated them as the models in academia. In a word, Quan Zuwang made a great contribution to *Scholarly Annals of the Song and Yuan Dynasties*.

Jieqiting Collection and *A Supplement to Jieqiting Collection* (《鲒埼亭集外编》) were also two of his masterpieces. After the death of Quan Zuwang, his student Dong Bingchun (董秉纯) collected his poems and essays and compiled them into 38 volumes of *Jieqiting Collection*, and 50 volumes of *A Supplement to Jieqiting Collection*, 88 volumes in total. Quan Zuwang's poetic and literary theories, as well as his views and methods of historical studies were all demonstrated in the above books.

He had seven volumes of *Continued Collection of Ancient Yongshang*

Poems as well. Quan made great efforts in compiling this book which, continuing Hu Wenxue and Li Yesi's *Collection of Ancient Yongshang Poems* (《甬上耆旧诗》), contains the Siming poets from the Wanli and Longqing periods of the Ming dynasty to the early Qing dynasty with both their biographies and representative poems. In total, the book covers up to 700 authors and more than 16,000 poems, and it combines the poems complementarily with the biographies of their authors, having a high academic value.

Besides, Quan Zuwang emendated *Commentary on the Water Classic* seven times, annotated *Reading Notes about Difficulties in Learning* three times, and finished works including *Answers to Questions on Confucian Classics and History* (《经史答问》), *Doubts about the Geographical Treatise of The Book of Han* (《汉书地理志稽疑》), and *Chronology through Ages* (《古今通志年表》), etc.

Quan Zuwang was a follower of Wang Yangming and an adherent of Huang Zongxi. Meanwhile, he was academically influenced by his contemporary scholars. He had a broad academic horizon, and despised academic sectarianism. As he said, "Academic sectarianism is the worst thing constraining people's minds. What sages value is not words but practice." Therefore, Quan viewed the scholarship of different schools from a practical perspective, and he claimed to integrate the ideas of different schools, especially the contrary theories of Zhu Xi's *lixue* and Lu Jiuyuan's *xinxue*. Zhu Xi's learning derived from the study of Yang Shi (杨时), teaching people to start their study through exhaustive inquiry into principle (*li*), and believing that the accumulated mastery of principles would lead to acquisition of knowledge, and that only when what is heard or known is put into practice, can it be called a significant thing instead of sapping the spirit by merely seeking pleasures; while Lu Jiuyuan's learning was close to the study of Shangcai School[①],

---

① Shangcai School was founded by Xie Liangzuo, a philosopher of the Northern Song dynasty. Xie was a native of Shangcai (now in Henan Province), hence the name of the school.

teaching people to start their study by discovering their original heart-mind, and believing that only one has a determined mind can he respond to the changes of things between heaven and earth and that a scholar should keep reading so as to avoid rootless talks. Zhu's and Lu's theories have their respective emphases in learning, so Quan Zuwang believed that only a complementary study of the two theories can lead to the complete learning rather than "accepting one and discarding the other". Quan thought it was also true to the learning of Wang Yangming (in line with Lu) and that of Huang Zongxi (in line with Zhu). For example, Quan fully affirmed the theory of Yangming, considering it "good medicine to cure the disadvantages", but he thought the problem appeared in the process of the spread of Wang Yangming's learning.

Quan Zuwang's most outstanding academic contributions were mainly reflected in his collating local documents and historical writing. He spared no effort in collecting documents with a broad and extensive view and can be called a master. He loved his hometown and particularly valued the collection of the documents left by famous local scholars. As for collecting and sorting out the documents of the local scholars in eastern Zhejiang and commending the loyal people, Quan regarded them as his due duty and a mission entrusted by the times to which he dedicated himself without any hesitation. The basic method of Quan Zuwang's literature sorting and historical writing was to synthesize the ideas from different sources and form them into a systematic frame. He paid special attention to those righteous and loyal martyrs in the late Ming dynasty. His *Jieqiting Collection* is full of articles about them, including tomb inscriptions, narratives, annals, prefaces and postscripts of biographies. The purpose of these writings was to let the later generations know their fame, deeds and writings so as to console these righteous and loyal martyrs and show their merits and virtues to the world. Quan faithfully and vividly depicted the moving tragic scenes of the anti-Qing struggles at all levels of society at the end of the Ming dynasty, and commended the deeds of a large number of anti-Qing warriors and martyrs such as Sun Jiaji (孙嘉绩), Qian Sule (钱肃乐), Zhang Huangyan, Shi Kefa, Huang Zongxi and Gu Yanwu. Besides, Quan mercilessly disclosed and denounced the ugly behavior of Xie Sanbin (谢三宾), Mao Qiling and others who lost their dignity as scholars.

In addition to commendation, Quan Zuwang took into account and recorded the knowledge about geography, calendar, local scenery, system evolution, and even architecture like academy buildings and pavilions. When sorting out documents, he was "ashamed of not knowing a certain thing", paying attention to the examination of its authenticity. He valued the first-hand documents obtained by himself, and he would even personally investigate whatever in doubt. In this sense, Quan's literature sorting and historical research had incomparable authenticity and reliability.

Quan Zuwang's *Jieqiing Collection, Continued Collection of Ancient Yongshang Poems* and *Scholarly Annals of the Song and Yuan Dynasties* are all masterworks, and his great masterpieces of textual criticism are three-time annotated *Reading Notes about Difficulties in Learning* and seven-time emendated *Commentary on the Water Classic*. He had extremely high attainments and views in the learning of Confucian classics and Neo-Confucianism, and was comparable in the textual research of Confucian classics, history and geography. His articles were lively, magnificent and unforgettable. Along with the publication and circulation of Quan's writings and with more and more researchers participating in the study, the evaluation of Quan Zuwang has been gradually enhanced.

Quan Zuwang, a great scholar worthy of eternal memory, should be learned by scholars of later generations.

IV. Yaojiang Academy School and Shao Tingcai

The spread of Wang Yangming's *xinxue* thought in his hometown gave rise to the foundation of Yaojiang Academy, whose purpose was to study and teach *xinxue*. Yaojiang Academy was the base for the dissemination of Wang Yangming's theory in eastern Zhejiang at the turn of the Ming and Qing dynasties. The academic group with Yaojiang Academy as its center was called "Yaojiang Academy School".

Yaojiang Academy was formerly called "Banlin Charity School" which was founded in the twelfth year of Emperor Chongzhen's reign in the Ming dynasty (1639). It was in the early Qing dynasty that the academy got its present name. Originally, Banlin School was in the southern suburb of Yuyao, and then it was moved to a place named Jiaoshengyuan inside the city so as to make it convenient for the students to go to school. The founders of the academy were "Four Masters", namely, Shen Guomo, courtesy name Shuze; Guan Zongsheng, courtesy name Yunzhong; Shi Xiaoxian, courtesy name Zixu; and Shi Xiaofu, courtesy name Zifu. Apart from their common social identity as *zhusheng* (诸生)[①], they had consanguineous or affinal kinship. For example, Shi Xiaoxian and Shi Xiaofu were brothers, while Guan Zongsheng was their brother-in-law.

When Banlin Charity School was founded, the four masters were all in their fifties or sixties. With the identity of *zhusheng*, they were excellent both in academic education and personal character. They were enthusiastic about the scholarship of their outstanding local forerunners, especially about Yangming

---

[①] *Zhusheng*, alias *xiucai*, refers to those who passed the county-level imperial civil service examination.

xinxue, and therefore, they devoted themselves to the study and spread of the learning, which became their common life pursuit. In his *Chinese Academic History of Recent Three Hundred Years*, Liang Qichao commented, "In the Qing dynasty, *Wangxue* gradually declined in other places, while in eastern Zhejiang, it was still disseminated and developed for a long period."

From the twelfth to fourteenth year of Emperor Chongzhen's reign (1639–1641), Yaojiang Academy was in its prime days. But soon after that, due to the death of scholars like Guan Zongsheng and Shi Xiaofu, as well as the Qing army's invasion to eastern Zhejiang in the third year of Emperor Shunzhi's reign, the teachers and students of the academy scattered everywhere, making the school in a state of suspension.

In the sixth year of Emperor Shunzhi's reign (1649), along with the gradual stabilization of the political situation in eastern Zhejiang, Banlin Charity School was re-opened with Shi Xiaoxian as the head of the school. In the middle spring of the ninth year of Emperor Shunzhi's reign (1652), the "Academy Meeting Regulations" (《书院会则》) was revised, which still implemented the system of a monthly meeting. In the fourteenth year of Emperor Shunzhi's reign (1657), the charity school was rebuilt before it was officially named "Yaojiang Academy". The head Shi Xiaoxian still adhered to the consistent principle of the academy—scholarship is above everything else. Besides, Shi attended in person every monthly and quarterly meeting of the academy. Around the sixteenth year of Emperor Shunzhi's reign, Shi Xiaoxian died. Subsequently, no one kept in charge of the academy affairs, and thereby the lectures were suspended.

In the eighth year of Emperor Kangxi's reign, Han Kongdang, a disciple of Shen Guomo, became the head of Yaojiang Academy. Han Kongdang (1599–1671), courtesy name Renfu, was respected as Master Yihan by his followers who thought him a responsible scholar with an independent mind. In the sixth year of Emperor Kangxi's reign, Han established Chengyu Club "where excellent scholars all went to consult with Han Kongdang about their learning". Han's teaching achievements attracted the attention of Yaojiang

Academy, so he was hired as the director of teaching affairs. During his tenure, Han restored the monthly meeting system of the academy, and revised the "Academy Regulations" (《书院规约》). Unfortunately, Han died of serious disease in the tenth year of Emperor Kangxi's reign (1671), only 2 years after he became the head of the academy.

Yu Changmin (俞长民) and Shi Biao (史标) were two successors of Han Kongdang. Yu Changmin (1597–1682), courtesy name Wuzhi, was a native of Yuyao. He was *zhusheng* of Renhe County, Hangzhou, and a disciple of both Shen Guomo and Han Kongdang. As the head of the academy, Yu Changmin continued to hold monthly meetings, writing articles to encourage students to study hard and make a difference.

Shi Biao (1616–1693), courtesy name Xianchen, was a native of Yuyao and a disciple of Shen Guomo. He once assisted Han Kongdang in giving lectures. In the twenty-second year of Emperor Kangxi's reign (1683), with the joint recommendation of Shao Tingcai and the disciples of the academy, Shi started to serve as the head of the academy until he passed away at the age of 78 in the thirty-second year of Emperor Kangxi's reign (1693).

Following Shi Biao, Shao Tingcai served as the head of the academy from the thirty-third year to the fiftieth year of Emperor Kangxi's reign (1694–1711). After Shao Tingcai, Yaojiang Academy was rebuilt several times during the period of Emperor Yongzheng and Emperor Qianlong, during which there were occasional lectures. The last repair of the academy was in the years of Emperor Guangxu (1875–1908).

In terms of Wang Yangming's *xinxue* studies, Yaojiang Academy School was obviously different from "Jishan School". While the former was represented by scholars from Wang Ji to Zhou Rudeng and then to Shen Guomo, the latter from Liu Zongzhou to Huang Zongxi. Shi Xiaofu and Dong Biao (董标) from Yaojiang Academy once debated repeatedly with Liu Zongzhou over the relationship between "making sincere intention" and "extension of [innate] knowledge" and that between "heart-mind" (*xin*) and "intention" (*yi*). Since Han Kongdang, a disciple of Shen Guomo's, became the head of Yaojiang Academy, he himself had accepted Liu Zongzhou's view of "idea of being on the right way" (*zhengren zhizhi*, 证人之旨). Thereafter, the views of both sides were getting closer. In addition, Huang Zongxi also rectified some views of his mentor Liu Zongzhou. Later, Shao Tingcai, as a later representative of Yaojiang Academy School, adopted an inclusive attitude towards the different theories of Zhu Xi, Lu Jiuyuan, Wang Yangming, Liu Zongzhou and Huang Zongxi. In the development process of Yaojiang Academy School, Shao Tingcai could be called a terminator. Although he called himself "the last one of Yaojiang Academy School", Shao insisted on holding the theories of different schools. All in all, he was an important academic scholar with a broad horizon in eastern Zhejiang in the early Qing dynasty.

Shao Tingcai (1648–1711), courtesy name Nianlu, was a native of Yuyao. The Shao family, where Shao Tingcai was born, was a prestigious family only following the Sun, the Wang and the Xie families on the list of famous Yuyao families. Shao Zengke (邵曾可), Shao Tingcai's grandfather, gave up his desire of becoming an official through *keju*, and made a living by teaching all his life. Shao Zhenxian (邵贞显), Shao Tingcai's father, was born at the turn of the Ming and Qing dynasties, and it was impossible for him to take the *keju* due to the war-period instability here and there. According to their life traces of several generations, the Shao family originally had a tradition of taking *keju* before Shao Tingcai's grandfather and father, who both made a living though teaching instead.

As a six-month infant, Shao Tingcai lost his mother who was only 21 years old, while at the age of 10, Shao lost his stepmother. Therefore, he was brought up by his aunt-in-law, Lady Sun. Shao was very smart since his childhood and taught by his father academically and socially. Besides, Shao Tingcai respected his grandfather Shao Lugong (Shao Zengke), hence his courtesy name "Nianlu" (literally, missing Lugong).

In the sixteenth year of Emperor Shunzhi's reign, when Shao Zhenxian was invited to teach in Shimen (now Tongxiang) in western Zhejiang, no one left at home to look after Shao Tingcai after his stepmother's death of illness. Therefore, the 12-year-old boy was sent to his maternal grandfather's home, where his maternal grandfather Chen Shu'an (陈蜀庵) taught him such traditional Chinese classics as *Commentary of Zuo* (《左传》), *Discourses of the States* (《国语》), *Records of the Grand Historian of China*, *The Book of Han*, *The Book of Changes*, *The Book of Songs* and *The Book of History*. In the next year, at the age of 13, Shao Tingcai began to study *shiwen* (时文)[①]. However, because what he first learned was Yangming *xinxue*, he was repellent to *shiwen*, and his academic progress was therefore limited.

In the sixth year of Emperor Kangxi's reign, Shao Tingcai officially became a disciple of Han Kongdang's, studying in Chengyu Club and Yaojiang Academy. "After years of learning from Han Kongdang, Shao made great progress in his study." Originally, he gained nothing from reading Wang Yangming's *Instructions for Practical Living* (《传习录》), and then he read Liu Zongzhou's *Human Schemata* (《人谱》) by which he got a sudden comprehension. He claimed that "I know that only by practice in person, can my mind and nature be discovered". From then on, he kept abiding by this rule.

In the ninth year of Emperor Kangxi's reign, his father Shao Zhenxian died in Shimen. Afterwards, the burden of the family was on Shao Tingcai's shoulders. He had no choice but to follow the path of teaching that his grandfather and father had taken. He went to a Zhang family in Daoxu, Kuaiji where he taught their two boys. In his spare time, Shao was engaged in reading and writing, and he finished his *One Hundred Principles of Reading History* (《读史百则》) in more than one year. During this period, he occasionally returned to his hometown Yuyao to participate in the lectures of Yaojiang Academy.

In the thirteenth year of Emperor Kangxi's reign, Shao Tingcai was invited to teach at a Tao family in Nanhu Village, Kuaiji, where he stayed for 6 or 7 years. At the age of 33, Shao married a daughter of Tao's family, becoming a son-in-law living in his bridge's family. After marriage, Shao's wife gave birth

---

① *Shiwen*, eight-legged essay, a kind of essay prescribed for the imperial civil service examination.

to four sons and a daughter. Thus, he had a heavier burden, still living a life of poverty. He depicted his life as "no house, no land, I study and teach all year round. A family of more than ten members is supported only by teaching. Once I lie ill, there would be no food for my family". Except a short period of time in the twenty-fourth year of Emperor Kangxi's reign (1685) when he worked as a secretary in Guide Prefecture of Henan Province, Shao's main way of making a living was still teaching. Teaching failed to bring him wealth, but during the process of his teaching, his knowledge and character were increasingly recognized by the society. In the thirty-third year of Emperor Kangxi's reign (1694), Wei Zhongzao (韦钟藻), the magistrate of Yuyao County, sent a letter to hire him as an instructor of Yaojiang Academy. Shao Tingcai replied that he agreed to teach in Yuyao. That year, he was 47 years old. Soon, Shao Tingcai went to Yuyao, giving lectures at Yaojiang Academy, meanwhile drafting "Yaojiang Academy Regulations" (《姚江书院训约》). Shao's teaching was highly praised by the people of the time.

In his later years, Shao Tingcai traveled to places like Qi, Lu, Yan and Zhao. Although he was poor all his life without any extra income, his learning was getting better, his behavior more sincere, and his character higher. In the fiftieth year of Emperor Kangxi's reign (1711), Shao Tingcai died of intestinal disease at the age of 64.

Shao Tingcai never worked as an official all his life, only making a living by teaching. Although leading a poor life and only known within the confine of his hometown, Shao Tingcai exerted huge impacts on the later scholars of Zhedong scholarship for his love and achievements in historical studies, for his collection and collation of documents of local scholars, and for his development and promotion of Wang Yangming's and Liu Zongzhou's learning. Firstly, Shao's knowledge and character were highly praised by Wan Jing (the son of Wan Sida). Secondly, his thought of historical studies inspired Quan Zuwang who, in his learning, focused on "the classic literature of southeastern China and the historical events of the Ming dynasty". Thirdly, the learning of Shao Jinhan, a grandchild of Shao Tingcai's family, came from the education of the Shao family, and was especially influenced and inspired by Shao Tingcai. Fourthly, Zhang Xuecheng and his father Zhang Biao (章镳) admired and thought highly of Shao Tingcai's learning of historical studies, Neo-Confucianism and literature. In particular, Zhang Xuecheng, an acknowledged modern master of historical studies, claimed that his academic source was from Shao Nianlu (Shao Tingcai). Later scholar Ye Ying (叶瑛), when commenting the relationship between Zhang Xuecheng's and Shao Tingcai's learning, argued, "Master Zhang Xuecheng's scholarship derived from the learning of Wang Yangming and (Liu Zongzhou in a far perspective and from the studies of Huang Zongxi and Sifu (Shao Tingcai). In "Zhedong Scholarship" by Zhang Xuecheng, the author told the origin of his learning. Zhang's studying of nature and destiny combined with historical studies was in line with the thought of Zhedong scholarship. In all his life, Zhang Xuecheng admired Shao Tingcai, believing the *Sifutang Collection* (《思复堂集》) by Shao Tingcai "a precious work in 500 years", "therefore Zhang's study followed Shao's" (quoted from the Preface of *Annotations of General Interpretation of Historiography* [《文史通义校注·题记》] by Ye Ying). All the above indicate that Shao Tingcai made great contributions to the inheriting and development of Zhedong scholarship.

Admiring the learning of the outstanding predecessors of his hometown, Shao Tingcai wrote "An Account of Yaojiang Academy" (《姚江书院记》), which affirmed the efforts of Shen Guomo, Guan Zongsheng and Shi Xiaofu in preaching the learning of Wang Yangming; due to his academic relationship with Wang Yangming, he wrote the "Biography of Master Wang Yangming" (《王子传》), expressed Wang Yangming's contributions in participating in worldly affairs and supporting Confucianism; he finished the "Biography of Master Liu Zongzhou" (《刘子传》) to record his learning of "*shendu*" and praise his loyalty and righteousness; when Wang Yangming's learning prevailed, Zhezhong (the middle Zhejiang) became its academic center, for which Shao Tingcai completed the "Biographies of Wang Yangming's Disciples" (《王门弟子传》); Liu Zongzhou's disciples, including Qi Biaojia (祁彪佳), Zhang Zhao'ao (张兆鳌) and Huang Zongxi, inherited and developed their teacher's theory, for which Shao wrote "Biographies of Liu Zongzhou's Disciples" (《刘门弟子传》). As seen from above, Shao had a special interest in the Zhedong scholarship following Wang Yangming and Liu Zongzhou, and aimed at clarifying its academic purpose and tracing back to its origin.

Shao Tingcai's learning focused on historical studies in particular so he wrote scores of historical essays like "On Authenticity" (《正统论》) and "A Summary of Farm Tax" (《田赋略》). Based on the anecdotes of those adherents of a former dynasty like the Song, Yuan and Ming dynasties, Shao completed his *Anecdotes of the Loyalists to the Song and Ming Dynasties* (《宋明遗民所知录》). He also wrote *Chronicles of Southeast* (《东南纪事》) and *Chronicles of Southwest* (《西南纪事》), narrating the anti-Qing events led by the princes in the late Ming dynasty. Apart from the above, Shao Tingcai wrote a book titled *Sifutang Collection* and compiled *Accounts and Annals of Yaojiang Academy* (《姚江书院志略》).

In terms of the influence of Shao Tingcai's scholarship at that time, it was limited to the confines of Yuyao and Kuaiji area, but his academic horizon was broad. He not only blended the different views of Zhedong *Wangxue*, but also tried to bridge the differences between Zhu Xi's Neo-Confucianism and Yangming's *xinxue*. It pointed directly to the basic characteristics of Zhedong scholarship summarized by Zhang Xuecheng: "[Zhedong scholarship] follows Lu Jiuyuan's ideas without deviating from Zhu Xi's theory"; "those who study human nature and destiny must resort to history".

Shao Tingcai developed the learning of the famous scholars in his hometown, highlighted the deeds of Yaojiang Academy School, expounded the origin of Liu Zongzhou's Jishan School, analyzed and summarized Liu Zongzhou's inheritance and revision of Yangming *xinxue*, and also tried to distinguish between Wang Yangming's *xinxue* and Zhu Xi's *lixue*, and between Wang Yangming's and Lu Jiuyuan's *xinxue*. Thereby, he correlated the theories after researching their origins and development paths by tracing them back to the learning of Confucius and Mencius in the pre-Qin period as well as the ancient books *The Great Learning* and *The Doctrine of the Mean*. Shao

Tingcai's theory actually oriented Zhedong scholarship from the perspective of historical evolution from Confucianism to Neo-Confucianism and to *xinxue*. Shao's integration, summary, inheritance and development of Zhedong scholarship was of great significance and far-reaching influence.

Chapter Six

Inheritance of Familial Learning:
A Selection of Academic Families in Siming

Family, or clan, was the most basic social unit in the agricultural patriarchal society of ancient China. It, meanwhile, played an important role in the academic and educational system dominated by Confucian culture. Thus, there repeatedly appeared a phenomenon that sons followed their fathers' business, which resulted in the emergence of many cultural and academic families featuring the prominent tradition of "familial learning".

In the process of evolution and development of Zhedong scholarship, some famous cultural and academic families emerged. During the period of Six Dynasties (222–589), there were families like the Yus, the Hes, the Kongs and the Xies; in the Song and Yuan dynasties, there were the Shis and the Yuans. In the Ming and Qing dynasties, more academic families emerged, including the Shaos (represented by Shao Tingcai and Shao Jinhan), the Huangs (Huang Zongxi, Huang Zongyan and Huang Baijia), the Wans (Wan Tai, Wan Sitong and Wan Sixuan), the Zhengs (Zheng Liang and Zheng Xing), the Huangs (Huang Shisan and Huang Yizhou) and the Suns (Sun Yiyan [孙 衣 言] and Sun Yirang). All these families made great contributions to the prosperous development of Zhedong academic culture.

This chapter aims at exploring the academic inheritance in Siming area by selecting and introducing three great academic families, namely, the Yus, the Huangs and the Wans.

I. The Yu Family

Yuhuan Street, now called Xinjian Road, is a thousand-year-old street in downtown Yuyao. After a fire in 1929, it was rebuilt and given its present name to commemorate Wang Yangming by his rank of nobility "Count of Xinjian". More than 700 meters from south to north, the road is just located in the center of Yuyao, on the east side of Longshan Park. Along the street are many shops on both of its sides, in hustle and bustle. This street, together with Longshan Park, is the commercial and cultural center of Yuyao, viewed as a treasure land of the city. Then why was it called "Yuhuan Street"? Actually, the name literally means "a street where an official surnamed Yu lives", and the official was Yu Fan (虞翻) who lived more than 1,700 years ago. He was a high-ranking official of the Wu State (222–280) during the period of the Three Kingdoms (220–280) and the leading figure of the Yu family, the most famous Yu gentry family of Yuyao at that time. It was he who took a fancy to that place and started to live there. In the subsequent 500 years from the period of the Three Kingdoms to the early Tang dynasty, Yuhuan Street was filled with luxurious mansions and manors, in which were officials and gentry in all their finery, surrounded by guards or family retainers here and there. During several centuries, the Yu family maintained their tradition of learning and official career, in spite of the periods of war or turmoil. Some of their family members took positions in the imperial court, some enjoyed their secluded life in forest, and some became famous scholars in their learning. As *History of the Southern Dynasties* (《南史》) says, Yuyao "has more than 1,000 families surnamed Yu… with their descendants in different positions, helping each other and cultivating their own force". In *A General History of China* (《中国史稿》) compiled by Guo Moruo (郭沫若), the Yu family of Yuyao was ranked top one among the three gentry families of Kuaiji[①], namely, the Yus, the Kongs and the Hes. It was a true "gentry family of Jiangzuo[②]".

From the Eastern Han dynasty to the Tang dynasty, more than 20 people of the Yu family in Yuyao were recorded in the official histories like *Annals of the Three Kingdoms*. In addition, more than 50 people were found in other historical books. Today, more than 70 members of the Yu family in Yuyao can still been found in relevant historical documents, including 7 marquises, more than 10 highest-ranking imperial officials, and a larger number of local heads like prefects or magistrates. Throughout the eras including the Eastern Han dynasty, the period of the Three Kingdoms, the Jin dynasty, the Southern dynasties, the Sui dynasty (581–618), the Tang dynasty, and the period of Five Dynasties and Ten Kingdoms, so many people made great academic and artistic achievements, and all of whom were the best talents in their own epochs.

The cultural and academic activities of the Yu family were not only an important extension of the culture of the ancient Yue area[③], but also a symbol and microcosm of the academic culture of the scholar-bureaucrat families in the Wei, Jin, as well as the Southern and Northern dynasties. They were also an organic part of the cultural and academic activities in eastern Zhejiang and even the southeast coastal areas of China in the Han and Tang dynasties, and also an important source of the prosperous scholarship of the southeastern China during the Song, Yuan, Ming and Qing dynasties.

The Yu family was not natives of Yuyao, but immigrants from Dongjun[④] in the north of China in the middle of the Eastern Han dynasty. After they moved to Yuyao following Yu Yi (虞意), the family gradually ascended

---

① Yuyao once belonged to Kuaiji before it was incorporated into Ningbo in June, 1949.

② Jiangzuo, alias Jiangdong, refers to a region on the left (east) side of the lower reach of the Yangtze River in ancient times. It has been renamed as Jiangnan since the Tang dynasty (*cf.* the preface of the book).

③ The ancient Yue area, in a narrow sense, covered today's Zhejiang Province, while in a broad sense, it covered the lands of present-day southern Jiangsu, Shanghai, Zhejiang, southern Anhui and northeastern Jiangxi.

④ Dongjun refers to the prefectures on the east of the capital (now Luoyang) of the Eastern Han dynasty.

into high social rank through the management and development of several generations led by Yu Guang (虞光), Yu Cheng (虞成), Yu Feng (虞凤) and Yu Xin (虞歆). However, the clan remained virtually unknown throughout the country in the Eastern Han dynasty. In the period of Three Kingdoms, the scholar-bureaucrat families of Wujun and Kuaiji prefectures were specially privileged by Sun Quan, the king of the Wu State, thanks to their support for Sun's throning. Therefore, many descendants of the Yu family were appointed official positions by the court of Wu State. In particular, with the efforts of Yu Fan, the Yu family won their status among the national scholar-bureaucrat families.

From the Eastern Han dynasty, the Yu family flourished for more than 500 years, going through the period of the Three Kingdoms, the Jin, Song, Qi, Liang, Chen and Sui dynasties, until the Tang dynasty when it fell along with the decline of the scholar-bureaucrat landlord class of imperial China.

During the hundreds of years from the Wu State during the period of the Three Kingdoms to the early Tang dynasty, the Yu family had a large number of famous cultural figures with great works published one after another. Among them, the well-known ones included Yu Fan, Yu Xi (虞喜), Yu Yu (虞预) and Yu Shinan, who made great achievements in Confucian classics, history, astronomy, literature and calligraphy.

Yu Fan (164–233), courtesy name Zhongxiang, first took the official post *gongcao* (功曹)[1] of Kuaiji, and later followed Sun Ce (孙策) to attack Shanyue[2]. Subsequently, when Sun Ce wanted to take Yuzhang (now Nanchang, Jiangxi Province), Yu Fan recommended himself to lobby, so that Sun Ce captured it without fighting. Later, he served as the magistrate of Fuchun County (in Wujun Prefecture). When Sun Ce was succeeded by his

---

[1] *Gongcao*, an official in charge of personnel affairs, subordinate of prefect. Here, Yu Fan was appointed as *gongcao* by Wang Lang (王朗), the prefect of Kuaiji Prefecture in the Eastern Han dynasty.

[2] Shanyue, a general name for the local armed bandits in the south of the Yangtze River in the late Han dynasty and the period of Three Kingdoms.

younger brother Sun Quan (孙权), Yu Fan was appointed as *qiduwei* (骑都尉)[①]. Well-known for his study of *The Book of Changes*, Yu Fan was a representative who interpreted the book through hexagram symbols. He also made achievements in the research of astronomy, calendar, and works of various pre-Qin schools of thought. During his tenure in Jiaozhou (now Guangzhou), he gave lectures to hundreds of students, and created an academic atmosphere in Lingnan area[②]. All his life, Yu Fan wrote a lot of works, of which more than ten kinds can still be seen today, including *Annotations to The Book of Changes* (《易注》) and *Laws of Solar and Lunar Changes in The Book of Changes* (《周易日月变律》). His works were highly praised by scholars of the same era. Later, Shao Jinhan, the great historian of Yuyao in the Qing dynasty and official compiler of *Complete Library in the Four Branches of Literature*, acclaimed him in his *Yangjiang River Boatman's Songs* (《姚江棹歌》):

> Such a talented man, precious and unparalleled,
>
> Who inspired a town of valuable literature and outstanding scholars.

Yu Xi (281–356), courtesy name Zhongning, was commented in "Confucian Scholars" of *The Book of Jin* (《晋书·儒林》) with the words that he "set up his rules of behavior and morality even in his childhood and grew into an erudite man enthusiastic about ancient books". Besides, "he kept behaving as a self-constrained and moral man even in his old age... With a good memory, he extended his learning largely and meticulously". For three times, Yu rejected the recommendations to serve the imperial court as *boshi*. Instead, he conducted learning in seclusion until his death.

Yu Xi's studies mainly focused on astronomy. His greatest achievement and contribution lay in the discovery of "precession of the equinox" (the difference between "celestial revolution" and "year cycle or year revolution") in the fifth year of the Xianhe period (330) in the Eastern Jin dynasty. After years

---

① *Qiduwei*, in charge of armed escort of cavalry.
② The Lingnan area is located on the southeast coast of China. Its unique geographical location and historical background make Lingnan culture rich in connotation.

of observation and calculation, Yu Xi argued that the sun moved westward against its original position from the first winter solstice to the second winter solstice by 1 degree every 50 years (71 years and 8 months, now calculated). This discovery was a major event in the history of Chinese astronomy and had a great impact on later astronomers. Zu Chongzhi (祖冲之) and Liu Zhuo (刘焯) applied "precession" into calendar and respectively created the Daming calendar (大明历) and Huangji calendar (皇极历), which opened a new era in the history of Chinese astronomy.

Yu Yu (ca. 285–340), courtesy name Shuning, was said in the "Biography of Yu Yu" of *The Book of Jin* (《晋书》) to be "engaged in study and rich in literary talent in his childhood" and "fond of Confucian classics and history and resentful at deliberate empty words". Yu Yu successively took such official posts as *gongcaoli* (功曹吏)[1], *zuo zhuzuolang* (佐著作郎)[2], and *sanqi changshi* (散骑常侍)[3]. Besides, he was granted the title "Marquis of Xixiang".

Yu Yu was one of the famous historians in the Eastern Jin dynasty, and he wrote 40 volumes of *The Book of Jin*. The book was written in biographic-thematic genre, recording the history of the Western Jin dynasty and the early Eastern Jin dynasty. It started the tradition of "contemporary historians writing contemporary history". A book of high historical value, it was highly acclaimed by Liu Zhiji (刘知几), a famous historian of the Tang dynasty. Paying special attention to the collection, collation and compilation of local literature, he compiled *Kuaiji Classic Records* (《会稽典录》), which was collected into the existing *The Siming Book Series* (《四明丛书》) by Zhang Shouyong (张寿镛). It recorded more than 80 figures in Kuaiji area from the period of Spring and Autumn to the Eastern Jin dynasty. As a book specialized in recording local figures of both ancient and contemporary periods, it was viewed as the origin of the writing of ancient local chronicles in Zhejiang. Besides, he wrote *Records of the Figures of the Yu Family* (《诸虞传》), which specially collected the

---

[1] *Gongcaoli*, head of personnel affairs.
[2] *Zuo zhuzuolang*, an official in charge of writing national history.
[3] *Sanqi changshi*, emperor's attendant.

meritorious deeds, words and articles by the figures of different generations in the Yu family of Yuyao. It was one of the annals of personages and the ancient genealogies in Zhejiang. In addition, he had 10 volumes collection of poems and essays, including dozens of his poems, versed-prose, inscriptions, eulogies, commentaries and debates.

It was Yu Shinan who wrote a brilliant page for the culture of the Yu family.

Yu Shinan (558–638), courtesy name Boyi, was a famous minister, calligrapher and poet in the early Tang dynasty. His former residence was in Dingshui Temple in Minghe Mountain (now Xiejia Village of Mijiadai), which was incorporated into Cixi in the late Tang dynasty. Therefore, he was viewed as a native of Cixi in the old annals of Ningbo and Cixi.

Born into a prosperous gentry family of high-ranking officials, Yu Shinan led an affluent way of life from his childhood. But he never treated himself as a well-born man, nor he had the bad habits of those playboys who often bullied others and enjoyed unhealthy pleasures. This might be related to the long-period good tradition and education of the Yu family where he was brought up. His great grandfather, Yu Quan (虞权), once served as *tingweiqing* (廷尉卿)[1] and the prefect of Yongjia in the Liang dynasty (502–557); his grandfather, Yu Jian (虞检), served as the counselor of Xiao Dan (萧憺), the Prince of Shixing in the Liang dynasty. His father, Yu Li (虞荔), was appointed as *taizi zhongshuzi* (太子中庶子)[2] in the Chen dynasty (557–589), and both Yu Jian and Yu Li were well-known for their erudite leaning; Yu Shinan's uncle, Yu Ji (虞寄), severed as *zhongshu shilang* (中书侍郎)[3] in the Chen dynasty. Yu Shinan was an adopted son of Yu Ji who had no sons. Hence Yu Shinan's courtesy name "Boyi" (伯施)[4].

Yu Shinan was a quiet an unambitious man, and his personality was

---

[1] *Tingweiqing*, the head of the Department of Justice.
[2] *Taizi zhongshuzi*, in charge of counseling and assisting the study of Crown Prince.
[3] *Zhongshu shilang*, the vice-minister of the Palace Secretariat.
[4] Boyi, literally, continuation of uncle's family.

largely influenced by the natural environment of Xiejia Village, where there were mountains and rivers, trees and bamboos, flowers and grass, and people there could enjoy the natural sounds, beautiful scenes, wonderful fragrance, and delicious food like fresh fish and fruit. It was just such a splendid landscape of his hometown that witnessed the growing up of Yu Shinan, cultivating his temperament and injecting vitality into his life.

In his boyhood, Yu Shinan, together with his older brother, Yu Shiji (虞世基), studied under the supervision of Gu Yewang (顾野王), an erudite scholar. For more than 10 years, he was tireless in his studies, and sometimes he even forgot to wash his face for a long period. Later, he learned the classic calligraphy of Wang Xizhi (王羲之), by which he gained his reputation after he absorbed the calligraphic essence of Monk Shi Zhiyong (释智永)[1], his teacher.

Yu Shinan lived in an era of frequent regime changes. He was born in the Chen dynasty and was assigned in his adulthood to be *facao canjun* (法曹参军)[2] of the Prince of Jian'an. Later, When the Chen dynasty was defeated by the Sui dynasty, he was granted the title of *mishulang* (秘书郎)[3] by the Sui emperor in the early Daye period (605–618). Then, he was transferred to the post of *qiju sheren* (起居舍人)[4]. In the fourth year of the Wude period (621) of the Tang dynasty, after Li Shimin, the Prince of Qin, destroyed the local rebellious force of Dou Jiande (窦建德), Yu Shinan was successively appointed as Li's *canjun, jishi, Hongwenguan xueshi*, and *taizi zhongsheren*. In the ninth year of the Wude period (626), when Li Shimin ascended to the throne of the Tang dynasty, Yu, as a trusted follower, was appointed as *zhuzuolang* (著作郎)[5] and meanwhile as *Hongwenguan xueshi*. Now, Yu Shinan was already in his seventies. He wanted to retire for a leisurely life in countryside but his request

---

① Monk Shi Zhiyong (释智永), a master of calligraphy of the Sui dynasty.
② *Facao canjun*, the head of Justice.
③ *Mishulang*, an official in charge of the "Four-branch Books" of the imperial state library.
④ *Qiju sheren*, a chief imperial chronicler, mainly in charge of recording the daily affairs of emperor and national events.
⑤ *Zhuzuolang*, the chief official in charge of the writing of national history.

was not approved by Li, which was really a regret in his late age. At this time, he was transferred to the office of *mishujian*, and granted the rank of nobility as the Viscount of Yongxing County. In the eighth year of the Zhenguan period (634), Yu's rank was promoted to the Marquis of Yongxing County. Hence the appellation "Yu Yongxing" for him. In the twelfth year of the Zhenguan period (638), he was conferred an honorific title *yinqing guanglu dafu* (银青光禄大 夫)[1]. One day of the fifth lunar month of this year, Yu Shinan bid his farewell to the great Tang dynasty and his contemporaries, and passed away lonely but gloriously. After his death, he was awarded the honorific title of Minister of Rites, given the posthumous title Wenyi, and buried in the imperial Zhaoling Mausoleum (now Jiujun Mountain, Liquan County, Shaanxi Province) according to the imperial edict. Such a privilege of being buried in an imperial cemetery was rarely seen in history, although it was just a posthumous glory. Several years later, he was listed as one of the "Twenty-four Meritorious Officials of Lingyan Pavilion"[2], and his portrait was displayed in the pavilion.

Yu Shinan and Li Shimin had both friendship and superior-subordinate relationship. They were in contact with each other from the time when Li was Prince of Qin. As an official, Yu Shinan was loyal and upright. He had strong will, held righteousness in his opinions and dared to give advice to the emperor in spite of his graceful appearance and weak build, while Li was a rare open-minded monarch in history who was thirsty for talents and willing to take advice. For example, one year, landslides appeared in Longyou area (now in Gansu Province). Subsequently, Yu Shinan, believing it might be related to the heavenly will for justice, suggested Li Shimin rectify injustices in prisons and relieve the victims. Li followed his words. Additionally, when Emperor Gaozu, Li Yuan (李渊), died, Li Shimin originally intended to hold a lavish burial to demonstrate the royal dignity, but Yu Shinan advocated him to hold a simple funeral as an example to demonstrate the disadvantages of the lavish funerals

---

[1] *Yinqing guanglu dafu*, an honorific title of no fixed duties awarded to emperor's intimate ministers. Literally, it means a glorious grand master with the silver badge and blue ribbon.

[2] Also known as "Twenty-four Heroes of Lingyan Pavilion".

of ancient emperors. Li Shimin adopted his advice. Furthermore, when Li Shimin was indulged in hunting in his old age, Yu Shinan advised him not to do it so frequently lest it disturb the people's life.

Li Shimin highly appreciated Yu's character and talent. He said, "If all the ministers are like Yu Shinan, then why should I be concerned about the disorder of the country?" Also, seeing Yu's excellence in "virtue, loyalty, erudition, writing and calligraphy", he honored Yu as the "contemporary famous official and ethic model".

Living through the three dynasties of Chen, Sui and Tang, Yu Shinan had rich experience. In addition, he was well-learned and good at thinking. Therefore, he had his unique and profound insight into the gains and losses of emperors in the past. For this reason, Li Shimin often summoned him to review the works of Confucian classics and history, discuss the ancient and contemporary issues, and evaluate the gains and losses of the emperors of different dynasties, so as to explore the way to govern the country.

The book *Accounts and Evaluations of Monarchs* by Yu Shinan might be a collection of his conversations with Emperor Taizong, Li Shimin. It was the first general historical work finished in the early Tang dynasty in chronological order and geographical division. In had five volumes, starting with Dayu's flood control of remote ages and ending with the unification of China by Emperor Wenof the Sui dynasty. Its title *Diwang Lüelun* means there are both "*lüe*" (略) and "*lun*" (论) in this work. "*Lüe*" refers to the biographical accounts of monarchs, i.e., the life experiences of the rulers of different dynasties; "*lun*" means the commentaries of the author on the virtues, talents and achievements of a certain emperor. For the monarchs before "The Three Dynasties" (namely, the Xia, Shang and Zhou dynasties), there are only introductions and no evaluations; while for the later rulers, there are both introductions and evaluations in this book; the author mainly focused on the monarchs at the time of rise and fall rather than those in peace time and without obvious blames or achievements. Thus, it was well-organized with clear ideas. Although it has less content than *Comprehensive Mirror in Aid of Governance* (《资治通鉴》)

by Sima Guang, it is more than 450 years earlier than the latter. The book was initially intended only for Emperor Taizong, but it was spread widely later and prevailed in the Tang dynasty. It might still exist in the Song dynasty (because it was introduced in *The History of the Song Dynasty: Bibliographical Treatise* (《宋史·艺文志》), but it was lost in the Yuan dynasty. Lu Xinyuan (陆心源), a Qing scholar, picked out the excerpts of this book compiled into *Monarch's Rulership* (《长短经》) by Zhao Rui (赵蕤) of the High Tang and *General History of State Governance* (《通历》) by Ma Zong (马总) of the Middle Tang, and compiled them into an article titled "Evaluations and Accounts" (《论略》) in his *Collection of Lost Works of the Tang Dynasty* (《唐文拾遗》). Now, only 58 remaining essays can be still seen.

Yu Shinan was not only respected as a knowledgeable politician for his demeanor of "famous official", but also for his outstanding cultural achievements. As an erudite scholar, he made multifaceted cultural achievements in such fields as literature, history and calligraphy.

Yu Shinan occupied an important position in the history of Chinese calligraphy.

After the Wei and Jin dynasties, the art of calligraphy reached its another peak in the Tang dynasty. It went through three stages from the Early Tang to the Middle Tang and then to the Late Tang. Among them, the early Tang was an important stage, which connected the former Wei-Jin (the Wei and Jin dynasties) tradition and the new prosperity of the middle Tang stage. Yu Shinan studied calligraphy from Monk Shi Zhiyong, the seventh-generation grandson of Wang Xizhi, in his early years and followed the tradition of Wang Xizhi and his son Wang Xianzhi (王献之). Yu Shinan, Ouyang Xun (欧阳询), Chu Suiliang (褚遂良) and Xue Ji (薛稷) were together called "Four Great Calligraphers of the Early Tang", and they played a very important role at the turning point from the Wei-Jin style to the Tang style, exerting a wide impact on later generations.

Moreover, Yu Shinan was a famous poet and a leader of the court literature① in the Zhenguan period. He made great achievements not only in poetry writing, but also in the composition of *ciqu* (词曲)② and prose. His Yuefu-style poems like "Frontier Soldiers" (《从军行》) and "Outside the Frontiers" (《出塞》), ornate and profound, depicted the scenes and events in the desolate and cold areas, and created a new style of the Tang dynasty for the flourishing of frontier-related poems in later periods.

Well-learned and erudite, Yu Shinan was a great compiler of encyclopaedic books. One of the books was *Collected Classics of Beitang* (《北堂书钞》), which was titled after the name of Yu Shinan's study, Beitang (North Hall), where he finished this book when he was serving as *mishulang* in the Sui dynasty. It is the earliest and relatively large-scale encyclopaedic book that can still be seen today. In spite of its shortcoming like incoherent citations and unclear sources, it has extremely high historical value, because it cites from more than 800 ancient books of the Chen and Sui dynasties (more than a half of the source books were lost). The book represents the outstanding contribution to China's philological culture made by Yu Shinan, such a great scholar of Siming.

---

① Court literature represented the artistic tastes of the highest class of society in feudal China.

② In the phrase, *ci* (词) is a type of Chinese poetry, in the form of songs characterized by lines of unequal length with prescribed rhyme schemes and tonal patterns, while *qu* (曲) is a type of classical Chinese poetry form, consisting of words written in a certain tone-pattern, based upon the tunes of various songs.

II. The Huang Family

Yuyao people have a tradition of admiring and commemorating their outstanding predecessors. In the city of Yuyao, many of the main streets, communities and parks are named after the local persons of virtue and talent in the past, such as Yangming Road, Xinjian Road, Shunshui Road, Ziling Road, Shinan Road, and Nanlei Road, as well as Yangming Park, Yangming Subdistrict, Lizhou Subdistrict, Shunshui Primary School and Ziling New Residential areas. However, sometimes, confusion would appear because of the overlapped naming of a certain place after different well-known persons and revolutionary martyrs of the past. For example, "Zhuqiao Huangshi" (literally, the Huang family of Zhuqiao) was once a well-known name in history because of its association with the Huang family, and it was also quite appropriate to name the township, to which Huangzhupu (Huang Zongxi's village) belonged, as "Lizhou Township" after Huang Zongxi's literary name. Nevertheless, after 1949, the township was renamed as "Mingwei Township" to commemorate Lou Mingshan (楼明山) and Zhou Zhiwei (周之伟), two revolutionary martyrs. Now, the names of both Huangzhupu and Lizhou Township are no longer used, while Mingwei Township, as an urban area of Yuyao now, has been renamed as "Lizhou Subdistrict". It should be regarded as the proper way to clarify the confusing names.

Nevertheless, the various traces about "Zhuqiao Huangshi" can still be seen everywhere in present-day Lizhou Subdistrict, especially in the local names of place such as Zhushan Bridge and "Zhushan Xia" (Zhushan mountain foot), as well as in corporate names like "Zhushan". Of course, there are also names related to "Mingwei", including Mingwei Bridge, Mingwei Primary School and Mingwei Clinic, etc. Now, no matter how these various names have changed, as long as you know the evolution of the name of "Zhuqiao

Huangshi", you'll be surely aware that once you set your foot on Lizhou Subdistrict, you are standing in the hometown of the Huang family, a clan widely renowned domestically.

The Huang family also immigrated from northern China. Before they moved to Yuyao, they lived in Jinhua. It was in the Jianyan period of the Southern Song dynasty that they moved to Ningbo when one of their ancestors served as *tongpan* in Qingyuan Prefecture. At that time, the Jin soldiers invaded Qingyuan territory and that ancestor died in the battle of defending the city. Then, in order to avoid military chaos, his son, Huang Wanhe (黄万河), moved their family to Zhudun, Fenghuang Mountain, Cixi (now Zhangting Township, Yuyao). Afterwards, the family moved the Zhuqiao, Yuyao and settled down forever.

Up to the Ming dynasty, the Huang family gradually rose in academic stature. According to the *Genealogy of the Huang Family of Zhuqiao* (《竹桥黄氏宗谱》), many members of the Huang family learned from Wang Yangming at that time, including Huang Ji (黄骥), Huang Wenhuan (黄文焕), Huang Jia'ai (黄嘉爱), Huang Yuanfu (黄元釜) and Huang Kui (黄夔), whose names were listed in the "Annals of Zhezhong Wangxue Scholars" of *The Records of Ming Scholars* (《明儒学案·浙中王门学案》). Among them, Huang Wenhuan, renowned as an excellent disciple of Wang Yangming, worked as family tutor of Wang Zhengxian (王正献), a son of Wang Yangming. Huang Wenhuan had a deep and thorough understanding of Wang Yangming's thought and he compiled Wang's words in to a book titled *Dongge Private Records* (《东阁私抄》) , which was lost unfortunately. By the time of Huang Zunsu of the late Ming dynasty, the Huang family had accumulated a lot of resources, especially in the study of Confucian classics and historiography, which laid a firm foundation for the great figures and achievements. In the words of their contemporaries, by the time of the eighteenth generation of the Huang family, they had cultivated the family tradition of "perfect etiquette and rites" and the family gradually turned into one of the famous families in Yuyao, and even in eastern Zhejiang.

From Huang Zunsu to his sons, Huang Zongxi, Huang Zongyan and Huang Zonghui, and then to Huang Baijia, the son of Huang Zongxi, these members from three generations were all the outstanding representatives of the Huang family of Zhuqiao for their achievements in both scholarship and thought.

Huang Zunsu (1584–1626), courtesy name Zhenchang, and literary name Bai'an. His father, Huang Yuezhong (黄曰中), was proficient in the "Five Classics", *Commentaries of Zuo* and *Records of the Grand Historian of China*, especially in *The Book of Changes* which he once taught in Wuxing. Huang Zunsu was enrolled as *jinshi* at the age of 33, and then served in the positions like *tuiguan* in Ningguo Prefecture (now in Anhui) and *yushi* of Shandong *Dao*. He was honest and upright, and took it as his duty to contribute to the country and improve the atmosphere of the scholars. He especially hated those powerful and imperious officials who manipulated their power and brought disasters to the country. In the fifth year of Emperor Tianqi's reign, because he impeached Wei Zhongxian, a high-ranking eunuch official, Huang was framed up and put into prison, where he died at the age of 43[1]. He was not rehabilitated until the reign of Emperor Chongzhen, and was posthumously awarded the title of minister of *taipu si* (太仆寺卿)[2]. Later, he was conferred the posthumous title Zhongduan by the Southern Ming regime of Prince of Fu. Because Huang Zunsu had a deep friendship with the thinker Liu Zongzhou, he asked his son Huang Zongxi to study as Liu's disciple in his will. Besides, as a leader of Donglin Fraction, he also had a good relationship with other leaders like Gu Xiancheng (顾宪成) and Gao Panlong. In his early years, he paid attention to the practice learning, well-learned in both Confucian classics and history, especially in contemporary history. Additionally, he was familiar with historical anecdotes and literary writing of *cifu* (辞赋)[3]. His works included 6 volumes of

---

[1] Actually, Huang Zunsu died at age of 42. But conventionally, Chinese usually count their age by adding one year to their actual age, and call it nominal age.

[2] Minister of *taipu si*, in charge of horses for transportation.

[3] *Cifu*, a sentimental or descriptive composition.

Zhongduan Collection (《忠端公集》), 8 volumes of *Notes on the Four Books* (《四书绒》), 2 volumes of *Chronicles of Ming Ministers in the Longqing and Wanli Periods* (《隆万两朝列卿记》), and *Annals of the late Ming Dynasty* (《说略》). Huang Zunsu collected many ancient historical books, especially the historical materials of the Ming dynasty, including unofficial history and notes.

Huang Zunsu had five sons: Huang Zongxi, Huang Zongyan, Huang Zonghui, Huang Zongyuan (黄宗辕) and Huang Zongyi (黄宗彝). In particular, the first three sons were all talented, who were called "Three Huangs of eastern Zhejiang". They belonged to the most brilliant generation of the Huang family, but also the most painful generation with most turmoil and hardships. With the agitation of the times, out of this generation of the Huang family, an outstanding thinker and historian finally appeared, and he was Master Lizhou, Huang Zongxi, one of the "Three Huangs of eastern Zhejiang".

In the first half of his life, Huang Zongxi was famous for his fight against the eunuch faction and the Qing army, while in the latter half of his life, he was devoted to research, writing, and cultivation of talents. He made unique findings in various academic fields, initiated Zhedong School, and wrote a large number of great works, and thereby was promoted as one of the three major domestic Confucian masters in the early Qing dynasty. As an enlightening thinker, he influenced other Chinese thinkers and historians for hundreds of years. His works, up to 110 kinds in 1,300 volumes, with 20 million Chinese characters in total, can be seen today in his *Complete Works of Huang Zongxi* (《黄宗羲全集》) (see Chapter Five).

Huang Zongyan (1616–1686), courtesy name Huimu, was respected as Master Zhegu. As the second son of Huang Zunsu, he was taught by his older brother Huang Zongxi in his early years and then recommended into Imperial Academy (*Taixue*) in the middle of the Chongzhen period (1628–1644). He participated in the anti-Qing battles after the demise of the Ming dynasty. Later, he also learned from Liu Zongzhou as Huang Zongxi did. With extensive knowledge and strong memory, he learned many disciplines such as *xiangwei* (astrology and divination), *lülü* (music theory) and *xiaoxue* (lesser or elementary learning). He was also good at writing poems and drawing Chinese Shanshui paintings[①]. His works are added up to seven kinds, including *Interpretations of the Hexagrams of The Book of Changes* and *Commentaries to the Interpretation of The Book of Changes* (《周易寻门余论》). Huang Zongyan had attainments in philosophy, and he advocated the "unity of principle and diagram" and valued the learning of practice.

Huang Zonghui (1622–1680), courtesy name of Zewang, was honored as Marster Shitian. He was also taught by his older brother Huang Zongxi before he was selected as *gongsheng* into the Imperial Academy (*Guozijian*). After the fall of the Ming dynasty, he converted to Buddhism. Erudite and indulged in learning, he was well-learned in the books of the "Four Branches", meanwhile familiar with the works of Buddhism and Taoism. His works included *Suozhai Collection* (《缩斋文集》), *Suozhai Diaries* (《缩斋日记》), *Records on Learning to Drive* (《学御录》), *Annotation to Discourse on the Perfection of Consciousness-only* (《成唯识论注》) and *Travelogue of Siming Mountain* (《四明游录》). Both Zonghui and Zongyan were authorities of Zhedong School on the Confucian classics.

Huang Zongxi had three sons, Huang Baiyao (黄百药), Huang Baijia and Huang Zhengyi (黄正宜). Among them, Huang Baijia was the most outstanding. Huang Baijia (1643–1709), given name Baixue, courtesy name Zhuyi, and literary name Leishi. Under the edification of his familial learning, Huang Baijia read extensively. He was particularly accomplished in astronomy, calendar and mathematics, and he absorbed a large number of new achievements of Western natural science. As a son, he did best in the inheritance of his father's learning, so he was also excellent in historical studies. In the nineteenth year of Emperor Kangxi's reign (1680), the Institution for the History of Ming was established, and Huang Zongxi was invited to join the compilation of this book. But Huang Zongxi, as a Ming loyalist, responded

---

① Chinese Shanshui Painting, a style of Chinese painting that involves the painting of scenery or natural landscapes with brush and ink.

with a firm refusal with the excuse of aging. Nevertheless, Huang permitted his son Huang Baijia and his excellent disciple Wan Sitong to participate in the project in the capital Beijing. There, Huang Baijia developed his specialty, and finished chapters like "Astronomical Records" (《天文志》) and "Calendrical Records" (《历志》). After returning to his hometown, Huang Baijia spent a period of time mainly in assisting his elderly father Huang Zongxi in writing, usually transcribing his father's oral accounts. He continued the writing of *Scholarly Annals of the Song and Yuan Dynasties, Collection of the Essays of Song* (《宋文案》) and *Collection of the Essays of Yuan* (《元文案》), which were left unfinished by Huang Zongxi, and finally completed Huang Zongxi's program of "Three *Wen'an*"[①]. What's more important, Huang Baijia was the first person in China to publicly introduce the Heliocentric Theory of Nicolaus Copernicus (1472–1543). In the article "'Rotation and Revolution' of *Unpleasant Words of Huangzhu Nongjia*" (《黄竹农家耳逆草·天旋篇》), he wrote, "During the Zhengde period (1506–1521) of the Ming dynasty, a man named Copernicus proposed that the Sun was the stationary center of the universe, while the Earth revolves outside around it." Additionally, Huang Baijia was also the first scholar to introduce into China the new discovery by Galileo and other scientists that the Sun is proved to rotate on its own axis by the movement of sunspots.

Huang Binghou (黄炳垕), the seventh-generation descendant of Huang Zongxi, continued the academic tradition of the Huang family. Huang Binghou (1815–1893), courtesy name Weiting, literary name Naiweng, was good at natural science. He wrote many astronomical, mathematical and geographical works, including *Rapid Calculation on the Solar and Lunar Eclipses* (《两太交食捷算》), *Rapid Calculation on Five Stars* (《五纬捷算》), *Records of Geographical Measurements* (《测地志要》), *Astronomical Measurement* (《方平仪象》) and *A Guide to Calendrical Studies* (《历学指南》). Due to his outstanding attainments in astronomy and mathematics, Huang Binghou was

---

① The *Collection of the Essays of Ming* had been finished by Huang Zongxi before he died.

invited to lecture in Bianzhi Academy, which was established by the governor of Ningbo, Zong Yuanhan, in the early years of Emperor Guangxu's reign. There, he served as head of the Branch of Astronomy & Calendar, giving lectures for more than 10 years, and was thereby praised as "the best scholar in astronomy and calendar of eastern and western Zhejiang".

His son, Huang Weihan (黄维翰), followed Huang Binghou's learning, and made certain achievements in geomatics and astronomy.

In his letter to *Yuyao Review* (《余姚评论》), modern scholar Liang Qichao commented, "From Yuyao, just one city, so many great scholars appeared during the 200 years from the middle of the Ming dynasty to the middle of the Qing dynasty, academically influencing whole China and even Japan. The Huang family had developed their spirit of integrity and nobility since the time of Zhongduan (Huang Zunsu, whose immediate family members Lizhou (Huang Zongxi), Huimu (Huang Zongyan) and Zhuyi (Huang Baijia) were all important figures bridging Ming and Qing scholarship." This is surely a sincere remark, which reflects the huge academic impacts of generations of outstanding scholars from the Huang family upon the society at that time.

III. The Wan Family

The Wans was a famous gentry family of Ningbo in the Ming and Qing dynasties. Many of their remaining relics can be seen in Ningbo, including the Wan's Mansion and Baiyun Manor in the urban area. The Wan's Mansion is located in Shangshu Street, Haishu District, Ningbo, and has been announced as one of Ningbo Municipal Protection Sites of Cultural Relics (the Second Batch). According to a survey, this building was constructed by Wang Chengxun (万承勋), the son of Wan Yan, during the Kangxi period (1662–1722) of the Qing dynasty. Wan Yan was the great grandson of Wan Bangfu who was the owner of Baiyun Manor, the academic center of Zhedong scholarship. Besides, Wan Yan was the nephew of Wan Sitong, and they were both invited to compile the *History of Ming*.

As a state-level protection unit of cultural relics, Baiyun Manor is not only well protected and repaired in itself, but also beautified outside with Baiyun Park. With shady green trees around and antique flavor here and there, this quiet and graceful place brings comfort and tranquility to people, and now it has become a good place for people to take a rest and sightseeing, and meanwhile to cherish the memory of the excellent former scholars of Zhedong School.

The Wan family of Ningbo had a deep relationship with the Ming dynasty. The Wan's ancestral hometown in Dingyuan County, Haozhou, Anhui Province. During the turmoil at the end of the Yuan dynasty, Wan Guozhen (万国珍), the ancestor of the Wans, together with his troop, joined Zhu Yuanzhang, the founder and the first emperor of the Ming dynasty, and then he was renamed as Wan Bin by Zhu. Wan Bin was the initial ancestor of the Wans family of Ningbo, but it was Wan Zhong (万钟), a son of Wan Bin, who moved their family to Ningbo wherein he worked. From Wan Bin to his son Wan Zhong, and then to his grandsons Wan Wu (万武) and Wan Wen (万文), they all died for their country, and were therefore called "Four Martyrs in Three Generations". They were highly praised in Ningbo, and brought great pride to their family. Since their ancestral time, the Wan family had developed their intellectual and martial tradition. Up to the time of Wan Biao (万表), the great-great-grandfather of Wan Sitong, this tradition was further promoted, and Wan Biao became a great general with both excellent literary talent and martial arts. Furthermore, it was Wan Biao that turned their family group with glorious honors into a well-known gentry clan. Later, in the era of Wan Tai, the family "abandoned the legacy of military arts and substituted them with literary and historical talents", and thereby shifted their focus from sword to pen.

Wan Biao (1497–1556), courtesy name Minwang, literary name Luyuan, was a key figure at the turn of the development of the Wan family. In the fifteenth year of Emperor Zhengde's reign (1520), he was enrolled as *wu jinshi* (武进士)[①] as his hereditary post. Later, he consecutively served as Jin *duzhihui* (都指挥)[②], *caoyun canjiang* (漕运参将)[③], Guangxi *fu zongbing* (副总兵)[④], Huai'an *zongbing* (总兵)[⑤], and *dudu tongzhi* (都督同知)[⑥] of Nanjing Central Military Division. Due to Wan Biao's high official rank and great social influence, the status of the Wan family had gradually grown until it turned into a gentry clan. Meanwhile, Wan Biao was a disciple of Wang Yangming's, and he kept close contact with scholars like Wang Ji, Qian Dehong, Luo Hongxian, Tang Shunzhi (唐顺之) and Wang Gen (王艮). He was more influenced by Wang Ji's thought. Wan Biao, as a *xinxue* scholar pursuing both learning and *shigong* (practical utility), was listed in the "Annals of Zhezhong Wangxue Scholars" of *The Records of Ming Scholars*. His works included the

---

① The term *wu jinshi* refers to the highest-rank title for the candidates of imperial examination in martial arts. It is a term relative to *jinshi* (*cf.* the preface of this book).
② *Duzhihui*, the commander of Shanxi Military Department.
③ *Caoyun canjiang*, subordinate of governor, in charge of transporting provisions by rivers or canals.
④ *Fu zongbing*, deputy military governor.
⑤ *Zongbing*, military governor.
⑥ *Dudu tongzhi*, high-ranking military official, subordinate of military governor.

Interpretation of The Great Learning and The Doctrine of the Mean (《学庸志略》), *A Xinxue Perspective on The Analects of Confucius* (《论语心义》, *The Doctrines of The Mencius* (《孟子摘义》), *Essays of Wangluting* (《玩鹿亭稿》), and *Collection of Essays on Governance of the Ming Dynasty* (《皇明经济文录》).

Following Wan Biao, the Wan family rose in prominence in Confucian studies, especially Wan Biao's son Wan Dafu (万达甫) and his grandson Wan Bangfu, and both of them had intellectual talents. Up to the time of Wan Tai, the son of Wan Bangfu, the focus of the clan was changed to pen from sword.

Wan Tai (1598–1657), courtesy name Lü'an, literary name Hui'an, was a disciple of Liu Zongzhou's. In the ninth year of Emperor Chongzhen's reign (1636), he passed the provincial-level imperial examination, and was appointed as *zhushi* in the Ministry of Revenue (户部主事). He hated evil things, and signed on the "Notice on Prevention Upheavals in the Old Capital (Nanjing)" together with others including Huang Zongxi, so as to expulse Ruan Dacheng, a remaining partisan of "Eunuch Faction". After the demise of the Ming dynasty, he participated in the anti-Qing battles but failed. Afterwards, he had to take refuge in the mountains of Fenghua before he returned to Ningbo when the situation regained its stability. In order to avoid the interference of the Qing court, Wan Tai traveled around in his later years and finally died in Jiangxi. Wan Tai wrote *Xusaotang Collection* (《续骚堂集》) and *Hansongzhai Collection* (《寒松斋集》). Although he was not buried in the cemetery of this family in Ningbo, his reputation was branded in the hearts of Zhedong scholars. This is not just because he "shifted the focus of his clan from sword to pen", advocated the learning of Siming, or had eight handsome sons called "Eight Dragons of the Wan family", but more because he invited his good friend Huang Zongxi to lecture in Ningbo, and thereby turned to a new page in the history of thought in eastern Zhejiang and even in the entire country.

As mentioned above, Wan Tai had eight sons, namely, Wan Sinian (万斯年), Wan Sicheng (万斯程), Wan Sizhen (万斯祯), Wan Sichang, Wan Sixuan, Wan Sida, Wan Sibei (万斯备) and Wan Sitong. With different talents, they were honored as "Eight Dragons of the Wan Family". Among them, Wan Sixuan, Wan Sida and Wan Sitong obtained the most outstanding achievements.

Wan Sixuan (1629–1694), courtesy name Gongze, was known as Master Baiyun. He made achievements in Neo-Confucianism. In the ninth year of Emperor Chongzhen's reign (1636), he was enrolled as *juren*. After the demise of Ming, he led a life in seclusion and refused to serve as an official. Wan Sixuan attended the lectures of Liu Zongxi, who was invited to Ningbo by Wan Tai, and then became one of Huang's 18 best disciples. He was well-known for the title of "Noble Man of Practice", viewed by his peers as model, and by Huang Zongxi as a friend who could give forthright admonition. Taking teaching as his career for his whole life, he conducted teaching in different places, including Hangzhou, Yuxi (now in Tongxiang) and Huainan. *Baiyun Collection* is his representative work.

Wan Sida (1633–1683), courtesy name Chongzong, gave himself a literary name Boweng (lame old man) due to his foot disease. Living in troubled times, Wan Sida didn't prepare for the imperial civil service examination, and took teaching as his career instead. Wan took his young child Wan Jing to Hangzhou, where he run a school at Wulin, meanwhile researching Confucian classics. From the sixth year of Emperor Kangxi's reign, Wan, together with more than ten peers, studied under the supervision of Huang Zongxi, and established a seminar on Confucius classics, which attracted many friends. They exchanged ideas by questioning and debating and promoted the seminar to its prime. He deeply studied various Confucian classics and often made prominent performance in the seminar. He claimed, "A certain classic could not be mastered until all classics are mastered, none of the classics could be mastered unless the losses in the interpretation or annotation to classics are found out, and none of the losses in the interpretation or annotation to classics could be found out unless a classic is interpreted based on another classic." These were his well-known words on the study of Confucian classics and also what he learned from the study. In his life, he was a man of determination and principle, and when seeing violation, he would show his indignation on his face. His works included two volumes of *Questions on the Learning of Rites* (《学礼质疑》), three volumes of *Annotations for the Learning of Rites* (《学礼偶笺》), and two volumes of *Textual Criticism on Ancient Rites* (《仪礼商》).

Among Huang Zongxi's disciples of Ningbo, Wan Sitong was the most outstanding in learning the Confucian classics and history. At the seminar, although he was the youngest, his words were very influential. When his peers were encountered with difficulties, they often asked him for advice, and he could always "convince them in a few words". Because of his excellent achievements in the study of "Sanli", he was invited by Xu Qianxue of Kunshan to join the compilation of *General Study of Rites*. Later, he joined the compilation of *The Manuscript of the History of Ming* and become the genuine chief compiler. Thereby, his historical achievements were widely acknowledged.

Among the grandsons of Wan Tai, Wan Yan and Wan Jing were relatively outstanding. Wan Yan (1637–1705), courtesy name Zhenyi, was the son of Wan Sinian. In his childhood, Wan Yan learned from Huang Zongxi together with his uncles Wan Sida and Wan Sitong, and was appreciated by the teacher. He was good at ancient prose, with a high ability of writing, and his composition was thought by his contemporaries to boast the "merits of the articles of both Shanyuan and Zhenchuan"[1], two outstanding ancient prose writers. His teacher Huang Zongxi commented, "Only Wan Yan and Zheng Liang[2] of Cixi did the best among the young scholars." In the fourteenth year of Emperor Kangxi's reign, Wan Yan was enrolled as *juren*, and then he started teaching. Years later, he was appointed as magistrate. In the eighteenth year of Emperor Kangxi's reign, he was invited to the Institution for the History of Ming together with his uncle Wan Sitong by Compiling Supervisor Xu Yuanwen and General Director

---

[1] Shanyuan (剡源) is the literary name of Dai Biaoyuan (戴表元, 1244–1310), the "Master of Prose in Southeastern China"; Zhenchuan (震川) is the literary name of Gui Youguang (归有光, 1507–1571), whose prose writing was honored as "The Best of the Ming Dynasty".

[2] Zheng Liang (郑梁, 1637–1713), courtesy name Yumei, literary name Hancun, a disciple of Huang Zongxi's and member of Zhedong School of historical studies, born in the Zheng family, a gentry clan of Cixi.

Ye Fang'ai (叶方蔼), who learned that they were both knowledgeable, especially proficient in historical studies. Then, Wan Yan went to Beijing together with Wan Sitong, where he participated in the compiling of *History of Ming*, and meanwhile joined the compiling of *Annals of the Unification of the Great Qing* (《大清一统志》). In Beijing, Wan Yan worked in the Bureau of History for up to 10 years as a compiler of Hanlin Academy with a salary equivalent to that of seventh-rank officials. He compiled all the historical material about the Chongzhen period of Ming into the *Drafted Chronicles of Chongzhen* (《崇祯长编》). Meanwhile, he compiled the *Gazetteers of Shengjing (Mukden)* (《盛京通志》) and *Annals of the Unification of the Great Qing*. He works included *Commentaries on The Book of History* (《尚书说》) and *A Brief History of Ming* (《明鉴举要》/《明史举要》). His *Guancun Collection* (《管村集》), which was named after his literary name Guancun, can still be seen today.

Wan Jing (1659–1741), courtesy name Shouyi, was the son of Wan Sida. In his childhood, he attended the Seminar held by Huang Zongxi. In the thirty-sixth year of Emperor Kangxi's reign (1697), he went to Beijing, where he stayed in his uncle Wan Sitong's private residence and supervised by him in study. Later, after the death of Wan Sitong, Wan Jing joined his son Wan Shibiao to deal with his afterlife affairs. With Wan Sitong's manuscript of *History of Ming* as reference, Wan Jing co-complied *A Brief History of Ming* with his cousin Wan Yan. Wan Jing participated in the compilation of the *Kangxi Dictionary*[1] (《康熙字典》). Besides, he presided over the compilation of *Annals of Ningbo Prefecture* (《宁波府志》) in the Yongzheng period. In the forty-second year of Emperor Kangxi's reign (1703), Wan Jing was enrolled as *jinshi*, and then selected as *shujishi* to further his study. Afterwards, he was granted the office of compiler and then assigned to Guizhou as *xuezheng* (学政)[2]. Wan Jing's learning covered Confucian classics, history and epigraphy. He wrote tens of thousands of words in supplement to Wan Sida's

---

[1] The *Kangxi Dictionary*, published in 1716, was the most authoritative dictionary of Chinese characters from the 18th century through the early 20th century.

[2] *Xuezheng*, educational supervisor.

Collected Interpretation of The Book of Rites (《礼记集解》), revised Wan Yan's *Commentaries to The Book of History*, and re-complied Wan Sitong's *Chronological Tables of China's History*. Besides, he was good at calligraphy, especially at Clerical Script (*lishu*, 隶书), and wrote a work titled *Records of Calligraphers of Clerical Script* (《分隶偶存》). Wan Jing died at age of 83.

Wan Chengxun was a representative of Wan Tai's fourth-generation descendants. Wan Chengxun (1670–1735), courtesy name Kaiyuan, was the son of Wan Yan. Like the above-mentioned Wan Jing, he was also once a student in the Seminar. As a young man, he studied under the guidance of his grandfather Wan Sinian, covering knowledge of Neo-Confucianism, Confucian classics and history and ancient prose writing. He had been well-known for his talent in poet writing since his childhood, and his poems were highly acclaimed by famous Qing poet Zha Shenqing, who remarked on his *Poetry of Ice and Snow* (《冰雪集》): "So moving are the lines that they make people burst into tears, so refined are the words that they remind readers of his deep sorrows." He had a close relationship with other three scholars from gentry families of Ningbo, Li Tun (李暾), Zheng Xing and Xie Xuzhang (谢绪章), and they were called "Four Friends of Siming". Wan Chengxun was a man of forthrightness and sincerity, refusing sophisticated contacts with others. In 1727, he was assigned to Cizhou Prefecture (now Cixian County, Hebei Province) as governor. Later he died of illness due to overwork. His works were compiled into *Collected Works of Qianzhi Caotang* (《千之草堂编年文钞》) and *Poetry of Ice and Snow*.

Chapter Seven

Closing Words:
To Be Continued

If the abolishment of imperial civil service examination by the Qing government in 1905 and the establishment of modern schools are viewed as the mark dividing the old learning and the new learning, then the "Zhedong scholarship" described in previous chapters can be categorized into the former. In this sense, Zhedong scholarship had already ended by the beginning of 20th century. However, the inherent authentic spirit of "Zhedong scholarship" actually hasn't terminated. On the one hand, there are still a large number of scholars researching, developing and innovating Zhedong scholarship. They are now making more and more new academic achievements; on the other hand, the spirit of Zhedong scholarship has deeply merged into the life and production activities of eastern Zhejiang people. It is reflected vividly in every social aspect and even becomes an indispensable part of their daily life.

In the transitional period from Zhedong scholarship of Siming to the new learning, great scholars like Wang Zicai (王梓材), Xu Shidong, Dong Pei (董 沛) and Zhang Shouyong were very important figures that cannot be ignored. They continued the research of Zhedong scholarship and achieved a lot. First, Wang Zicai completed 100 volumes of *Supplements to the Scholarly Annals of the Song and Yuan Dynasties* (《宋元学案补遗》). He added nearly 800 pieces of information and made complete the issues left unfinished by Qing scholars Huang Zongxi, Huang Baijia and Quan Zuwang, which is of great significance. Second, Xu Shidong was a famous Ningbo bibliophile in the late Qing dynasty, and he had a private library on the Mist Islet (*Yanyu*) of the Moon Lake, which was once widely known. But unfortunately, it was destroyed by a fire. During the reign of Emperor Tongzhi (1856–1875), he served as the head of Ningbo Local Annals Bureau, and spent more than 10 years in collating

Six Annals of Siming in Song and Yuan Dynasties (《宋元四明六志》), which was honored as "first-rate annals". Also, he edited *Collected Works of Siming Old Annals* (《四明旧志诗文钞》) and published his *Yanyulou Collection* (《烟屿楼文集》) and *Yanyulou Poetry* (《烟屿楼诗集》). Third, Dong Pei was a good friend and successor of Xu Shidong, and he continued compiling annals after Xu. In the fifth year under the reign of Emperor Tongzhi of Qing (1866), he finished *Mingzhou Chronicles* (《明州系年录》), which was compiled chronologically, covering the historical facts of Mingzhou from the Zhou dynasty to the second year of Emperor Tongzhi of the Qing dynasty (1863). The book left valuable historical materials for later generations. He lectured for many years in Chongshi Academy and Bianzhi Academy of Ningbo, not only proficient with history but also renowned for his poetry and ancient prose. He compiled *Collected Poems of Yongshang in the Song and Yuan Dynasties* (《甬上宋元诗略》) and *Poetry of Liuyi Shanfang* (《六一山房诗集》).

Zhang Shouyong was an outstanding scholar of Siming area in the transitional period from the late Qing dynasty to the Republican period. He presided over the editing of the first eight sets of *The Siming Book Series*, which collected 178 kinds of works by Ningbo scholars in 1,177 volumes; during the period of The War of Resistance against Japanese Aggression, he cooperated with scholars He Bingsong and Zheng Zhenduo (郑振铎) to rescue the ancient books in the occupied areas by Japanese army in Shanghai and other places, and he collected more than 15,000 ancient books. Besides, he collected the books and transcripts from old gentry families, including 4,860 rare books, and 11,000 ordinary books. His total collection reached 160,000 volumes, which were respectively stored in 11 library buildings such as "Yueyuan" Library. This is his great contribution to the cultural undertakings of Siming and China.

From the perspective of modern scholarship, including natural sciences, social sciences and humanities, i.e., the so-called "new learning", Zhedong scholarship mainly belongs to the category of humanities, with some of its branches categorized into social sciences and even natural sciences, because its majority is composed of history of culture and thought. True, in terms of academic scope, the previous Zhedong scholarship is quite different from the modern academic studies, but history and culture are the root of our existence when we are facing the future. Therefore, it is of great significance to research, elucidate, inherit and innovate Zhedong scholarship, which has now become a duty of many scholars with unswerving devotion. Some scholars assert that a new Zhedong School is taking shape. Whether it be a truth or just a casual remark, it is a kind of expectation and hope, because genuine scholarship is supposed to have its academic origin, and more importantly, to have vitality in its development. In my opinion, an excellent tradition or academic research must have its essential vitality which enables it to withstand the test of time and history. It is certain that today's "Zhedong scholarship" is writing a new page.

Excellent scholarship is by no means an abstract dogma, because it originates from life and is higher than life. The inner spirit of Zhedong scholarship has been integrated into the daily life of the common people in eastern Zhejiang, and runs through each aspect of their life, including daily ethics, basic etiquette, daily necessities, and life rituals of each life stage such as wedding and funeral. That is a more important manifestation of the enduring vitality of Zhedong scholarship in contrast with its own academic development.

How to define the social influence and vitality of Zhedong scholarship depends on different perspectives, while in my opinion, the definition should be based on Zhedong scholarship's own spiritual characteristics, the unique and prominent characteristics of Zhedong people formed in their daily life and production which are different from those of the people in other regions, and the organic relationship between the two categories of characteristics. To make a definition in this way might be more convincing. Thereby, we can draw a conclusion that it is in four aspects that the inner spirit of Zhedong scholarship is closely related to the practice of daily life and production of the people in eastern Zhejiang, especially in Ningbo.

First, encouraging industry and commerce. Traditional China was a large agricultural country and it had a deeply rooted idea of "valuing righteousness over personal interests" and "emphasizing agriculture and restraining commerce". Both the policies of the imperial court and the doctrines of Confucianism demoted industry and commerce to the bottom of the society. Surrounded by mountains, rivers and sea, Ningbo area has a very advantageous geographical position for industrial and commercial activities. In addition, Ningbo people are hard-working and extremely talented in commerce. All these advantages contributed to the formation of Ningbo *bang*, the world-known group of merchants. It is worth noting that all the Ningbo people with either traditional or modern thinking naturally agree with the Confucian ethics, but at the same time, they are also convinced by, and have accepted the idea of "both industry (handicraft) and commerce as foundations" put forward by Huang Zongxi, the academic giant of Zhedong scholarship. Ningbo people are practical. They believe that as long as they can make a living, there is nothing to be ashamed of in the business of industry and commerce. This point just coincides with what Wang Yangming claimed. As early as the middle of the Ming dynasty, Master Wang Yangming proposed, "The people of four classes (i.e., scholars, farmers, craftsmen, and merchants) have their different trades, but they follow the common *dao* (heavenly principle), and their devotion to the efforts is the same," so as to oppose the discrimination against different sectors. That is to say, in terms of their duties, scholars are supposed to conduct learning and governance, farmers to feed the people, craftsmen to offer instruments, and merchants to circulate goods. Each member of the society tries his best to carry out his work chosen according to his own professional interest. All of them are needed by the society and all their jobs are very important. Their statuses are equal and there is no difference between different industries. Furthermore, from the perspective of national economic policy, Huang Zongxi emphasized "for people's practical use", and "both industry (handicraft) and commerce as foundations". Meanwhile, he opposed the traditional idea of "valuing the foundation [agriculture] over other trades". These statements of thinkers not only ideologically reflected the daily practice of life and production of the Siming people, but also spiritually supported their ideas of "valuing and encouraging industry (handicraft) and commerce".

Ningbo people have made great achievements in industry and commerce. In as early as the periods of Wanli and Tianqi of the Ming dynasty, Ningbo merchants were active in and outside the capital, and they were fruitful in pharmaceutical and garment industries; by the Qian-Jia period, Ningbo merchants had formed the famous Ningbo *bang*, which was one of the top ten commercial groups in the past; during the years around the outbreak of the Opium War in 1840, the top ten commercial groups evolved into four major competitive groups, namely, Jin *bang* (merchant group of Shanxi), Yue *bang* (merchant group of Guangdong), Min *bang* (merchant group of Fujian) and Ningbo *bang*, with Ningbo *bang* being the most potential one. After Shanghai was opened for foreign trade, Ningbo *bang* quickly became the backbone of its industry and commerce, and along with the trend, a large number of business tycoons emerged. The century-old Ningbo *bang* made outstanding contributions to the development of China's modern industry and commerce, while Zhedong scholarship was just the spiritual foundation of this great commercial success, which was closely related to the characteristics of Ningbo merchants: honest and trustworthy character, rational management and prudent operation.

Second, venerating learning and encouraging the good. The development and evolution of Zhedong scholarship was closely related to education, and many thinkers were also well-known educators. For example, most of the "Five Scholars of the Qingli Period" took teaching as their lifelong career. Among them, Lou Yu headed the Prefecture School and County School of Ningbo for more than three decades, and he was affectionately respected as "Master Lou" by the local people. Yan Jian not only developed his profound *xinxue* thought, but also made outstanding achievements as a great educator. Up to the Ming dynasty, Wang Yangming, a versatile talent as thinker, politician and military strategist, also had prominent performance in teaching. The reason why his *xinxue* theory was widely spread lay not only in the convincingness of the theory itself, but also in his wonderful teaching, and even some well-educated officials and scholars became his followers. It was just because of the unremitting efforts of the great Zhedong scholars from generation to generation that Siming area became a fertile land for education. Its tradition of advocating learning has lasted for hundreds of years.

Ningbo people like collecting and reading books. In old days, they were proud of their family tradition of farming and reading. They admired scholarly family, respecting knowledge and valuing propriety. Even ordinary people from destitute families would send their children to school; when businessmen earned money outside and had some savings, they would be willing to make a donation for the development of education in their hometown; of course, it should be remembered that local officials also offered their support to the education of Ningbo. Among them, Wang Anshi and Shi Hao set up the best models. It was just the profound tradition of advocating learning that nourished the talents of Siming area, and made Ningbo the "Land of Academicians" of modern times.

What matches the tradition of venerating learning of Ningbo people is their pursuit of the good, and therefore, Ningbo is a well-known "caring land". From the perspective of culture inheritance, Ningbo people integrate the glorious tradition of pursuing the good from ancient culture, such as Confucius and Mencius's the theory of "benevolence and righteousness" and their teaching of "not to impose on others what you yourself do not desire", Wang Yangming's theory of "extension of innate knowledge of the good" and his statement that "the benevolent views himself a unity with the myriad things between heaven and earth", and even Buddhist doctrines like "nothing is valid except compassion" and "to help people in distress". Most Ningbo people believe in Yangming's theory of *liangzhi*, agreeing on the idea that people should be conscientious. Also, they like to go to Tiantong Temple and Ashoka Temple to worship Bodhisattvas. They deeply believe "people are doing, and the divine is watching" and "divinity is over the head of everyone" and they are good at keeping the bottom line when doing anything. At the same time, Ningbo people are extremely enthusiastic about doing good deeds and helping others, and they will warmheartedly offer a hand to those in difficulty or in need.

According to a piece of incomplete statistics, from 2000 to 2011, the charity organizations of Ningbo received donations of more than three billion yuan, which is a proud achievement of the caring city. Doing good deeds, the caring people always bring warm breeze of great love to the people. What's more, they are frequently reported over their goodness by media of different levels like local newspapers and state-level journalism institutions. This has become a beautiful sight of such a city full of care and love.

Third, open-mindness. Zhang Xuecheng claimed that Zhedong scholarship was specialized learning and one of its important features was that it could open up a new trend of times, correct errors and avoid one-sided views. That is to say, opening up and expanding was one of its major spiritual characteristics. According to its history, it can be concluded that this characteristic ran through the whole process of its evolution and development. For example, Wang Yinglin, a scholar in the late Southern Song dynasty, made a great contribution to the expansion of the research scope of Chinese philology through conducting the studies that were left untouched previously. Therefore, he could be viewed as the founding father of the later learning of textual research during Qian-Jia period. Another example is Wang Yangming's theory of "extension of innate knowledge" which was intended to rectify the academic shortcomings of his time. He pointed out that scholarship is a public tool for all people, and what makes it precious lies in the unique creation that is "obtained from the mind", which is higher than any given authority. Adhering to the spirit of *xinxue*, Huang Zongxi advocated "learning through various approaches and considerations", emphasizing a scholar's "personal acquisition" and "learning with an orthodox idea". By the "learning with an orthodox idea", a scholar realizes "what his conscious effort is aimed at" and then forms his academic characteristic(s), i.e., his own most precious academic creation.

Under the long-term edification and influence of Zhedong scholarship by its spirit of opening-up, expanding and innovating, Ningbo people are smart and flexible. With an open mind, they are willing to accept new things, and constantly make innovations that surpass their predecessors. In the process of China's modern industrial development, Ningbo *bang* created nearly 100 "China's firsts", and made pioneering contributions in many industrial and commercial fields. Today, Ningbo is still a famous "city of brands" in China, with remarkable achievements. Compared with the "Chinese Jews"[1]— Wenzhou people, Ningbo people are slightly reserved and introverted; on the contrary, Wenzhou people are bolder and more adventurous, and their economic development focuses more on private operation. The "Wenzhou Pattern" was once renowned nationwide for a time. However, from a long-term perspective, Ningbo people have kept their rationality and prudence in the process of opening-up and expanding. While maintaining their existing characteristic of private operation, they have built more contacts with the government and foreign businessmen. Therefore, their performance is a little better to some degree. But generally speaking, both of them are very valuable forces in the construction of the market economy with Chinese characteristics, and each has its own advantages.

Fourth, deep affection for hometown and country. The development of Zhedong scholarship was inseparable from Zhedong scholars' strong feelings to their hometown and country. The so-called "feelings to hometown and country" refers to people's deep affections and attachments to their hometown and country. One of the important reasons for the great reputation and long-term endurance of Zhedong scholarship or Zhedong School lies in the fact that generations of subsequent scholars, harboring admiration for their excellent local forerunners, deeply studied, promoted and passed down their learning, and wonderfully highlighted and maintained the regional features of their scholarship. This phenomenon is rare in other parts of China. As seen in Qing scholar Quan Zuwang's *Jieqiting Collection*, the lines are full of the author's endless attachment to the landscape of his hometown, his admiration for and praise for the anti-Qing heroes, and his sincere inheritance of the predecessors'

---

[1] Wenzhou people are usually compared to the Jews who are good at business due to their resemblance to them in financial circles. Hence the title "Chinese Jews" for Wenzhou people.

learning. As for the later Ming scholar Zhu Zhiyu, during his stay in Japan, he gave himself the literary name "Shunshui". That's because, in his own words, "Shunshui is the name of a river in my town." It was in this way that Zhu cherished the memory of his hometown. In addition, the Yaojiang Academy, which lasted for nearly 100 years, was initiated and established out of the admiration for Yangming *xinxue* by Yuyao scholars like Shen Guomo, Guan Zongsheng, Shi Xiaoxian and Shi Xiaofu, who were all devoted to the study and dissemination of the learning of Wang Yangming, the famous and outstanding forerunner from their hometown.

This kind of feeling to hometown and country was believed in and followed by the common people in Ningbo. It has formed an excellent tradition. Among them, the most prominent are the group of merchants called Ningbo *bang*. Due to the professional demand of commercial activities, the Ningbo merchants in the past had to travel north and south, keep contacts with society, and they were separated from their hometown in time and space. On the one hand, the feeling of this separation enhanced their yearning for their hometown called "homesickness"; on the other hand, it produced a more hazy and beautiful impression of their hometown called "beauty at a distance". As an old Ningbo saying goes, "Going east and west, I like Jiangxia (downtown Ningbo) the best," which typically reflects the feeling of those traveled afar. Therefore, among the group of Ningbo merchants, a large number of models with deep feeling to hometown and country emerged. They went through ups and downs and finally achieved success in their business, and therefore, they knew clearly the value of the feeling to the people of their hometown. They were totally aware of what to do and how to do it. Thus, they took out their savings one after another and donated them to their hometown to build schools, run hospitals, help those in distress and grant awards to teachers and students, etc. With their sincere heart, they contributed very much to the development of their hometown.

The inner spirit of Zhedong scholarship, namely, encouraging industry and commerce, venerating learning and encouraging the good, opening-up consciousness, and affections to home and country, influences the ideas and values of Ningbo people from generation to generation, and promotes the advancement of regional economy and society. The outstanding predecessors have long gone, their traces disappearing gradually, but their spiritual power never withers, and remains fresh and nutritious forever. Today, the research, development and advocation of Zhedong scholarship and its spirit is not only a necessity for academic development, but also an internal demand for the regional social progress and civilization construction.

Bibliography

Chai Ying (ed.). *The Culture of Eastern Zehjiang (Symposium)*. Shanghai: Shanghai Ancient Books Publishing House, 2005. [柴英，编 . 浙东文化：集刊 . 上海：上海古籍出版社，2005.]

Chen Guoqing. Huang Zongxi's academic style. *Journal of Zhejiang Wanli University*, 2005(1): 1-6. [陈国庆 . 黄宗羲的学术风格 . 浙江万里学院学报，2005(1)：1-6.]

Chen Que. *Chen Que Collection*. Beijing: Zhonghua Book Company, 2009. [陈确 . 陈确集 . 北京：中华书局，2009.]

Chen Zuwu. *Studies on Eastern Zhejiang Academic Culture of the Ming and Qing Dynasties*. Beijing: China Social Sciences Press, 2004. [陈祖武 . 明清浙东学术文化研究 . 北京：中国社会科学出版社，2004.]

Cheng Hao & Cheng Yi. *Collected Works of Cheng Hao & Cheng Yi*. Beijing: Zhonghua Book Company, 2004. [程颢，程颐 . 二程集 . 北京：中华书局，2004.]

Chinese Society of Practical Learning. *Scholarship of Eastern Zhejiang and Practical Learning of China*. Ningbo: Ningbo Publishing House, 2007. [中国实学研究会 . 浙东学术与中国实学 . 宁波：宁波出版社，2007.]

Collection of Various Pre-Qin Schools of Thought. Vols. 1–8. Beijing: Zhonghua Book Company, 2002. [《诸子集成》（1—8）. 北京：中华书局，2002.]

CPPCC Haishu District Committee. *A Resplendent Pearl: The Moon Lake*. Beijing: Central Party Literature Press, 2002. [宁波市海曙区政协 . 璀璨明珠——月湖 . 北京：中央文献出版社，2002.]

Dai Songyue. Great Confucian scholar Wang Yinglin of the Song dynasty. *Journal of the Party School of CPC Ningbo Municipal Committee*, 2007(5): 106-112. [戴松岳 . 宋代鸿儒王应麟 . 中共宁波市委党校学报，2007(5)：106-112.]

Fan Lizhou. Wan Sitong's inheritance and development of Huang Zongxi's thought. *Zhejiang Academic Journal*, 2001(6): 153-156. [范立舟 . 万斯同对黄宗羲思想的继承与发挥 . 浙江学刊，2001(6)：153-156.]

Fang Rujin, Fang Tongyi & Chen Guocan. *A Study on Chen Liang and Eastern Zhejiang School in the Southern Song Dynasty*. Beijing: People's Publishing House, 1996. [方如金，方同义，陈国灿 . 陈亮与南宋浙东学派研究 . 北京：人民出版社，1996.]

Fang Tongyi, Chen Xinlai & Li Baogeng. *A Study on Eastern Zhejiang Academic Spirit*. Ningbo: Ningbo Publishing House, 2006. [方同义，陈新来，李包庚 . 浙东学术精神研究 . 宁波：宁波出版社，2006.]

Fang Xiaoru. *Xunzhizhai Collection of Master Fang Zhengxue*, collected in the *First Volume of Four-branch Book Series*. [方孝孺 . 方正学先生逊志斋集，四部丛刊初编本 .]

Fang Zuyou. *Biography of Huang Zongxi*. Hangzhou: Zhejiang University Press, 2011. [方祖猷 . 黄宗羲长传 . 杭州：浙江大学出版社，2011.]

Fang Zuyou. *Commentaries on Wan Sitong*. Nanjing: Nanjing University Press，1996. [方祖猷 . 万斯同评传 . 南京：南京大学出版社，1996.]

Feng Qi. *An Exploration of Wisdom*. Shanghai: East China Normal University Press, 1996. [冯契 . 智慧的探索 . 上海：华东师范大学出版社，1996.]

Feng Youlan. *A New History of Chinese Philosophy*. Beijing: People's Publishing House, 1999. [冯友兰 . 中国哲学史新编 . 北京：人民出版社，1999.]

Feng Youlan. *The Spirit of Chinese Philosophy*. Beijing: The Commercial Press, 1945. [冯友兰 . 新原道 . 北京：商务印书馆，1945.]

Fu Xuancong. *A General History of Ningbo*. Ningbo: Ningbo Publishing House. 2009. [傅璇琮 . 宁波通史 . 宁波：宁波出版社，2009.]

Guan Minyi. *The Academic History of Eastern Zhejiang*. Shanghai: East China Normal University Press, 1993. [管敏义 . 浙东学术史 . 上海：华东师范大学出版社，1993.]

He Bingsong. *The Origin of Zhedong School*. Beijing: Zhonghua Book Company, 1989. [何炳松 . 浙东学派溯源 . 北京：中华书局，1989.]

Hou Wailu. *A History of Song-Ming Neo-Confucianism*. Vols. I, II & III. Beijing: People's Publishing House, 1984. [侯外庐 . 宋明理学史（上、中、下）. 北京：人民出版社，1984.]

Huang Zhen. *Huang Zhen's Daily Records*, a reprinted version by *Xin'an Wangshi* (The Wang's in Xin'an) during the Qianlong period of Qing. [黄震 . 黄氏日抄 . 清乾隆间新安汪氏覆元刻本 .]

Huang Zongxi. *Scholarly Annals of the Song and Yuan Dynasties*. Vols. 3–6. Hangzhou: Zhejiang Ancient Books Publishing House, 2004. [黄宗羲 . 宋元学案（3—6）. 杭州：浙江古籍出版社，2004.]

Huang Zongxi. *The Records of Ming Scholars*. Hangzhou: Zhejiang Ancient Books Publishing House, 2004. [黄宗羲 . 明儒学案 . 杭州：浙江古籍出版社，2004.]

Institute of Ancient History of Chinese Academy of Social Sciences. *Quan Zuwang and Eastern Zhejiang Academic Culture*. Beijing: China Social Sciences Press, 2010. [中国社会科学院古代史研究所 . 全祖望与浙东学术文化 . 北京：中国社会科学出版社，2010.]

Ji Xueyuan. *Yaojiang Cultural History*. Ningbo: Ningbo Publishing House, 1998. [季学原 . 姚江文化史 . 宁波：宁波出版社，1998.]

Jin Yuelin. *Ontology*. Beijing: The Commercial Press, 1985. [金岳霖 . 论道 . 北京：商务印书馆，1985.]

Li Dingfu. *Wenzhou Merchants and Wenzhou People's Spirit*. Hong Kong: CHINA NEWS MEDIA INT'L GROUP LIMITED, 2004. [李丁富 . 温州商人与温州人精神 . 香港: 中国新闻传媒国际集团有限公司, 2004.]

Li Mingyou. *Diversity Begotten by One Origin: Huang Zongxi's Philosophy and Philosophical Outlook on History*. Beijing: People's Publishing House, 1994. [李明友 . 一本万殊: 黄宗羲的哲学与哲学史观 . 北京: 人民出版社, 1994.]

Li Yesi. *Gaotang Collection*. Hangzhou: Zhejiang Ancient Books Publishing House, 1988. [李邺嗣 . 杲堂诗文集 . 杭州: 浙江古籍出版社, 1988.]

Liang Qichao. *Chinese Academic History of Recent Three Hundred Years*. Beijing: China Bookstore Publishing House, 1985. [梁启超 . 中国近三百年学术史 . 北京: 中国书店, 1985.]

Liu Zongzhou. *Complete Works of Master Liu Zongzhou*, the Xiaoshan version in the Daoguang period of Qing. [刘宗周 . 刘子全书 . 清道光年间萧山刊本 .]

Lu Jiuyuan. *Collection of Lu Jiuyuan*. Beijing: Zhonghua Book Company, 2008. [陆九渊 . 陆九渊集 . 北京: 中华书局, 2008.]

Lü Zuqian. *Collection of Master Lü Donglai*. Yangzhou: Guangling Ancient Books Publishing House, 1983. [吕祖谦 . 东莱吕太史集 . 扬州: 广陵古籍刻印社, 1983.]

Luo Zheng & Qin Jiajun. Huang Zongxi's thought of "both industry and commerce are fundamental" in his *Waiting for the Dawn: A Plan for the Prince. Guangxi Social Sciences*, 2005(6): 124-126. [罗政, 秦加军 . 黄宗羲《明夷待访录》中的 "工商皆本" 思想 . 广西社会科学, 2005(6): 124-126.]

Pan Fu'en & Xu Yuqing. *Commentaries on Lü Zuqian*. Nanjing: Nanjing University Press, 1992. [潘富恩, 徐余庆 . 吕祖谦评传 . 南京: 南京大学出版社, 1992.]

Pan Pingge. *Edition of Master Pan's Records of Pursuing Benevolence*. Beijing: Zhonghua Book Company, 2009. [潘平格 . 潘子求仁录辑要 . 北京: 中华书局, 2009.]

Pan Qizao & Liang Yiqun (eds.). *Symposium of Ningbo Culture Studies (2007)*. Hong Kong: Hong Kong International Academic Cultural Information Publishing Company, 2008. [潘起造，梁一群，编. 宁波文化研究论文集：2007 卷. 香港：香港国际学术文化资讯出版公司，2008.]

Pan Qizao. Regional cultural origin and cultural spirit of Eastern Zhejiang scholarship. *Zhejiang Academic Journal*, 2006(4): 105-110. [潘起造. 浙东学术的地域文化渊源及其文化精神. 浙江社会科学，2006(4)：105-110.]

Qian Maowei. *A History of Eastern Zhejiang Scholarship*. Ningbo: Ningbo Publishing House, 1999. [钱茂伟. 浙东学术史话. 宁波：宁波出版社，1999.]

Qian Maowei. *A Study on Yaojiang Academy School*. Beijing: China Social Sciences Press, 2005. [钱茂伟. 姚江书院派研究. 北京：中国社会科学出版社，2005 年 .]

Qian Ming. *The Formation and Development of Yangming Studies*. Nanjing: Jiangsu Ancient Books Publishing House, 2002. [钱明. 阳明学的形成与发展. 南京：江苏古籍出版社，2002.]

Qian Mu. *Academic History of China in Recent 300 Years*. Beijing: Zhonghua Book Company, 1984. [钱穆. 中国近三百年学术史. 北京：中华书局，1984.]

Quan Zuwang. *Collected Works of Quan Zuwang with Annotation and Collation*. Shanghai: Shanghai Ancient Books Publishing House, 2000. [全祖望. 全祖望集汇校集注. 上海：上海古籍出版社，2000.]

Ruan Yuan. *Thirteen Classics Explanatory Notes and Commentaries*. Vols. I & II. Beijing: Zhonghua Book Company, 2009. [阮元. 十三经注疏（上、下）. 北京：中华书局，2009.]

Shan Chun. On Confucian outlook of integrity and its modern value. *Oriental Forum*, 2002(4): 11-22. [单纯. 论儒家的气节观及其现代价值. 东方论坛，2002(4)：11-22.]

Shao Tingcai. *Sifutang Collection*. Hangzhou: Zhejiang Ancient Books Publishing

House, 1987. [邵廷采 . 思复堂文集 . 杭州：浙江古籍出版社，1987.]

Sun Yirang. *Chronicle of Wenzhou Classics*. Hangzhou: Zhejiang Province Library, 1921. [孙诒让 . 温州经籍志 . 杭州：浙江图书馆，1921.]

Teng Fu. Chen Liang and the spirit of Zhejiang studies. *Zhejiang Daily (Theoretical Horizon)*. Oct. 25, 2004. [滕复 . 陈亮与浙学精神 . 浙江日报（理论视野），2004 年 10 月 25 日 .]

Wan Sitong. *Shiyuan Collection*, collected in *The Siming Book Series*, 1935. [万斯同 . 石园文集,《四明丛书》1935 刻本 .]

Wang Fengxian & Ding Guoshui. *A Study on Zhedong School*. Hangzhou: Zhejiang People's Publishing House, 1993. [王凤贤，丁国顺 . 浙东学派研究 . 杭州：浙江人民出版社，1993.]

Wang Gen. *Complete Works of Master Xinzhai*. Yangzhou: Guangling Publishing House, 2008. [王艮 . 心斋先生全集 . 扬州：广陵书社，2008.]

Wang Ji. *Complete Works of Master Wang Longxi*, photocopied from the version of Renwu Year (1822) in the Daoguang period of Qing of Huawen Publishing House. [王畿 . 王龙溪先生全集 . 华文书局影印道光壬午年刻本 .]

Wang Yangming. *Complete Works of Wang Yangming*. Vols. I & II. Shanghai: Shanghai Ancient Books Publishing House, 1992. [王阳明 . 王阳明全集(上、下). 上海：上海古籍出版社，1992.]

Wang Yinglin. *Reading Notes about Difficulties in Learning*. Shenyang: Liaoning Education Press, 1998. [王应麟 . 困学纪闻 . 沈阳：辽宁教育出版社，1998.]

Wu Guang (ed.). *Collected Papers of the International Symposium on Huang Zongxi's Scholarship*. Hangzhou: Zhejiang Ancient Books Publishing House, 1987. [吴光，编 . 黄宗羲论：国际黄宗羲学术论文讨论会论文集 . 杭州：浙江古籍出版社，1987.]

Xiao Shafu & Li Jinquan. *A History of Chinese Philosophy*. Vols. I & II. Beijing:

People's Publishing House, 1983. [肖萐父，李锦全 . 中国哲学史（上、下）. 北京：人民出版社，1983.]

Xu Dingbao. *Commentaries on Huang Zongxi*. Nanjing: Nanjing University Press, 1996. [徐定宝 . 黄宗羲评传 . 南京：南京大学出版社，1996.]

Xu Shixing. A review on Wan Sitong's scholarship and character. *Journal of Anhui Normal University*, 2003(6): 695-699. [徐世星 . 万斯同学行述论 . 安徽师范大学学报，2003(6)：695-699.]

Yang Guorong. *An Introduction to Wang Yangming's Philosophy*. Shanghai: East China Normal University Press, 2003. [杨国荣 . 王学通论 . 上海：华东师范大学出版社，2003.]

Yang Jian. *Posthumous Works of Yang Cihu*, from *Complete Library in the Four Branches of Literature* of Qing dynasty. [杨慈湖 . 慈湖遗书 . 清《四库全书》本 .]

Ye Jianhua. On the historical thought of the early-Qing historiographers of the institution for the history of Ming. *Studies on the History of Historical Science*, 1994(4): 24-34. [叶建华 . 论清初明史馆馆臣的史学思想 . 史学史研究，1994(4)：24-34.]

Zhan Haiyun. *Collected Papers on the Early-Qing Scholarship*. Taipei: Taiwan Wenjin Publishing House, 1992. [詹海云 . 清初学术论文集 . 台北：台湾文津出版社，1992.]

Zhang Jiajun. *A Great Historiographer of Zhejiang: Symposium Dedicated to the 300th Anniversary of the Birth of Quan Zuwang*. Ningbo: Ningbo Publishing House, 2005. [张嘉俊 . 越魂史笔——全祖望诞辰三百周年纪念文集 . 宁波：宁波出版社，2005.]

Zhang Liwen. *A History of the Development of Categories in Chinese Philosophy*. Beijing: China Renmin University Press, 1986. [张立文 . 中国哲学范畴发展史 . 北京：中国人民大学出版社，1986.]

Zhang Ru'an. A brief summary of the cultural contributions of the Northern Song "Five

Masters of the Qingli Period" to Ningbo. *Journal of the Party School of CPC Ningbo Municipal Committee*, 2008(2): 110-116. [张如安 . 略论北宋 "庆历五先生" 对宁波的文化贡献 . 中共宁波市委党校学报，2008(2)：110-116.]

Zhang Shouyong. *The Siming Book Series*. Yangzhou: Guangling Publishing House. 2006. [张寿镛 . 四明丛书 . 扬州：广陵书社，2006.]

Zhang Shuwang. On the death of Fang Xiaoru and its implication in Confucian history. *Chuanshan Journal*, 2010(2): 119-121. [张树旺 . 论方孝孺之死的儒学史意蕴 . 船山学刊，2010(2)：119-121.]

Zhang Xuecheng. *General Interpretation of Historiography*. Vols. I & II. Beijing: Zhonghua Book Company, 1994. [章学诚 . 文史通义（上、下）. 北京：中华书局，1994.]

Zhang Xuecheng. *Posthumous Works of Zhang Xuecheng*. Beijing: Cultural Relics Publishing House, 1982. [章学诚 . 章氏遗书 . 北京：文物出版社，1982.]

Zhu Shunshui. *Complete Works of Zhu Shunshui*. Beijing: China Bookstore Publishing House, 1991. [朱舜水 . 朱舜水全集 . 北京：中国书店，1991.]

Zhu Xi. *Collected Works of Zhu Xi*. Beijing: National Library of China Publishing House, 2006. [朱熹 . 朱文公文集 . 北京：国家图书馆出版社，2006.]

Zhu Xi. *Commentaries on the Four Books*. Changsha: Yuelu Publishing House, 1985. [朱熹 . 四书集注 . 长沙：岳麓书社，1985.]

Zi Zhongyun. Death of Fang Xiaoru and Giordano Bruno. *Guoxue*, 2009(8): 6-7. [资中筠 . 方孝孺与布鲁诺之死 . 国学，2009(8)：6-7.]

Glossary

Chinese	English
《安南供役纪事》	*Chronicle of Services in Annam*
《白云集》	*Baiyun Collection*
《百家姓》	*Hundred Family Names*
《北堂书钞》	*Collected Classics of Beitang*
《碧沚龙神庙碑铭》	"The Stele Inscription on the Longshen Temple on Bizhi"
《碧沚杨文元公书院记》	"An Account on Yang Wenyuan Academy on Bizhi"
《辨二氏之学》	*Commentaries on Buddhism and Taoism*
《冰雪集》	*Poetry of Ice and Snow*
《补历代史表》	*Supplementary Chronological Tables of China's History*
《沧天记》	*Cangtianji*
《测地志要》	*Records of Geographical Measurements*
《禅障》	"Zen Barriers"
《陈确集》	*Chen Que Collection*
《成唯识论注》	*Annotation to Discourse on the Perfection of Consciousness-only*
《崇礼说》	*On Exalting the Rules of Rites*
《崇祯长编》	*Drafted Chronicles of Chongzhen*
《出塞》	"Outside the Frontiers"
《传习录》	*Instructions for Practical Living*
《春秋》	*The Spring and Autumn Annals*
《春秋释》	*Interpretation of The Spring and Autumn Annals*
《淳熙四先生祠堂碑阴文》	"An Inscription on the back of the Tablet for the Temple of Four Masters of the Chunxi Period"
《慈湖遗书》	*Posthumous Works of Yang Cihu*
《从军行》	"Frontier Soldiers"
《大清一统志》	*Annals of the Unification of the Great Qing*
《大日本史》	*The History of Great Japan (Dai Nihonshi)*
《大学》	*The Great Learning*

《大学辨》 "Criticism on The Great Learning"

《帝王基命录》 *Records of Emperor's Ascending to Throne*

《帝王略论》 *Accounts and Evaluations of Monarchs*

《定川遗书》 *Dingchuan Posthumous Works*

《东发学案》 "The Records of Dongfa Scholars"

《东阁私抄》 *Dongge Private Records*

《东南纪事》 *Chronicles of Southeast*

《东南纪闻》 *Records of Southeast*

《读礼通考》 *General Study of Rites*

《读史百则》 *One Hundred Principles of Reading History*

《读书分年日程》 *Graded Learning Schedule*

《读书小记》 *Notes on Reading*

《尔雅》 *Erya*

《尔雅正义》 *Semantic Annotations to Erya*

《二陆先生祠记》 *An Account of the Memorial Temple of Masters Lu Jiuling and Lu Jiuyuan*

《方平仪象》 *Astronomical Measurement*

《方舆金石编目》 *Bibliography of Geography and Epigraph*

《方正学年谱》 *Fang Zhengxue's Chronicle*

《方正学先生逊志斋集》 *Xunzhizhai Collection of Master Fang Zhengxue*

《分隶偶存》 *Records of Calligraphers of Clerical Script*

《冯京第小传》 "The Brief Biography of Feng Jingdi"

《复礼说》 *On Obeying the Rules of Rites*

《鄮城集》 *Houcheng Collection*

《公羊传》 *Commentaries of Gongyang*

《古今纪要逸编》 *A Sequal to the Brief Chonicles of Ancient and Contemporary Dynasties*

《古今纪要》 *Brief Chronicles of Ancient and Contemporary Dynasties*

《古今通志年表》 *Chronology through Ages*

《谷梁古注》	*Ancient Annotations to Guliangzhuan*
《谷梁正义》	*Semantic Annotations to Guliangzhuan*
《谷梁传》	*Commentaries of Guliang*
《瞽言》	"Unreasonable Remarks"
《管村集》	*Guancun Collection*
《广平类稿》	*Classified Essays of Guangping*
《国朝汉学师承记》	*Origin and Development of the Han Studies in the Qing Dynasty*
《国语》	*Discourses of the States*
《果斋训语》	*Guozhai's Instructions on Learning*
《海涵万象录》/《南山杂录》	*Records of Daily Remarks on Diverse Issues / The Records of Nanshan's Remarks*
《寒松斋集》	*Hansongzhai Collection*
《汉书》	*The Book of Han*
《汉书地理志稽疑》	*Doubts about the Geographical Treatise of The Book of Han*
《汉艺文志考证》	*Text-critical Commentaries on the Bibliographical Treatises of The Book of Han*
《汉志》	*Treatises of The Book of Han*
《杭州府志》	*Annals of Hangzhou Prefecture*
《贺公逸老堂碑铭》	"The Stele Inscription on the Yilao Hall of He Zhizhang"
《弘光实录抄》	*Records of the Hongguang Period of Ming*
《洪范口义》	*Oral Records of the Great Norm*
《洪范统一》	*General Instruction to the Great Norm*
《后汉书》	*The Book of the Later Han*
《湖语》	"Dialogues at the Moon Lake"
《皇明表忠纪》	*Memorial Records of Loyal Ministers of the Ming Dynasty*
《皇明经济文录》	*Collection of Essays on Governance of the Ming Dynasty*
《黄氏日抄》	*Huang Zhen's Daily Records*

《黄氏塾课》　　　　　　*Huang Zhen's Instructions on Learning*

《黄竹农家耳逆草·天旋
篇》　　　　　　　　　"Rotation and Revolution" of *Unpleasant Words of
Huangzhu Nongjia*

《黄宗羲全集》　　　　　*Complete Works of Huang Zongxi*

《回乡偶书》　　　　　　"On My Way Home"

《会稽典录》　　　　　　*Kuaiji Classic Records*

《急就篇补注》　　　　　*Supplementary Annotations to the Quick Access to
Chinese Characters*

《絜斋毛诗经筵讲义》　　*Jiezhai's Notes of Lectures in the Imperial Palace on
Mao's Version of The Book of Songs*

《鲒埼亭集》　　　　　　*Jieqiting Collection*

《鲒埼亭集外编》　　　　*A Supplement to Jieqiting Collection*

《晋书》　　　　　　　　*The Book of Jin*

《晋书·儒林》　　　　　"Confucian Scholars" of *The Book of Jin*

《经史答问》　　　　　　*Answers to Questions on Confucian Classics and History*

《经书补注》　　　　　　*Supplementary Annotations to Confucian Classics*

《经说略》　　　　　　　*Introduction and Commentaries on Confucian Classics*

《经义通诂》/《经训比
义》　　　　　　　　　*General Interpretation of Confucian Classics*

《儆季杂著》　　　　　　*Jingji Miscellaneous Writings*

《儆居集经说》　　　　　*Commentaries on the Confucian Classics* in *Jingju
Collection*

《儆居遗书》　　　　　　*Jingju Posthumous Writings*

《静清书院记》　　　　　"An Account of Jingqing Academy"

《静清学案》　　　　　　"The Records of Jingqing Scholars"

《九国志》　　　　　　　*Annals of Nine States*

《旧五代史》　　　　　　*The Old History of the Five Dynasties*

《军礼司马法考征》　　　*Textual Research of Methods of the Minister of War
Concerning Military Rituals*

《康熙字典》　　　　　　*Kangxi Dictionary*

《困学纪闻》	*Reading Notes about Difficulties in Learning*
《嬾堂记》	"On (Shu Dan's) Lantang Hall"
《类要》	*Encyclopedia of Important Issues*
《梨洲末命》	"Lizhou in Remaining Days"
《礼记》	*The Book of Rites*
《礼记集解》	*Collected Interpretation of The Book of Rites*
《礼书通故》	*The History of Life Ritual*
《礼书通故序》	"Preface of The History of Life Rituals"
《历学指南》	*A Guide to Calendrical Studies*
《历志》	"Calendrical Records"
《两朝纲目备要》	*Chronicles of Emperor Gaozong and Emperor Xiaozong of the Song Dynasty*
《两太交食捷算》	*Rapid Calculation on the Solar and Lunar Eclipses*
《列代纪年》/《历史年表》	*Chronological Tables of China's History*
《临安集》	*Lin'an Collection*
《刘门弟子传》	"Biographies of Liu Zongzhou's Disciples"
《刘子传》	"Biography of Master Liu Zongzhou"
《刘子全书》	*Complete Works of Master Liu Zongzhou*
《刘子全书遗编》	*Supplementary Compilation of Complete Works of Master Liu Zongzhou*
《留都防乱公揭》	"Notice on Prevention Upheavals in the Old Capital (Nanjing)"
《留书》	*Advice for the Future Generations*
《六一山房诗集》	*Poetry of Liuyi Shanfang*
《隆万两朝列卿记》	*Chronicles of Ming Ministers in the Longqing and Wanli Periods*
《论衡》	*Disquisitions or Discourses Weighted in the Balance*
《论略》	"Evaluations and Accounts"
《论语》	*The Analects of Confucius*

《论语后案》	*Commentaries on The Analects of Confucius*
《论语集解》	*Collected Interpretations of The Analects of Confucius*
《论语集注》	*Collected Annotations to The Analects of Confucius*
《论语心义》	*A Xinxue Perspective on The Analects of Confucius*
《毛诗》	Mao's version of *The Book of Songs*
《梅花岭记》	"Records of Meihualing"
《蒙训》	*Instructions on Enlightenment*
《孟子》	*The Mencius*
《孟子述义》	*Interpretation of The Mencius*
《孟子摘义》	*The Doctrines of The Mencius*
《梦溪笔谈》	*Dream Pool Essays*
《明鉴举要》/《明史举要》	*A Brief History of Ming*
《明乐府》	*Yuefu Poetry of Ming*
《明儒学案》	*The Records of Ming Scholars*
《明史》	*History of Ming*
《明史案》	*The Records of Ming History*
《明史稿》	*The Manuscript of the History of Ming*
《明文案》	*Collection of the Essays of Ming*
《明文海》	*Anthology of the Essays of Ming*
《明夷待访录》	*Waiting for the Dawn: A Plan for the Prince*
《明州系年录》	*Mingzhou Chronicles*
《南都事略》	*Records of the Capital of the Southern Song Dynasty*
《南江诗钞》	*Nanjiang Poetry*
《南江文钞》	*Nanjiang Essays*
《南江札记》	*Nanjiang Reading Notes*
《南史》	*History of the Southern Dynasties*
《宁波府志》	*Annals of Ningbo Prefecture*

《潘先生传》	"Biography of Master Pan Pingge"
《潘子求仁录辑要》	*Edition of Master Pan's Records of Pursuing Benevolence*
《平桥水则记》	"On Pingqiao Shuize Tablet"
《泊姚江》	"Mooring on Yaojiang River"
《契圣录》	*Records of Word Corresponding to Sage's Thought*
《千之草堂编年文钞》	*Collected Works of Qianzhi Caotang*
《千字文》	*Thousand-Character Text*
《清初浙东学派论丛》	*Collected Papers on the Early-Qing Zhedong School*
《清代学术概论》	*Intellectual Trends in the Ch'ing Period*
《庆历五先生书院记》	"An Account of the Academy of Five Masters of the Qingli Period"
《求仁录》	*Records of Pursuing Benevolence*
《全谢山先生年谱》	*Chronicle of Master Quan Xieshan*
《群经说》	*Commentaries on Confucians Classics*
《人谱》	*Human Schemata*
《容斋随笔》	*Rongzhai Essays*
《三国志》	*Annals of the Three Kingdoms*
《三太誓考》	*Textual Criticism on the Three Chapters of Great Declaration in The Book of History*
《三字经》	*Three-Character Classic*
《丧礼》	*Funeral Rituals*
《丧俗》	"Customs of Burial Rites"
《尚书》	*The Book of History*
《尚书·说命下》	"Charge to Yue III" of *The Book of History*
《尚书启蒙》	*Basic Knowledge of The Book of History*
《尚书说》	*Commentaries on The Book of History*
《尚书逸汤誓记》	*Textual Criticism on the Lost Speech of Tang in The Book of History*
《深宁集》	*Collected Works of Shenning*

《盛京通志》	*Gazetteers of Shengjing (Mukden)*
《诗丛说》	*Commentaries on The Book of Songs*
《诗经》	*The Book of Songs*
《诗考》	*Textual Researches on the Three Versions of The Book of Songs*
《诗礼讲解》	*Interpretation of The Book of Songs and The Book of Rites*
《诗序通说》	*Comprehensive Interpretation of the Preface and Introductions in The Book of Songs*
《诗学发微》	*Explorations of Poetics*
《石龙集》	*Shilong Collection*
《史记》	*Records of the Grand Historian of China*
《史说》	*Commentaries on History*
《史说略》	*Accounts and Commentaries on History*
《授时历》	*Season-Granting Calendar*
《授时历法假如》	*Calculation of Season-Granting Calendar*
《授时历故》	*Annotation to Season-Granting Calendar*
《水经注》	*Commentary on the Water Classic*
《水云亭记》	*"On Shuiyun Pavilion"*
《说略》	*Annals of the late Ming Dynasty*
《思复堂集》	*Sifutang Collection*
《四部丛刊初编》	*First Volume of the Four-branch Book Series*
《四库全书》	*Complete Library in the Four Branches of Literature*
《四库全书总目提要》	*Descriptive Catalogue of the Complete Library in the Four Branches of Literature*
《四库史部提要》	*Abstracts of the Historical Records in Complete Library in the Four Branches of Literature*
《四明丛书》	*The Siming Book Series*
《四明丛书·甬上水利志》	*The Siming Book Series: Water Conservancy of Yongshang*

《四明旧志诗文钞》	*Collected Works of Siming Old Annals*
《四明山志》	*Chronicles of Siming Mountain*
《四明游录》	*Travelogue of Siming Mountain*
《四书发明》	*Interpretation of the Four Books*
《四书绒》	*Notes on the Four Books*
《四书章句集注》	*Collected Commentaries to the Four Books*
《宋明遗民所知录》	*Anecdotes of the Loyalists to the Song and Ming Dynasties*
《宋儒学案》	*The Records of Song Scholars*
《宋史》	*The History of the Song Dynasty*
《宋史·艺文志》	*History of the Song Dynasty: Bibliographical Treatise*
《宋史就正编》	*Corrections to The History of the Song Dynasty*
《宋史新编》	*A New History of the Song Dynasty*
《宋史要言》	*Important Issues in the History of the Song Dynasty*
《宋文案》	*Collection of the Essays of Song*
《宋元四明六志》	*Six Annals of Siming in Song and Yuan Dynasties*
《宋元学案》	*Scholarly Annals of the Song and Yuan Dynasties*
《宋元学案补遗》	*Supplements to the Scholarly Annals of the Song and Yuan Dynasties*
《宋志》	*Treatises of the History of Song*
《缩斋日记》	*Suozhai Diaries*
《缩斋文集》	*Suozhai Collection*
《太祖实录》	*Veritable Records of Emperor Taizu*
《泰西历》	*Western Calendar*
《唐文拾遗》	*Collection of Lost Works of the Tang Dynasty*
《桃花堤记》	"Taohua (Peach Blossom) Causeway"
《天文志》	"Astronomical Records"
《田赋略》	"A Summary of Farm Tax"
《通历》	*General History of State Governance*

《玩鹿亭稿》	*Essays of Wangluting*
《万贞文先生传》	"Biography of Master Wan Zhenwen"
《王门弟子传》	"Biographies of Wang Yangming's Disciples"
《王文成公全集》	*Complete Works of Master Wang Wencheng*
《王阳明年谱》	*Wang Yangming's Chronicle*
《王子传》	"Biography of Master Wang Yangming"
《畏斋集》	*Weizhai Collection*
《文史通义》	*General Interpretation of Historiography*
《文史通义校注·题记》	Preface of *Annotations of General Interpretation of Historiography*
《文统》	*Civil Administration*
《吴丞相水则碑阴》	"An Inscription on the Back of Wu Qian's Shuize Tablet"
《五纬捷算》	*Rapid Calculation on Five Stars*
《五箴》	*Five Admonitions*
《武王戒书注》	*Annotations to the Self-guarding Words of King Wu of the Zhou Dynasty*
《戊辰修史传》	*Records of History Compiling in Wuchen Year*
《西湖引水记》	"Water Diversion of Ningbo West Lake"
《西南纪事》	*Chronicles of Southwest*
《小学》	*The Lesser Learning*
《小学讽咏》	*Satirical Ballads of the Lesser Learning*
《小学绀珠》	*A Deep Blue Pearl for the Lesser Learning*
《孝经发明》	*Interpretation of The Classic of Filial Piety*
《行朝录》	*Records of the Exiled Regime*
《性解》	"Interpretation of Nature"
《性情集》	*Collection on Nature and Emotions*
《姓氏急就篇》	*Quick Access to Surnames*
《续三通》	*Continued Compilation of Three Comprehensive Historical Works*

《续骚堂集》	*Xusaotang Collection*
《续通典》	*Continued Compilation of Comprehensive Statutes*
《续通志》	*Continued Compilation of General Treatises*
《续通志·金石略》	"Chapters on Epigraphy" of *Continued Compilation of General Treatises*
《续文献通考》	*Continued Compilation of General Study of the Literary Remains*
《续甬上耆旧诗》	*Continued Collection of Ancient Yongshang Poems*
《学礼偶笺》	*Annotations for the Learning of Rites*
《学礼质疑》	*Questions on the Learning of Rites*
《学谱》	"Notes on Learning"
《学庸志略》	*Interpretation of The Great Learning and The Doctrine of the Mean*
《学御录》	*Records on Learning to Drive*
《荀子·天论》	"*Tianlun*" ("Discourse on Heaven") in *Xunzi*
《周易寻门余论》	*Commentaries to the Interpretation of The Book of Changes*
《逊志斋集》	*Xunzhizhai Collection*
《烟屿楼诗集》	*Yanyulou Poetry*
《烟屿楼文集》	*Yanyulou Collection*
《阳九述略》	*A Brief Account of Unfortunate State Destiny*
《姚江书院记》	"An Account of Yaojiang Academy"
《姚江书院训约》	"Yaojiang Academy Regulations"
《姚江书院志略》	*Accounts and Annals of Yaojiang Academy*
《姚江棹歌》	*Yangjiang River Boatman's Songs*
《仪礼》	*Etiquette and Rites*
《仪礼笺》	*Annotations to Etiquette and Rites*
《仪礼商》	*Textual Criticism on Ancient Rites*
《忆龙泉山》	"Longquan Mountain Recalled"

《易经》	*The Book of Changes*
《易释》	*Interpretation of The Book of Changes*
《易注》	*Annotations to The Book of Changes*
《鄞西湖十洲志》	"On the Ten Islets of Xihu Lake (the Moon Lake) at Yinxian County"
《甬上耆旧诗》	*Collection of Ancient Yongshang Poems*
《甬上宋元诗略》	*Collected Poems of Yongshang in the Song and Yuan Dynasties*
《余姚评论》	*Yuyao Review*
《余姚县志》	*Annals of Yuyao County*
《玉海》	*Jade Sea*
《玉堂类稿》	*Yutang Encyclopaedical Manuscripts*
《元儒学案》	*The Records of Yuan Scholars*
《元文案》	*Collection of the Essays of Yuan*
《袁正献公遗文钞》	*Yuan Zhengxian's Posthumous Works*
《约礼说》	*On Self-restraining by Rites*
《葬书》	"On Books of Burials"
《葬约》	"Conventions on Burials"
《长短经》	*Monarch's Rulership*
《浙东学派溯源》	*The Origin of Zhedong School*
《浙东学派研究》	*A Study on Zhedong School*
《浙江通志》	*Annals of Zhejiang*
《明儒学案·浙中王门学案》	"Annals of Zhezhong Wangxue Scholars" of *The Records of Ming Scholars*
《真隐观洞天古迹记》	"On the Relic of Siming Dongtian/Zhenyin Temple"
《正统论》	"On Authenticity"
《中国近三百年学术史》（梁启超）	*Chinese Academic History of Recent Three Hundred Years*
《中国近三百年学术史》（钱穆）	*Academic History of China in Recent 300 Years*

《中国史稿》	*A General History of China*
《中庸》	*The Doctrine of the Mean*
《忠端公集》	*Zhongduan Collection*
《众乐亭》	"Zhongle Pavilion"
《重修十洲阁记》	"An Account on the Rebuilding of Shizhou (Ten Islets) Pavilion"
《重修众乐亭记》	"An Account on the Rebuilding of Zhongle Pavilion"
《周官》/《周礼》	*The Rites of Zhou*
《周季编略》	*A Brief Chronicle of the Late Zhou Dynasty*
《周礼考次目录》	*Contents of the Rites of Zhou*
《周易·十翼后录》	*Elucidation on the Ten Commentaries in The Book of Changes*
《周易日月变律》	*Laws of Solar and Lunar Changes in The Book of Changes*
《周易象辞》	*Interpretations of the Hexagrams of The Book of Changes*
《周易郑康成注》	*Zheng Kangcheng's Annotations to The Book of Changes*
《周易枝辞》	*Florid Language in the Book of Changes*
《朱舜水先生文集》	*Collected Works of Master Zhu Shunshui*
《朱熹读书法》	"Zhu Xi's Principles of Reading"
《诸虞传》	*Records of the Figures of the Yu Family*
《竹桥黄氏宗谱》	*Genealogy of the Huang Family of Zhuqiao*
《竹洲三先生书院记》	"An account on the Academy of Three Masters of the Bamboo Islet"
《竹洲晏尚书庙碑》	"The Tablet Inscription on Yan Dunfu Temple on the Bamboo Islet"
《著道录》	*Records on the Teachings of Confucius and Mencius*
《资治通鉴》	*Comprehensive Mirror in Aid of Governance*
《子刘子祠堂配享碑》	"Inscriptions for Those Worshiped in Master Liu Zongzhou's Temple"
《子思子辑解》	*Interpretation of Collection of Master Zisi*

《左传》	*Commentaries of Zuo*
安定"湖学"	learning of Master Anding (Hu Yuan) / "*Huxue*" (the learning of Huzhou)
半殖民地半封建社会	The semi-colonial and semi-feudal society
北方王学	Beifang *Wangxue* (in northern China)
本体	*benti* (original substance)
本体和工夫的统一	unity of "*benti*" (original substance) and "*gongfu*" (conscious effort)
本心	*benxin* (original mind)
边缘性文化	marginal culture
兵部尚书	Minister of War
兵部武选清吏司主事	administrative director [an official in *wuxuan qingli si* (a department mainly in charge of the affairs of military officers) of Ministry of War]
兵部职方司主事	*zhushi* (subordinate of the director) of *zhifang si* (a department of the Ministry of War, in charge of military fortifications)
兵部主事	*zhushi* (administrative director) in the Ministry of War
伯府第	Mansion of the Count (*Bo Fu Di*)
博士制度	*boshi* system
博学鸿词科	*boxue hongci ke* (a specialty for scholars who are erudite and excellent in writing)
博雅之学	extensive learning
不名一师	not limited to just one school
布衣史官	historiographer as a common man
参军	*canjun* (administrative assistant)
藏书楼	book-collecting buildings (private libraries)
漕运参将	*caoyun canjiang* (subordinate of governor, in charge of transporting provisions by rivers or canals)
常平属官	subordinate of the head of *changping si* (a department in charge of grain storage, welfare, water conservancy, etc.)
诚意说	Theory of Sincere Intention

程朱复出	Latter-day Cheng-Zhu
程朱理学	Cheng-Zhu School of Neo-Confucianism
处士	*chushi* (literally, recluse, refers to a scholar who doesn't seek any official position)
楚中王学	Chuzhong *Wangxue* (now in Hubei and Hunan)
辞赋	*cifu* (a sentimental or descriptive composition)
刺史部	*cishi bu* (department of regional inspection)
词曲	*ciqu.* In the phrase, *ci* is a type of Chinese poetry, in the form of songs characterized by lines of unequal length with prescribed rhyme schemes and tonal patterns, while *qu* is a type of classical Chinese poetry form, consisting of words written in a certain tone-pattern, based upon the tunes of various songs.
从事郎	*congshilang* (a sub-eighth-rank official title among the imperial official system of nine ranks)
大明历	Daming calendar
大学士	grand academician
大浙东	Greater Eastern Zhejiang; Greater Zhedong
大中至正之道	impartial way
道不离器	*qi* is indispensable to *dao*
道器合一	unity of *dao* (ideal method) and *qi* (definite thing)
道器相因	reciprocal causation of *dao* (ideal method) and *qi* (definite thing)
道心	*daoxin* (the heart-mind of *dao*)
道学	*daoxue* (the learning of way), a branch of Confucianism
道因器显	*dao* is demonstrated through *qi*
道在日用之间	*dao* is conveyed in the daily practice
道在事中	*dao* is in the things and affairs
迪功郎	*digonglang* (a ninth-grade official rank)

东林党	Donglin Faction, a Confucian group of scholar-officials in the Ming dynasty. They pushed relentless for the national moral rearmament under Emperor Tianqi's reign (1621–1627). Later, they suffered gruesome political repression by the Eunuch Faction led by high-ranking eunuch official Wei Zhongxian, and many of them were purged from key positions in the imperial court.
东浙三黄	Three Huangs of eastern Zhejiang
都察院	the Censorate
都督同知	*dudu tongzhi* (high-ranking military official, subordinate of military governor)
都指挥	*duzhihui* (the commander of the Military Department)
督学	educational inspector
恩贡生	*en gongsheng*. In the Ming and Qing dynasties, in the year when an imperial edict of kindness was issued for a new emperor ascending the throne or other great celebrations, an additional batch of *gongsheng* would be selected, and these group of students were called *en gongsheng*.
二十四史	*The Twenty-four Histories*
法曹参军	*facao canjun* (the head of Justice)
浮屠老氏	Buddhism and Taoism
府尹	prefect
复社	Fushe Society, also known as The Revival Society, was the largest literary movement of the late Ming dynasty that had political intentions.
副总兵	*fu zongbing* (deputy military governor)
纲常	ethical code
高丽使馆	Koryŏ Embassy
格物致知	investigating things to extend knowledge
各有事事	*ge you shi shi* (literally, every scholar has his practical affairs to tackle)
给事中	*jishizhong* (in charge of giving suggestions, expostulations and supervisions)
工夫	*gongfu* (conscious effort)

工商皆本	both industry (handicraft) and commerce are foundations
功曹	*gongcao* (an official in charge of personnel affairs, subordinate of prefect)
功曹吏	*gongcaoli* (head of personnel affairs)
宫廷文学	court literature
贡士	*gongshi* (candidates who passed the imperial metropolitan examination, the national-level imperial examination)
古文	ancient prose
故国遗事	the scattered records of the lost country
故国忠义	loyalist to the lost country (the Ming dynasty)
国史院编修官	historiographer in the Academy of National History
国学	*guoxue (*the study of ancient Chinese culture, especially Confucian culture, including language, literature and etiquette, etc.)
国子学	*Guozixue* (the Imperial Academy, the highest-level education institution in some Chinese feudal dynasties)
汉学	*Hanxue* (the Han studies)
翰林侍讲	*shijiang* (imperial tutor, in charge of interpreting the Confucian classics for the emperor) at Hanlin Academy
翰林学士	Hanlin academician
翰林院庶吉士	*shujishi* of Hanlin Academy, a scholastic title during the Ming and Qing dynasties for those selected *jinshi* who would further their study instead of working as officials
和会朱陆	combination of *Zhuxue* (Zhu Xi's *lixue*) and *Luxue* (Lu Jiuyuan's *xinxue*)
河图洛书	*Hetu and Luoshu.* By *Hetu and Luoshu*, literally, the former means "the Yellow River chart" and the latter "the inscription of Luo River". As two cosmological or numerological diagrams, they were employed by both Daoists and Confucians to explain the correlation of the hexagrams of *The Book of Changes* with the universe and human life.
贺秘监祠	He *Mijian Ci* (Temple of He Zhizhang)

弘文馆学士	*Hongwenguan xueshi* (member of the Institute for the Advancement of Literature)
户部主事	*zhushi* (administrative director) in the Ministry of Revenue
皇极历	Huangji calendar
会试	*huishi* (the metropolitan imperial examination)
即物求理	seeking the principle by investigating things
辑佚学	*Jiyixue*, literally, the studies on the collecting of lost literature. It involves the act of collecting and sorting out the lost literature materials recorded in other surviving documents in the form of quotation, so that the lost books and documents can be restored entirely or partially. As a discipline, it studies the history, methods, principles and other related issues of the edition of lost books or materials.
记室	*jishi* (secretary)
家天下	*jia tianxia* (hereditary monarchy)
监仓	*jiancang* (grain warehouse supervisor)
监修	*jianxiu* (compiling supervisor)
践履之学	doctrines on practice
鉴真大师	Master Jianzhen (a great Chinese monk of the Tang dynasty who propagated Buddhism in Japan)
江户学派	Edo school
江右王学	Jiangyou *Wangxue* (in Jiangxi)
将仕郎	*jiangshilang* (a low-level official rank)
鷓林六子	Six Poets of Jiaolin, a group of Ming loyalists
教授	*jiaoshou* (an official title, in charge of educational affairs of a certain region)
教谕	*jiaoyu* (director of education)
节度判官	*jiedu panguan* (assistant to the Military Commissioner)
节度使	local military governor
借儒谈禅	preaching Zen by way of Confucianism

进士	*jinshi* [literally, advanced scholar, a title for the nominees who passed *dianshi* (imperial court examination), the highest-level imperial civil service examination]
进士出身	*jinshi chushen* (second-rate *jinshi*)
进士及第	*jinshi jidi* (among the top three in the highest imperial examination)
经史并重	emphasizing both Confucian classics and historical studies
经史传记	Confucian classics, history, as well as commentaries and records
经史互通	association between Confucian classics and historical studies
经世之学	practical learning
经世致用	learning for practical use
经书纬书	*jingshu* and *weishu*. The former refers to the Confucian classics; while the latter, also called "*yizhoushu*" (逸周书), refers to the rest Zhou-dynasty books which were not chosen into Confucian classics.
经术史裁	studying Confucian classics through historical studies
经学	the learning of Confucian classics
靖难	Pacification of National Calamity (*jingnan*)
旧学与新学	the old learning and the new learning
举人	*juren* [literally, recommended scholar, a title granted to a scholar who passed the provincial-level imperial civil service examination (*xiangshi*)]
君权	monarchical power
开国文臣之首	The Leading State-founding Civil Official
考据学	textual research (*kaojuxue*)
考证学	textual criticism (*kaozhengxue*)
科举	*keju* (the imperial civil service examination)
类书	encyclopaedic books
礼部郎官	subordinate of the Minister of Rites

礼部尚书	Minister of Rites
礼部主事	*zhushi* (administrative director) in the Ministry of Rites
理气合一	unity of *li* (principle) and *qi* (vital force)
理象合一	unity of principle and diagram
理性	principle and nature
理学	*lixue* (the learning of heavenly principle)
立德、立功、立言	*lide* (establishing virtues), *ligong* (establishing accomplishments) and *liyan* (establishing words)
立言宗旨	orthodox ideas in writing
良能	*liangneng* (innate ability)
良知现成	*liangzhi xiancheng* (the innate knowledge of the good is in a constant state of readiness and fullness)
两浙斯文冠冕	Scholarly Model of Eastern Zhejiang and Western Zhejiang
凌烟阁二十四功臣	Twenty-four Meritorious Officials of Lingyan Pavilion
龙场悟道	Longchang Enlightenment
陆海交融文化	blended land-sea culture
陆王心学	Lu-Wang *xinxue*
陆学	Lu Jiuyuan's Neo-Confucian philosophy of the mind (*xinxue*)
秘监	*mijian* (short for *mishujian*, director of the Palace Library)
秘书郎	*mishulang* (an official in charge of the Four-branch Books of the imperial state library)
秘书省校书	*jiaoshu* (collator) of the Imperial Library
勉励工商	encouraging industry and commerce
妙悟	*miaowu* (spiritual perception)
民意	the mind of people (people's will)
闽学	*Minxue* (Fujian scholarship)
明觉之心	the mind of clear awareness
明史馆总裁	general director of the Institution for the History of Ming

明体达用之学	learning of Confucian doctrines for practical service
明之学祖	Father of the Scholarship of Ming
明治维新	Meiji Restoration
明州刺史	governor of Mingzhou Prefecture
明州郡守	prefect of Mingzhou
明州杨杜五子	Five Great Scholars of Mingzhou
明州知州	Governor of Mingzhou
南明永历政权	the Yongli regime of Southern Ming
南中王学	Nanzhong *Wangxue* (in the area nearby Nanjing)
内阁大学士	grand academician of the Grand Secretariat
内阁中书	*zhongshu* (secretary, in charge of drafting, recording, translating and hand-copying official documents) of the Grand Secretariat
宁波帮	Ningbo *bang*
宁波海上丝绸之路	Ningbo Maritime Silk Road
农商并举的杂文化	mixed culture of agriculture and commerce
农商皆本	both agriculture and commerce are essential
骑都尉	*qiduwei* (in charge of armed escort of cavalry)
起居舍人	*qiju sheren* (a chief imperial chronicler, mainly in charge of recording the daily affairs of emperor and national events)
气禀	*qibing* (vital life energy in man)
清节	moral integrity
清君侧	Ridding the Emperor of Evil Ministers (*qingjunce*)
清末三先生	Three Masters of the Late Qing Dynasty
庆历五先生	Five Masters of the Qingli Period
穷尽万理	exhaustively seeking myriad principles
求仁	pursuing benevolence
人民性	affinity to the people

仁义	benevolence and righteousness
仁政	benevolent governance
认识论	epistemology
儒家文化	Confucian culture
入世精神	*rushi* (concerning the worldly affairs)
瑞龙山	Zuiryusan Mountain
三礼	Sanli (Three Rites, namely, *The Rites of Zhou, Etiquette and Rites*, and *The Book of Rites*)
散骑常侍	*sanqi changshi* (emperor's attendant)
杀身成仁	dying for supreme virtue
山水画	Chinese Shanshui Painting, a style of Chinese painting that involves the painting of scenery or natural landscapes with brush and ink.
舍人	*sheren* (imperial secretary)
舍生取义	sacrificing for righteousness
慎独	*shendu* (vigilant solitude)
圣王之治	reign of sage monarch
胜国宾师	*Shengguo Binshi. Shengguo*, literally, a lost country, refers to the Ming dynasty defeated by the Qing dynasty, while *Binshi* means a person who has no official title/position but is respected by a sovereign.
市舶司	*shibo si* (Maritime Trade Supervising Department, also known as the Trading-ship Office, functioned as customs at that time)
时文	*shiwen* (eight-legged essay, a kind of essay prescribed for the imperial civil service examination)
实事实功	practical efficacy and utility
事功	practical utility
事其当事	to do the things that one is supposed to do
事其所事	to do one's own things to be coped with
使院	*Shiyuan* (office of local military governor's agents)

银青光禄大夫	*yinqing guanglu dafu* (an honorific title of no fixed duties awarded to emperor's intimate ministers, which literally means a glorious grand master with the silver badge and blue ribbon)
殊途百虑之学	learning through various approaches and considerations
庶常馆	*shuchang guan* (a department for newly-enrolled high-ranking *jinshi* to further their study)
水户历史学派	Mito School of history
水户学派	Mito School (Mitogaku)
水则碑	Shuize Tablet
舜水热	craze for Shunshui Studies
舜水学	Shunshui Studies
私意	*siyi* (selfish intention)
思田之乱	Si-Tian Rebellion
四句教	Four-sentence Teaching
四明儒学	Confucian learning in Siming
四明逸老	Siming yilao (an old man of leisure)
四书	Four Books
四无说	Fourfold Nothingness (*siwushuo*)
宋初三先生	Three Masters of the Early Song Dynasty
宋明理学	Song-Ming Neo-Confucianism
宋学	*Songxue* (the Song Studies)
素位之学	the learning of *suwei*. *Suwei* literally means to be satisfied with the current state/position. The learning of *suwei* emphasizes practical principle, practical action, practical effect and practical learning.
岁差	precession of the equinox
岁贡生	*Sui gongsheng*, literally, annually selected *gongsheng*. In the Ming and Qing dynasties, every year or every two or three years, students were selected from the official public schools of various levels into *Guozijian/Guozixue* (the Imperial Academy) for their further study. Those selected were called *sui gong* or *sui gongsheng*.

太常博士	*taichang boshi* [a post of *taichang si* (Office of Imperial Sacrifices), mainly in charge of teaching Confucian classics]
太常寺卿	Minister of the Office of Imperial Sacrifices (*taichang si*)
太常寺主簿	*zhubu* (official registrar, in charge of secretarial affairs) of the Office of Imperial Sacrifices (*taichang si*)
太仆寺卿	Minister of *taipu si* (in charge of horses for transportation)
太学	the Imperial Academy (*Taixue*)
太子中舍人	*taizi zhongsheren* (attendant of Crown Prince)
太子中庶子	*taizi zhongshuzi* (in charge of counselling and assisting the study of Crown Prince)
泰州王学	Taizhou *Wangxue* (in Jiangsu)
唐初四大书法家	Four Great Calligraphers of Early Tang
天机	heavenly mystery
天理	heavenly principle
天泉证道	Tianquan Zhengdao (Debate on *Dao* on Tianquan Bridge)
天人合一	unity of heaven and man
天下为主君为客。	The people are the hosts, while the monarch is the guest.
天一阁	Tianyi Pavilion (private library)
廷尉卿	*tingweiqing* (the head of the Department of Justice)
通判	*tongpan* (a subordinate of county magistrate, in charge of administering lawsuit)
推官	*tuiguan* (in charge of justice and evaluation of officials)
万氏八龙	Eight Dragons of the Wan family
万物一体	unity of myriad things
王道	kingly way
文武全才第一	top one of intellectual and martial talents
文献名邦	a famous place with valuable literature and outstanding scholarly talents
文学博士	*wenxue boshi* (a post in Hanlin Academy, literally refers to an erudite scholar of Confucian classics and history)

无名天地之始。	The nameless is the beginning of heaven and earth.
无形本寂寥。	Formlessness is infinite stillness.
五经	Five Classics
五征君	Five Summoned Men of Noble Character
武进士	*wu jinshi* (a highest-rank title for the candidates of imperial examination in martial arts. It is a term relative to *jinshi*)
务明体以达用	to apply the Confucian principles into practical service
务实之学	learning of practice
悟修并进。	Perception goes side by side with cultivation.
西乡侯	Marquis of Xixiang
习心	*xixin* (idea/knowledge learned from what is seen and heard)
先验唯心论	transcendental idealism
县试	*xianshi* (the county-level imperial civil service examination)
县尉	*xianwei* (subordinate of the magistrate, in charge of public security)
乡试	*xiangshi* (the provincial-level imperial examination)
小浙东	Lesser Eastern Zhejiang; Lesser Zhedong
心外无理	no principles outside the mind
心外无物	no things outside the mind
心性之学	learning of *xinxing* (heart-mind and human nature)
心学	*xinxue*, the learning of heart-mind. It refers to the Neo-Confucian philosophy of the mind, one of the two major branches of Neo-Confucianism. The other major branch is *lixue*, the learning of *li* (heavenly principle).
心之万殊	diversity of mind
新建伯	Count of Xinjian (*Xinjian Bo*)
刑部尚书	Minister of Justice
行朝	exiled regime

行道有功	Neo-Confucian learning for practical utility
性情	*xingqing* (nature and emotion)
学术世家	academic families
学有宗旨	learning with orthodox idea
学政	*xuezheng* (educational supervisor)
训导	*xundao* (assistant director of education)
衙推	*yatui* (subordinate of local governor)
阉党	eunuch faction
言性命者必究于史。	Those who study human nature and destiny must resort to history.
阳明洞	*Yangmingdong* (Yangming Grotto)
阳明心学	Yangming *xinxue*
阳明学	Yangming studies
一本万殊	*yiben wanshu* (literally, diversity begotten by one origin)
一偏之见	one-sided views
移植创新性文化	innovative transplanted culture
以工夫见本体	seeking "*benti*" through "*gongfu*"
以利和义	promoting righteousness by interest
以民为本	people-oriented
以人心为本	human-mind-oriented
义利双行	stressing both righteousness and interest
驿丞	head of the Post House
因果报应	karma (retribution for sin)
隐逸	seclusion
永嘉九先生	Nine Masters of Yongjia
永兴县子	Viscount of Yongxing County
甬上四先生	Four Masters of Yongshang
甬上望族	gentry family of Yongshang

甬上证人书院	Yongshang (Ningbo) Zhengren Academy
由工夫以悟本体	understanding *benti* through *gongfu*
由器而道	to realize *dao* (ideal method) through *qi* (definite thing)
由虚转实	from *xu* (emptiness) to *shi* (reality)
御史	*yushi* (investigating censor)
越魂史笔	*yuehun shibi* (a great historian with the spirit of Zhedong School of historical studies)
粤闽王学	Min-Yue *Wangxue* (in Fujian and Guangdong)
宰相	prime minister
长史	*zhangshi* (subordinate of the governor)
哲学本体论	philosophical ontology
浙东史学	Zhedong historical studies
浙东史学派	Zhedong School of historical studies
浙东文献学	Zhedong School of philology
浙东心学	Zhedong philosophy of the mind
浙东学派	Zhedong School
浙东学术	Zhedong scholarship
浙东朱学	Zhu Xi's Neo-Confucianism in Zhedong
浙东朱子学派	Zhedong *Zhuxue* School
浙学	*Zhexue* (Zhejiang scholarship)
浙中王学	Zhezhong *Wangxue* (in central Zhejiang)
证人之旨	idea of being on the right way
正学	*zhengxue* (upright learning)
知府	prefect
知先行后。	Knowledge goes before action.
知县	magistrate
知行合一	unity of knowledge and action

直学士院	*zhixueshiyuan* (literally, auxiliary Hanlin academician, a title of concurrent post for an official who worked partly for Hanlin Academy but not as a Hanlin Academician)
制置史	*zhizhishi* (in charge of military affairs on border defense)
致良知	*zhiliangzhi* (extension of innate knowledge of the good)
致命遂志	adhere to one's belief through death
致知之功	effort in the extension of *liangzhi*
中官御史	*zhongguan yushi* (investigating censor of the imperial court officials)
中书舍人	*zhongshu sheren* (mainly in charge of drafting imperial mandates)
中书侍郎	*zhongshu shilang* (the vice-minister of the Palace Secretariat)
中原	Central Plains
中浙东	Middle Eastern Zhejiang
重农抑商	emphasizing agriculture and restraining commerce
朱熹理学	Zhu Xi's Neo-Confucianism (*lixue*)
朱学	*Zhuxue*, Zhu Xi's Neo-Confucianism
诛十族	ten familial exterminations
诸生	*zhusheng* (alias *xiucai*, referring to those who passed the county-level imperial civil service examination)
诸子百家	various pre-Qin schools of thought
主编	chief compiler
主簿	*zhubu* (official registrar, in charge of secretarial affairs)
主讲	lecturer
主意说	Theory of Subjective Intention
著作郎	*zhuzuolang* (the chief official in charge of the writing of national history)
专家之学	specialized learning
自得	personal acquisition

自得之学	learning of personal acquisition
自家准则	personal norms
自作主宰	self-dominance
宗陆而不悖于朱	following the learning of Lu Jiuyuan without contradicting Zhu Xi's thought
总兵	*zongbing* (military governor)
总裁	general director
邹鲁	Zou-Lu (a place with prosperous culture and education)
左都御史	censor-in-chief of the Censorate
左副都御史	vice censor-in-chief of the Censorate
佐著作郎	*zuo zhuzuolang* n official in charge of writing national history)

Translator's Note

穿针引线合中西

——《千年文脉：浙东学术文化》译后记

千年文脉，上溯千年，更及先秦百家。

浙东学术，根植浙东，载誉华夏内外。

月湖如镜，鉴照古今，盛观宋元明清。

三江汇聚，贯通天下，泽被千秋万古。

方同义教授的《千年文脉：浙东学术文化》（简称为《千年文脉》）是一本跨越千年的学术历史著作，旁征博引，气势恢宏。该书从北宋浙东学术之缘起述及民国时期"旧学"之终结，涵盖浙东朱学、心学、文献学、史学的巨大成就和历史贡献，并以四明虞氏、黄氏、万氏三大家族为轴，探析了浙东学者的家学传承。时间上，虽言千年，溯至北宋，但行文所及，无不关乎两周先秦；地域上，虽在浙东，聚于月湖，然话题所至，无不推及华夏内外。该书资料之翔实、叙论之周密、心怀之宽阔、视角之广博，无一不令人拍案。

待到译文登场，当头三问：信乎？达乎？雅乎？正所谓严复所言译事三难，于本书英译而言，尤为如此。信，难在回归历史语境、文本语境，而非作现代阐释或个体性解读；达，难在穿针引线、和合中西，以重构原文的内在逻辑；雅，难在复现原文娓娓道来却又不失厚重的行文风格。且不论译"雅"，单就"信""达"二字已非易事。跨语移译，旨在桥连源语作者与译语读者的沟通。关联翻译理论提出，"译者的责任是努力做到使原文作者的意图（intention）与译文读者的企盼（expectation）相吻合"。换言之，译者的任务在于确保目的语读者免于不必要的努力，便可得到足够的语境效果。①

通观《千年文脉》全书，引经据典，洋洋洒洒十万言，可谓浙东学术之四库提要。览读此书，母语读者尚需"努力"，遑论译语读者。关联理

---

① 林克难. 关联翻译理论简介. 中国翻译，1994(4)：7.

论不把翻译看成是源语与译语间的直接交流，而是充分强调译者在翻译中的重要作用。① 因此，若要译语读者 "免于不必要的努力"，自然责在译者。下文将围绕 "信" 和 "达" 两个层面，探究《千年文脉》的英译。

"信" 在还原语境的感知与理解

《千年文脉》一书，行文所至必涉典籍，而典籍文献断不可贸然取义。所谓 "信" 者，实为忠实于特定语境下的特定含义。故而，译语传达，必以训字为先。例如：

> 梨洲先生秉承心学的精神，竭力倡 "殊途百虑之学"，强调学者需 "自得" "学有宗旨"。所谓 "学有宗旨" 就是学者的 "工夫所致" 的得力处，从而形成自己的学术特色，也就是最可宝贵的创造。②

一代宗师黄宗羲，可谓史学大柱，其提出的诸多概念，至今仍在学界广泛应用。通读该段对梨洲先生心学思想的总结，会发现 "自得" 显然不是 "洋洋自得"，"宗旨" 也并非现代意义所指的 "主要目的和意图"，因而绝非某些篇章英文摘要所用的 content 或 purpose。那么，黄宗羲的本义作何理解？据其《明儒学案·发凡》："学问之道，以各人自用得著者为真，凡倚门傍户、依样葫芦者，非流俗之士，则经生之业者。此编所列，有一偏之见，有相反之论，学者于其不同之处，正宜著眼理会，所谓一本万殊也，以水济水岂是学问？"③ 由此可见，所谓 "自得" 是学者对学问的自我领悟，而非人云亦云，旨在强调个体在学术修习中的自我习得。故而，本文将其译为 personal acquisition（个人的习得）或 personal comprehension（个人的领悟）。

再谈 "宗旨"，黄宗羲在《楚中王门学案》一章评价道："楚学之盛，惟耿天台一派，自泰州流入。当阳明在时，其信从者尚少。……然道林实得阳明之传，天台之派虽盛，反多破坏良知学脉，恶可较哉！"④ 他认为天台一派的阳明心学 "多破坏良知血脉"，从而背离了师门 "宗旨"。所

---

① 顾韵. 从关联理论解读翻译策略. 大连大学学报, 2006(3)：67-70.
② 方同义. 千年文脉：浙东学术文化. 宁波：宁波出版社, 2014：171.
③ 黄宗羲. 明儒学案. 北京：中华书局, 1985：18.
④ 黄宗羲. 明儒学案. 北京：中华书局, 1985：627.

谓"学有宗旨"，指的是学问不可信手拈来，而是学问必有所宗。因而，"宗旨"并非现代意义上的"目的""定位"，而是 orthodox idea（正统的思想）。由此可见学贵"自得"的"自得"是一种强调主体意识的治学精神，是黄宗羲编著《明儒学案》时选案的重要参考；"宗旨"不但是对"自得"的肯定和提升，还体现了黄宗羲的学术脉略和治学精神。① 故而，本段英文处理如下：

> Adhering to the spirit of *xinxue*, Huang Zongxi advocated "learning through various approaches and thinking pattens", emphasizing a scholar's "personal acquisition" and "learning with an orthodox idea". By "learning with an orthodox idea", a scholar realizes "what his conscious effort is aimed at" and then forms his academic characteristic(s), i.e., his own most precious academic creation.

典籍文献英译，不仅需要对学术概念做好训释，还要对句子层面的内在衔接进行训读，否则就会译出"拧巴"的句子，导致译语读者对原文信息的错误领会。例如：

> 浙东之学，虽出婺源，然自三袁之流，多宗江西陆氏，而通经服古，绝不空言德性，故不悖于朱子之教。至阳明王子，揭孟子之良知，复与朱子抵牾……②

众所周知，婺源虽现属江西省，但在 1949 年之前隶属"徽州府"，即现在的安徽省。再依照史学大家章学诚所处的清代来看，该句极易解读为："浙东学术，虽然出自徽州婺源县，然而自袁燮、袁肃、袁甫之后，大多推崇江西陆氏（陆九渊、陆九龄），并且精通经学，熟谙传统文化，绝不空口谈论道德性情，所以不违背朱熹的教诲。等到王阳明，阐发孟子的良知观念，又和朱熹的学说相矛盾。"

若据此训读，则句子的内在逻辑是，浙东学术虽然出自徽州婺源县，后来却改为推崇江西的陆氏兄弟。这显然无法与后面的"不违背朱熹的教

---

① 姚文永，宋晓伶."自得"和"宗旨"——《明儒学案》一个重要的编撰方法与原则.大连大学学报，2010(3)：7-11.
② 转引自：方同义.千年文脉：浙东学术文化.宁波：宁波出版社，2014：25.

诲""又和朱熹的学说相矛盾"等表述形成逻辑关联。因而可以断定,婺源并非指代地名,而且必然与朱熹相关。那么,远在福建的"闽学"代表人物朱熹和婺源又有怎样的渊源呢? 答案在于朱熹虽然出生于福建尤溪,但其祖籍为徽州府婺源县,即婺源是朱子的故乡。另据李江辉所述:"'浙东学术'虽然源于朱熹理学思想的影响,但自从袁燮、袁肃、袁甫父子宗奉陆九渊'心学'以来,又有浙东学者如吕祖谦、陈亮、叶适等反对空谈'心''理''性''命'。"^① 由此可以印证,章学诚此处所谓"婺源",其实是指代宋代理学家"朱熹"。照此理解,本段的逻辑衔接便会豁然开朗,即,浙东学术虽然出自朱熹理学,但后来转向了陆九渊、陆九龄兄弟的心学。简而言之,这句话实际上是说浙东学术从理学到心学的转向。这就充分应合了浙东作为中国古代心学大本营的论断。综上所述,译文处理如下(本段译文其他译注暂未列出):

> Although Zhedong scholarship derived from Wuyuan*, most of its scholars, from the time of Yuan Xie and his two sons Yuan Su and Yuan Fu, began to follow Lu Jiuyuan and his brother Lu Jiuling of Jiangxi Province. Zhedong scholars were proficient in Confucian classics, familiar with traditional culture but unwilling to talk about virtue and human nature in empty words, so their learning was still compatible with Zhu Xi's teachings. However, the ideas of Wang Yangming started to deviate from Zhu Xi's theory in the process of developing Mencius's concept of *liangzhi*...

> * Note: Wuyuan, the name of Zhu Xi's hometown, is here used to refer to Zhu Xi and his learning of *lixue*.

无独有偶,因为古今政区划分不同,地名不仅容易引起名称指代的误解,也容易导致读者对所叙内容的疑惑。例如:

> 郭沫若主编的《中国史稿》将余姚虞氏列为会稽三大家族虞、孔、贺之首,是名副其实的"江左豪族"。^②

依照区域划分,四明即是宁波,会稽即是绍兴。那么,宁波的虞氏

---

① 李江辉. 章学诚与浙东学派. 西安电子科技大学学报(社会科学版),2006(5):80-84.
② 方同义. 千年文脉:浙东学术文化. 宁波:宁波出版社,2014:146-147.

缘何位列绍兴的三大家族之首？当然，面对这样的疑惑，译者只需添加一个简单的背景注解就可以了。译文处理如下（本段译文其他译注暂未列出）：

> In *A General History of China* compiled by Guo Moruo, the Yu family of Yuyao* was ranked top one among the three gentry families of Kuaiji, namely, the Yus, the Kongs and the Hes. It was a true "gentry family of Jiangzuo".
>
> * Note: Yuyao once belonged to Kuaiji (Shaoxing) before it was incorporated into Ningbo in 1949.

"达"在穿针引线合中西

"达"，即译文通达，旨在使译语读者能顺畅理解。换言之，能让译文读者通过最佳关联形成完整的理解逻辑链。例如在下例中，由于英汉语言本身的差异，容易导致源语中本来前后关联的信息在译入语中失去关联。因而译者务必以穿针引线之功重构关联。

余姚城中有一条千年古街——虞宦街，现在称为新建路，这是民国18 年（1929）火灾后重建，为纪念王阳明封"新建伯"而改的名。[①]

中文读者对"新建路""新建伯"均能通畅理解，且能轻松关联两者的含义。诚然，若单以拼音方式将两者音译为 Xinjian Road 和 Count of Xinjian，译文也能靠 Xinjian 形成关联，但疑问也会随之而来："新建"为何物？

据《明史本纪第十六·武宗》载："六月丙子，宁王宸濠反……丁巳，守仁败宸濠于樵舍，擒之。"樵舍，就是王阳明擒获宁王朱宸濠的地方，此地位于江西南昌西北部的新建县，因而王阳明以此地为名受封"新建伯"，以表彰其平叛之功，其逝后又获追封"新建侯"。伯，即伯爵，侯，即侯爵。可见，"新建伯"的源头来自"新建"县这样一处地名。故而，译者的责任，除了通过音译形成文字表层的关联之外，还需补充语境信息，以实现译语读者对文字的深层理解。因此，译文尝试处理如下：

---

① 方同义. 千年文脉：浙东学术文化. 宁波：宁波出版社，2014：146.

Yuhuan Street, now called Xinjian Road, is a thousand-year-old street in downtown Yuyao. After a fire in 1929, it was rebuilt and given its present name to commemorate Wang Yangming by his rank of nobility "Count of Xinjian"*.

*Note: Count of Xinjian is actually the Count of Xinjian County. It was just in this county that Wang Yangming captured the head of a rebellion against the emperor's sovereignty. That's why he was granted the rank of nobility with "Xinjian" in the title when he was awarded for his great military contributions to the country.

此外，在本书第六章关于虞氏家族巨子虞世南的描述中，也出现了类似的表述。详见下文：

这时他［虞世南］改任秘书监，封爵永兴县子。唐贞观八年（634年）晋封县公，故有"虞永兴"之称。[1]

传统上，中国古代文人的称谓，不仅包括名、字、号，还有根据其所居之处、所属官位或为官所在地所起的名号，例如杜甫杜工部、韩愈韩昌黎、柳宗元柳柳州。因此，对中国读者而言，虞永兴即是虞世南，没有理解障碍。但在跨文化翻译中，虞永兴之称则需借助背景信息才能与虞世南形成关联。当然，本处原文已经做出解释，因而仅需音译便可将虞世南——永兴县子——虞永兴关联起来。译文处理如下：

At this time, he [Yu Shinan] was transferred to the office of *mishujian*, and granted the rank of nobility as the Viscount of Yongxing County. In the eighth year of the Zhenguan period (634), his rank was promoted to the Marquis of Yongxing County. Hence the appellation "Yu Yongxing" for him.

如前所述，跨语言的语义关联，需要建基于充分的语境或背景信息。虽然在源语中有时会因行文需要而对相关概念进行解释，但解释往往局限于语内而非语际，若单纯在译入语中复制这一解释，仍然难以实现语际间的有效关联。例如：

为什么叫"虞宦街"？这是 1700 多年前余姚最有名的世家大族

---

[1] 方同义．千年文脉：浙东学术文化．宁波：宁波出版社，2014：150.

虞氏家族的领军人物——东吴高官虞翻所相中的地方。①

原文对"虞宦街"的解释，对源语读者而言可谓一目了然。简言之，虞宦就是虞姓官宦，虞宦街就是虞姓官宦居住的街道。再看英译，"虞宦街"属于政区地名类词语，自然需要音译为 Yuhuan Street。"高官虞翻"是人名，自然也需音译为 high-ranking official Yu Fan。但是，两者除了"Yu"之外，没有任何共通之处，即便是语言表层也无法形成关联。可见人名、地名英译，采用音译方式并非一劳永逸。就本例而言，还需要译者在两者之间穿针引线，缝合两者的语义缝隙。为此，译文采用了文内加注方式，整体译文处理如下：

> Then why was it called "Yuhuan Street"? Actually, the name literally means "a street where an official surnamed Yu lives", and the official was Yu Fan who lived more than 1,700 years ago. He was a high-ranking official of the Wu State (222–280) during the period of the Three Kingdoms (220–280) and the leading figure of the Yu family, the most famous Yu gentry family of Yuyao at that time. It was he who took a fancy to that place and started to live there.

为确保译文通达，译者的穿针引线不仅体现在上述例证所示的词汇层面上，而且还体现在篇章层面上。例如：

> 他 [杨简] 说："学者当知，夫举天下万古之人心皆如此也。孔子之心如此……复斋之心如此，象山先生之心如此，金溪王令君之心如此，举金溪一邑之心如此。"这一"同心"能够"范围天地，发育万物"，天地、万物、四时、风霆雨露霜雪等无不在"心"之中。②

本段文字中，"甬上四先生"之一、陆学重要代表人物杨简阐发了心学之"心"。孔子之心、陆九龄之心、陆九渊之心，一脉相承，都容易理解。但金溪王令君是何许人也？他与心学有何关联？显然，Magistrate Wang 这样一个单一的称谓并不能传达原文之全貌。这就需要还原历史语境，一探究竟。

① 方同义 . 千年文脉：浙东学术文化 . 宁波：宁波出版社，2014：146.
② 方同义 . 千年文脉：浙东学术文化 . 宁波：宁波出版社，2014：78.

　　南宋绍熙四年（1193），陆九渊卒于荆门，后灵枢归于家乡金溪。仰慕陆九渊学识的时任金溪知县王有大，捐出薪俸在县学创设"二陆先生祠堂"，并请陆学大弟子杨简作记。而该段引述正是出自杨简为此所作的《二陆先生祠记》。由此可见，金溪王令君虽非陆九渊弟子，但对心学也颇有研究。杨简正是通过从孔子到陆氏兄弟到王令君再到金溪百姓这样一条逻辑线，来论证"人同此心"或"同心"。

　　基于此，译者有必要补足相关背景信息，以确保在译文中完整复现这条逻辑线，从而实现从源语到目的语的"意图"传达。译文处理如下：

　　He [Yang Jian] said, "Scholars are supposed to know that all men under heaven, whether they be men in the past or at present, have the same *xin*", so did Confucius, Master Fuzhai (Lu Jiuling) and Master Xiangshan (Lu Jiuyuan), so does Magistrate Wang (Youda) of Jinxi County, and so do all the people throughout the whole county."* This "shared *xin*" "contains heaven and earth, and conceive myriad things". Things like heaven and earth, myriad things, four seasons and all kinds of weather phenomena are all in "*xin*". In this way, the "*xin*" that Yang Jian realized through abstraction is actually the "shared *xin*" by all men, although he based "*xin*" on his subjective self-experience. In this sense, he actually drew an equal sign between the "*xin*" of an individual and that of a sage.

　　*Note: These words are cited from Yang Jian's *An Account of the Memorial Temple of Masters Lu Jiuling and Lu Jiuyuan*, which was written in 1193 at the invitation of Wang Youda, the magistrate of Jinxi County, to commemorate the completion of the temple.

结　语

　　如前所述，跨语移译，旨在桥连源语作者与译语读者的沟通。依照关联理论，译者还需做到尽量免除译文读者不必要的努力，这就需要译者对典籍文献做到逐字训释，并在译文中穿针引线，以确保词语之间、语句之间乃至篇章之间形成逻辑关联。正所谓信在还原语境的感知与理解，达在穿针引线合中西。

文章千古事，译作亦如此。译者也正是在这样的鞭策之下，愿拼尽全力以求事安、心安。承蒙师长同道不弃，三番五次倾囊相授。尤其感谢译审董铁柱教授，在译文审校过程中，事无巨细，不厌其烦，多次提点译文的粗鄙之处。感谢文献大家裴爱民先生，多次在译者迷惘之际，及时帮助译者找到所涉文献典籍的出处，并给予细致通透的解读。两位专家的学养实乃令人折服。感谢文字编辑黄墨老师，大到行文规范，小到年份转换，无不耐心审核，细致修订，更让译者感受了出版工作者对文字的精准把悟。感谢宁波大学科学技术学院各级领导对本书翻译和出版的深入关心与倾力支持，尤其感谢人文学院特聘院长周志锋教授、院长贺安芳教授，让译者有幸结识了本书原著者方同义教授，并在交流过程中进一步体会了原著的力量。还要感谢宁波大学科学技术学院人文学院 2016 级翻译专业本科生林靖雯，2017 级翻译专业本科生徐婷婷，2020 级翻译专业本科生董佳源、王慧敏、张璐宁、祝静，以及宁波大学外国语学院 2021 级翻译专业硕士研究生倪淑萍，他们为本书做了大量的资料查询、文字校对、术语整理等工作。

译者于教学课业之余，通译此书。译毕之际，满心欢喜。其间，体验过"吟安一个字"，感受过"狂搜海亦枯"，虽言历经寒暑，却也乐在其中。独乐乐，不如众乐乐。愿读者您也在阅读本书时感受到快乐。